The Cheap Bastard's Guide to
NEW YORK CITY

"A penny-pincher's nirvana—it's as if we wrote it!"
—*Arthur Frommer's Budget Travel Magazine*

"A book that reinforces one of the classic family values
that New Yorkers hold dear—never pay retail."
—Brian Lehrer, *WNYC New York Public Radio*

"But does it work? You bet. . . . Grader hilariously dissects
the city to come up with his innovative money savers."
—John Deiner, *The Washington Post*

"There are a lot of ideas worth considering. . . .
Plenty of attractions for the casual visitor."
—Richard P. Carpenter, *Boston Globe*

"The $14.95 you spend on this book
will be recouped in no time."
—*Brooklyn Parent Magazine*

"Brings on attitude and humor in its revelations
of how to obtain assorted freebies."
—*Publishers Weekly*

"The last word on living well and cheaply
in the Big Apple—and, no, it is not an oxymoron."
—June Sawyers, *Chicago Tribune*

"If you are planning a trip to the Big Apple, this book is a
must . . . You will enjoy the wit and humor Grader has
inserted into this delightful guide."
—*Gillette News–Record* (Gillette, Wyo.)

Help Us Keep This Guide Up to Date

Every effort has been made by the author and editors to make this guide as accurate and useful as possible. However, many things can change after a guide is published—establishments close, phone numbers change, facilities come under new management, and so on.

We would love to hear from you concerning your experiences with this guide and how you feel it could be improved and kept up to date. While we may not be able to respond to all comments and suggestions, we'll take them to heart and we'll also make certain to share them with the author. Please send your comments and suggestions to the following address:

The Globe Pequot Press
Reader Response/Editorial Department
P.O. Box 480
Guilford, CT 06437

Or you may e-mail us at:

editorial@GlobePequot.com

Thanks for your input, and happy travels!

INSIDERS' GUIDE®

The Cheap Bastard's Guide™ to
NEW YORK CITY

A NATIVE NEW YORKER'S SECRETS OF LIVING THE GOOD LIFE—FOR FREE!

THIRD EDITION

Rob Grader

INSIDERS' GUIDE®

GUILFORD, CONNECTICUT
AN IMPRINT OF THE GLOBE PEQUOT PRESS

The prices and rates listed in this guidebook were confirmed at press time. We recommend, however, that you call establishments to obtain current information before traveling.

To buy books in quantity for corporate use or incentives, call **(800) 962–0973, ext. 4551,** or e-mail **premiums@GlobePequot.com.**

INSIDERS' GUIDE®

Copyright © 2002, 2004, 2006 by Rob Grader

The Cheap Bastard's Guide is a trademark of Rob Grader.

Insiders' Guide is a registered trademark of Morris Book Publishing, LLC.

Text and map design: M. A. Dubé © Morris Book Publishing, LLC
Spot art: Image Club
Lyrics on page 27 from "Grand Central Station, March 18, 1977" by Steve Forbert, reprinted by kind permission of Welk Music (ASCAP, adm. Lichelle Music Co.).

ISSN 1549-5116
ISBN-13 978-0-7627-4063-5
ISBN-10 0-7627-4063-9

Manufactured in the United States of America
Third Edition/First Printing

For Dad, the one, the true, the Original Cheap Bastard,
and for Mom, though not always cheap,
one true original in her own right.

Contents

"Misers aren't fun to
to live with, but they
make wonderful
ancestors."

— David Brenner

ACKNOWLEDGMENTS

N **O ONE BECOMES** a Cheap Bastard on his own, and here are the names to prove it. There are many people I need to acknowledge who've helped me along the way. From the very beginning, I had training from the best, the ultimate Cheap Bastard himself, my dad, Jack Grader. Thanks also to Mom, Bernice Grader, and everyone in my family for their support, encouragement, and suggestions while I was putting this opus together. In particular, thanks to Scott Grader (with two t's, right?) for all the free legal counseling, to Trish Lande Grader for all the free publishing know-how, and to all the rest of the Graders: Jessica, Michelle, Emily, Sally, Jonas, Jeff, Lisa, Stu, and Ellen. Special thanks to Shari Springer Berman and Bob Pulcini for all the free writing advice and consultations. I am also indebted to Steve Harper for the free proofreading services (and the constantly free ear!), to Harry Mizrahi of American Spectrum Realty for the free use of the office equipment and for giving me plenty of free time while I was working for him, to Hans Kriefall and his mom for the free Latin lesson, and to Chiori Miagowa, Suzi Takahashi, Nilaja Sun, Ignacio Lopez, Ken Bolden, Danny Weiss, Patricia Kelley, Bill Quigley, Bill Driscoll, Mark Farnan, Sue Barret, Helen Mandlin, Karen Raksis (the best things in life are free!) for all giving so freely of their spirits. My gratitude also goes out to Mark S. Roy and Brian DeFiore of DeFiore and Company, and to Laura Strom, Shelley Wolf, Maureen Graney, Jennifer Quint, and everyone at The Globe Pequot Press for their invaluable assistance. There is also a nasty little secret about New Yorkers I must expose: Contrary to popular belief, they truly are the friendliest, smartest, most generous and helpful people in the world. Innumerable friends, acquaintances, associates, and strangers helped me out in countless ways throughout the development of this book. I'm sorry I cannot name you all, but please know you are appreciated. Thanks to all—you're a wonderful bunch of Bastards!

"Truly, our greatest blessings are very cheap."

—Henry David Thoreau

INTRODUCTION: THE LAND OF THE FREE

A FEW YEARS BACK WHILE I was visiting England, I found myself low on cash—but still wanting to see the sights. Not to be deterred by this minor detail, I proceeded to figure out ways to sneak into some of the Brits' most expensive and heavily guarded tourist attractions. My proudest feat was making my way into the impenetrable Tower of London. Take that, William the Conqueror! I was having such a good time getting around the system that I thought this would make a great first in a series of books—Getting Around London: How to Sneak into Anywhere. Upon further consideration (and after speaking with my brother the lawyer), it seemed there might be an array of legal problems with this kind of book. But somehow the idea wouldn't go away.

Then back home in New York, I watched the Pulitzer Prize–winning play *Wit* one evening for free (and legally!). After the show, I stopped by a favorite haunt of mine to get a little snack (free, thank you), and made it home to my spacious Upper West Side apartment (for which I pay $560 a month in rent and found without paying any broker's fee). As I sat relaxing in my leather easy chair (free, too!) and thinking about my yoga class the next morning (you guessed it, free), it dawned on me—I am one cheap bastard. I also understood that I have a mission in life to figure out how I can get or do practically anything I want without paying one red cent, and usually on the up and up. And I felt compelled to share this—my life's work—with the world. So I humbly offer to you *The Cheap Bastard's Guide to New York City*.

The *CB Guide* is not only a collection of specific destinations, listings, and tips on how to get almost anything imaginable for free or ridiculously cheap (more on my definition of these later), it's also a celebration of life on the cheap. The myth is that New York is a great place to live or visit if you have the money to enjoy it. The truth is, no place offers more for free than New York, but only if you know how to find it. And once you find it, oh the joy! Anyone can pay their way into a Broadway show, but when you get in for free, somehow the lights are brighter, the songs are sweeter, the drama so much more heartbreaking. There is no thrill in buying a dinner, but the taste of a free Buffalo wing is spiced with adventure, the crunch of a crisp free Granny Smith apple is the sound of triumph, and the kick of getting a free cup of coffee puts just that extra spring in your step.

A big part of the value of getting something for nothing is the story that goes with it—the history, the event. What can you tell me about any piece of furniture in your house that you bought? *I went to the store. I liked it. I bought it.* But everything in my house comes with a heritage. Every time I sit in my leather easy chair, I'm reminded of how I came to own this piece of furniture that by all rights I could never afford to buy. I was walking along a few blocks away from my apartment, my arms loaded down with books I was donating to my local library, when I saw a chair sitting on the curb waiting to be picked up by the next sanitation truck. While at first glance it looked like it might truly be ready for the trash heap, with its torn-up seat cushion, I knew right away I wanted it. Still, I couldn't stop to grab it then. I hurried to the library, dropped off my books, and rushed back to the chair. Of course, someone else was checking out the merchandise by the time I got back. I thought I had lost it. Who would pass up such a great find? I waited on the corner sending evil thoughts his way . . . and miraculously, he walked away. *Great, it's mine!* When I was in the middle of inspecting my chair, seeing if the cushion really was beyond repair, another guy walked up to offer his advice. "Eh, you don't want that, it's falling apart," he said. I thanked him for his words of wisdom and continued to poke and prod at the chair. He then walked away, and I noticed him heading back to his double-parked van just down the block. *Nice try, buddy,* I thought. I knew I had to grab it now or kiss it good-bye. I heaved it over my head, managed to lug it the few blocks home—and the rest is history. All I had to do was to fashion a new cover for the cushion, which cost me no more than $30. The chair has now served me well for more than five years.

Each and every listing in this book offers you an opportunity for something more valuable than money: a memory, an experience, a story (and of course, the chance to save a boatload of cash ain't such a bad thing, either).

The listings in this book can be split into two categories: "Free" and "Ridiculously Cheap," with the vast majority of the listings being free. So let's define what I mean by these terms.

Simply stated, *free* is getting something without having to pay any money for it. So, here are some of the things you will *not* find in this book: "Buy One, Get One Free"; "First Month Free"; "Mention the Cheap Bastard and get in for half price"; or any other scheme that is ultimately about getting cash out of your wallet. What kind of free listings *will* you find in this book? Two basic kinds: free-free and free-with-a-catch. *Free-free* is just that: no-strings-attached, give-it-to-me-but-I'm-not-giving-you-anything free. For example, you can get a professional facial for free at Shiseido Studio in Soho, no strings attached. *Free-with-a-catch* generally means you'll need to exchange some time or effort to get that something for free. For example, you can see almost any Off Broadway and some Broadway shows for free by being a volunteer usher. Show up an hour early, help seat the paying folks, and watch the show for nothing. I have tried to clearly lay out any catch you may need to know about by including the category "The Catch" (ingenious, eh?) wherever necessary.

"Ridiculously cheap" listings are those things that, yes, you will have to lay out some money to get. Still, the cost is so minimal that when you're asked to pay, you do it quickly for fear they'll realize their mistake. For example, does $75 a year for a gym membership sound pretty ridiculous to you?

Let me also mention what makes someone a Cheap Bastard. I see *Cheap Bastard* as a proud term referring to someone who enjoys the thrill of the hunt, not someone whose end-all and be-all is not spending money. This isn't someone who will deny himself or anyone else anything simply because it will cost some money. Most importantly, this isn't someone who is looking to cheat another person; nor is it to be confused with *stingy*. A Cheap Bastard is not out to beat another person out of a few cents; he is out to beat the system.

This book is intended for visitors and natives alike. Whether you're a backpacker from Australia who has just shown up in the city at the end of your round-the-world jaunt with less cash than you planned; a born-and-bred New Yorker who needs to stretch that paycheck a little farther; someone who's just moved to the city and working his first (low-paying) job out of college; a college student who needs to figure out how to make that student loan last all year; or even one of those folks for whom money is no worry, but, hey, you just like getting something for nothing (and who doesn't?)— this book is for you.

Finally, all the information in this guide is accurate as of press time, but things change quickly in New York, so I have included as much contact information as possible for each listing. Always call, check the Web site, or stop by to make sure all the information in this book is still accurate. If you have any thoughts, comments, corrections, or suggestions for future volumes, I would love to hear from you. Please send all correspondence to jivner@yahoo.com (you guessed it, that's a free e-mail address).

I've had a ball putting this book together, and I hope it helps you get the most out of the greatest city in the world.

Live well, live free,

Rob Grader
The Cheap Bastard
New York City
www.thecheapbastard.com

ENTERTAINMENT IN NEW YORK

"Of all men, physicians and playwrights alone possess the rare privilege of charging money for the pain they inflict on us."

—Santiago Ramón y Cajal

FROM THE BRIGHT LIGHTS of Broadway to the cutting-edge antics of the downtown performance world, New York is the undisputed capital of the theater world. Any day of the week, there are literally hundreds of performances going on in every corner of the city. And while the top ticket prices for a Broadway show have surpassed $400, you can spend endless evenings in the theaters of New York without spending a cent. By taking on the role of a volunteer usher, you can make your way into some Broadway shows and almost any Off Broadway show absolutely free. You can also keep yourself very busy attending any of the many just-plain-free performances at theaters throughout the city. These run the gamut from full productions to staged readings of new plays and musicals.

VOLUNTEER USHERING

Every time you walk into a theater to see a show, some kind person takes your ticket and shows you to your seat. Often you find that these folks are just thrilled to be doing this job. Ever wonder why? Well, this isn't their regular job; they're just there to see the show, like you. The only difference is, they haven't paid a cent to get in. Yes, they're volunteer ushers, and you'll find them at almost all Off Broadway and some Broadway theaters. Considering the ticket prices of these shows (from $25 to more than $400), volunteer ushers get "paid" very well for basically one hour's work, so why wouldn't they be pretty darn happy? And it's easy to join their ranks.

Each theater has its own protocol, but essentially all that's involved is making a reservation a week or two in advance, then showing up an hour before the curtain rises. The house manager will give you a quick rundown on the seating plan (warning: you do need to be able to count to twelve to understand this; sometimes you even need to count backward), then you help seat the paying folks. During the performance, enjoy the show. Ushers get to watch from seats that remain empty as the show is about to start. There are almost always good seats—many times the best seats in the house—for you to fill, even if the show is officially sold out. On the very rare occasion that there are absolutely no seats available, they will set up chairs for you, or in extremely rare cases, ask you to sit in the aisles. Occasionally you need to stay a couple of minutes after the show to help pick up stray playbills. It's as simple as that.

Dress the Part

While no special skills or training are needed to be a volunteer usher, a nice pair of black pants and a crisp white shirt are often required. Many theaters do ask you to look the role, even though you're only playing the part for one evening. The dress codes vary from black and white (black pants and a white shirt) to all-black; some just ask you to look respectable (don't worry, no ties required). Be sure to ask what to wear when making reservations. Most theaters are flexible in these requirements, but some do take them very seriously and will not let you usher if you aren't dressed properly.

Why do theaters do this? Economics. It's cheaper to let you in for nothing than it is to hire a full-time ushering staff. You can even bring a friend. Most theaters need at least two ushers per show (some as many as ten) and are happy to let you reserve more than one slot. Even some theaters that officially only use one usher per show will let you bring a companion to usher with you if you ask nicely. Talk about your cheap dates!

BROADWAY

THE ROUNDABOUT THEATRE COMPANY
The American Airlines Theater
227 West 42nd Street (between Eighth Avenue and Broadway)
(212) 719-9393, ext. 523 (usher hotline)
www.roundabouttheatre.org
Ushers per performance: 6
After years of hopping from theater to theater, one of New York's most renowned theater companies has found a permanent home on Broadway. And since they remain a not-for-profit theater, this is one of the few opportunities to volunteer-usher on Broadway. They also maintain productions at Studio 54 and the Off Broadway performances at the Laura Pells Theatre (see below for information on these theaters). Their productions often attract star performers and are almost always of a high caliber (particularly the musicals). To book a slot at the American Airlines Theater, go to the box office Monday through Friday between 10:00 A.M. and 5:00 P.M. (but just from 10:00 A.M. to noon on Wednesday) to sign up. They generally make dates available about a month in advance, and once those slots are filled they close the books till the next month. Call their hotline (listed above) to find out when they are accepting ushers. They are very serious about the black-and-white dress code for ushers.

STUDIO 54
254 West 54th Street (between Broadway and Eighth Avenue)
(212) 719-9393, ext. 523 (usher hotline)
www.roundabouttheatre.org
Ushers per performance: 10
The Roundabout Theatre Company has taken ownership of the legendary disco and turned it into its own permanent home for musicals and high-profile plays. After playing host to the longtime Broadway hit *Cabaret,* the Roundabout will now continue to fill this theater with its own brand of high-quality, often star-studded revivals and original musicals for both limited and extended runs. To nab yourself an ushering slot, stop by the theater on

specific Saturdays between 5:00 and 6:00 P.M. to sign up. Be sure to call the usher hotline before you head down there to find out on which Saturdays they will be signing folks up.

ASTOR PLACE THEATRE
434 Lafayette Street (between East 4th and 8th Streets)
(212) 254–4370, ext. 220
www.blueman.com
Ushers per night: 4
Home to the long-running Off Broadway industry Blue Man Group. You've seen them on the Intel commercials, Jay Leno, David Letterman, and every other talk show imaginable, and if you still haven't seen enough of them, come on down to the theater where the whole thing started and see them for free (they don't need any more money). They will also ask you to stay about fifteen minutes after the show is over to clean up. Warning: It's a messy show. To make an ushering reservation, call about a week in advance, Monday through Friday from 9:00 A.M. to 9:00 P.M.

ATLANTIC THEATER COMPANY
336 West 20th Street (between Eighth and Ninth Avenues)
(212) 645–8015
www.atlantictheater.org
Ushers per performance: 2
Founded by followers of the David Mamet school of acting and known for producing his works and others of the same ilk. Productions all have limited runs, and ushering slots fill quickly. They start taking ushering reservations three weeks prior to the start of performances and are usually "sold out" by the time the reviews come out.

CENTURY CENTER THEATRE
111 East 15th Street (between Union Square East and Irving Place)
(212) 982–6782, ext. 11
Ushers per performance: 2
This theater has been home to a number of popular Off Broadway plays, including *The Play about the Baby,* the Pulitzer Prize–winning *How I Learned to Drive,* and *The Complete Works of William Shakespeare (Abridged).* Call the house manager to make an ushering reservation. Call one week to a month in advance for reservations.

THE CHERRY LANE THEATRE

38 Commerce Street (between Bedford and Hudson Streets)
(212) 989–2020
www.cherrylanetheatre.com
Ushers per performance: 3

Since 1924 this theater has been home to many of the early works of such playwrights as Edward Albee, Beckett, Ionesco, Mamet, Pinter, Lanford Wilson, and Sam Shepard. In recent years it has played host to such successful Off Broadway shows as *Fully Committed, Nunsense, True West, Blown Sideways through Life,* and many others. Call a week to a month in advance. Very casual and easygoing atmosphere for ushers.

CLASSIC STAGE COMPANY (CSC)

136 East 13th Street (between Third and Fourth Avenues)
(212) 677–4210, ext. 56
cschousemanager@gmail.com
www.classicstage.org
Ushers per performance: 3

For more than thirty years, CSC has built a reputation for reinventing classic works of the theater—some well-known, others less so. They have attracted a loyal following by working with some of the best-known actors, directors, and writers from New York, Hollywood, and around the country. Call or e-mail for ushering reservations a week to a month in advance of the performance.

DODGER STAGES

340 West 50th Street (between Eighth and Ninth Avenues)
(646) 871–1730
www.dodgerstages.com

From the ashes of the World Wide Cinema (what used to be every cheap bastard's favorite $2.00 movie theater) comes a sparkling new complex of five state-of-the-art Off Broadway theaters. The theaters are owned and operated by The Dodgers, a producing organization that has been responsible for many of Broadway's biggest hits over the last twenty or so years. At this point they are still formulating their volunteer usher policy; they are currently using ushers on an as-needed basis. Stop by the box office or the stage door (on 49th Street) and leave your name, and they will contact you when they have an opening.

DRAMA DEPARTMENT

9 Desbrosses Street (between Hudson and Greenwich Streets)
(212) 633–9108
www.dramadept.org

This high-profile theater collective is the love child of actress Cynthia Nixon *(Sex and the City)* and playwright Douglas Carter Beane *(As Bees in Honey Drown)*. The members of this company are many of the most sought-after artists in film, TV, and the theater, and in turn tickets for their productions can be hard to come by (even if you are willing to pay for them). Fret not, if you are willing to donate an hour or two helping out around their offices, they will happily pay you with free tickets to their shows.

ENCORES
City Center
West 55th Street (between Sixth and Seventh Avenues)
(212) 247–0430, ext. 202
www.citycenter.org
Ushers per performance: 6–9
Presenting series of highly produced staged readings of musicals with star performers, Encores is considered one of the hottest tickets in town. Call far in advance to put your name on a list of volunteers to hawk CDs and other paraphernalia in the lobby to get into the shows.

ENSEMBLE STUDIO THEATRE
549 West 52nd Street (between Tenth and Eleventh Avenues)
(212) 247–4982
www.ensemblestudiotheatre.org
Ushers per performance: 2–3
They use ushers on an as-needed basis. They are always in need of ushers during their Octoberfest and Spring Marathon.

45 BLEECKER THEATER AND GALLERY/THE CULTURE PROJECT
45 Bleecker Street (between Bowery and Lafayette Streets)
(212) 253–9983
ushers@cultureproject.com
www.45bleecker.com
Ushers per performance: 2
Since opening its doors in 1999, 45 Bleecker/The Culture Project has played host to such shows as *Bombity of Errors, And God Created Great Whales,* and the star-studded hit *The Exonerated* in its two performance spaces. E-mail them a week or two in advance with the dates you are available, and they will call you back to make a reservation.

HERE PERFORMANCE ART CAFE

145 Sixth Avenue (between Spring and Domnich Streets)
(212) 647-0202
www.here.org
Ushers per performance: 1-2

Here is a downtown art center bringing together theater, performance art, music, dance, and visual art into one complex. With an ever-changing rotation of productions of all sorts in their three theaters and intriguing work on the walls and floors of their gallery, there is always something worthwhile to see Here. Call the box office manager a couple of days to a week in advance to reserve an ushering slot.

IRISH ARTS CENTER

553 West 51st Street (between Tenth and Eleventh Avenues)
(212) 757-3318, ext. 203
info@irishartscenter.org
www.irishartscenter.org
Ushers per performance: 1-2

Presents a full season of productions by and about the Irish experience, as well as playing host to many imports from Ireland. Call to add your name to the list of volunteer ushers and they will call when they need you.

IRISH REPERTORY THEATRE

132 West 22nd Street (between Sixth and Seventh Avenues)
(212) 255-0270
www.irishrepertorytheatre.com
Ushers per performance: 2

Call 10:00 A.M. to 6:00 P.M. Monday through Friday to schedule a date. This company has built a strong reputation for presenting the works of (believe it or not) Irish and Irish-American writers, both classical and contemporary. They have two theaters, and you may usher in either of them. Call at least two weeks in advance for an ushering reservation, more if you need a specific date.

JANE STREET THEATRE

113 Jane Street (between West and Washington Streets)
(212) 929-0060
Ushers per performance: 2

Call to set up a date, but you may have more luck if you drop by the box office and ask to speak to the house manager. The theater has been the home of such shows as *Hedwig and the Angry Inch, Tick, Tick . . . Boom!,* and *Debbie Does Dallas.*

JEAN COCTEAU REPERTORY (BOUWERIE LANE THEATRE)
330 Bowery (at 2nd Street)
(212) 677–0060, ext. 16
www.jeancocteaurep.org
Ushers per performance: 2

For more than thirty years, their resident acting company has presented a season of classics by the likes of Shakespeare, Shaw, Sophocles, Strindberg, Chekhov, Molière, Wilde, Tennessee Williams, Harold Pinter, and others. Call any time from a couple of days to a couple of months in advance to make an ushering reservation.

THE JOYCE THEATER
175 Eighth Avenue (at 19th Street)
(646) 792–8355
www.joyce.org
Ushers per performance: 8

The leading theater for dance companies, the Joyce plays host to practically every major company from around the country and around the world. They begin taking ushering reservations two weeks before each performance.

THE LAMB'S THEATRE
130 West 44th Street (between Sixth Avenue and Broadway)
(212) 575–0300, ext. 28
www.lambstheatre.org
Ushers per performance: 3

Designed by noted architect Sanford White in 1904 and as the original home to the Lambs, America's oldest theatrical club, this building has played a leading role in the development of the American theater. It was here that Lerner met Lowe *(My Fair Lady, Camelot)*, that Mark Twain wrote his first play, and here that Richard Rodgers set to work on a new musical called *Away We Go* (later renamed *Oklahoma!*). The upstairs residences were once home to the likes of John Wayne, Fred Astaire, and John Philip Sousa. These days, their two Off Broadway theaters have been hosts to such shows as *Smoke on the Mountain, Dames at Sea, Beau Jest,* and *The Countess.* Call for ushering reservations.

THE LAURA PELLS THEATRE
The Roundabout Theatre Company
111 West 46th Street (between Sixth and Seventh Avenues)
(212) 719–9393, ext. 523 (usher hotline)
www.roundabouttheatre.org

Ushers per performance: 6
The Roundabout Theatre Company has closed down shop at the Gramercy Theater and moved its Off Broadway productions into the old American Place Theater. Expect a season chock-full of classics, small-scale musicals, and new plays with cast lists punctuated with star names. Sign up for an ushering slot at the theater on Monday, Tuesday, Thursday, or Friday from 10:00 A.M. to 5:00 P.M.

LUCILLE LORTEL THEATER
121 Christopher Street (between Hudson and Bleecker Streets)
(212) 924–2817, ext. 207
www.lortel.org
Ushers per performance: 3
This venerable Off Broadway theater has been the home of many major productions over its fifty-year history, such as *Cloud 9, Steel Magnolias, Three Penny Opera, As Bees in Honey Drown,* and many others. Call anywhere from a few days to a few weeks in advance to make an ushering reservation, depending on the popularity of the show.

MANHATTAN ENSEMBLE THEATER (MET)
55 Mercer Street (between Broome and Grand Streets)
(212) 925–1900
www.met.com
Ushers per performance: 3
This Soho theater company founded by the former artistic director of Cocteau Rep has quickly established a name for itself with the well-received hits *Hank Williams: Lost Highway, Golda's Balcony,* and *9 Parts of Desire.* Call Monday through Friday between 10:00 A.M. and 6:00 P.M. to make an ushering reservation.

MANHATTAN THEATRE CLUB (MTC)
City Center (theater and box office)
West 55th Street (between Sixth and Seventh Avenues)
311 West 43rd Street, eighth floor (administrative offices)
(212) 247–0430, ext. 240
www.mtc-nyc.org
Ushers per performance: 4 on Stage 1, 1 on Stage 2
MTC is a major producer of new plays, many of which end up transferring to Broadway theaters, including *Proof, The Tale of the Allergist's Wife, Ain't Misbehavin',* and many others over the years. See them before they move, because you can't usher for them once they hit the Great White Way. Call Tuesday through Saturday after 9:30 P.M. anywhere from one to three

weeks in advance once the show is running. If you reach the voice mail, don't bother leaving a message; just keep calling back until you reach an actual human being on the other end to make an ushering reservation. Be persistent.

MCC THEATER
Lucille Lortel Theater
121 Christopher Street (between Hudson and Bleecker Streets)
(212) 924–2817
www.mcctheater.org
Ushers per performance: 3

MCC is a small but popular Off Broadway company that has made a name for itself by producing such plays as the Pulitzer Prize–winning *Wit* and has worked with such actors as Calista Flockhart, Bridget Fonda, Thomas Gibson, Kyra Sedgwick, Marisa Tomei, Allison Janney, and Lili Taylor over its more-than-twenty-year history. Make ushering reservations a week or two before performances begin. Slots fill up quickly.

MINT THEATER COMPANY
311 West 43rd Street, third floor (between Eighth and Ninth Avenues)
(212) 315–0231
www.minttheater.org
Ushers per performance: 1–2

This small, well-respected company concentrates on rediscovering lost classics from the nineteenth and twentieth centuries. Recent productions have included *The Voysey Inheritance, House of Mirth,* and *Mr. Pim Passes By.* Ushering slots do get filled quickly; call Monday through Friday noon to 6:00 P.M. two to three weeks before performances begin to be assured of a reservation.

THE NEW GROUP THEATER
410 West 42nd Street (between Ninth and Tenth Avenues)
(212) 244–3380, ext. 301
www.thenewgroup.org
Ushers per performance: 2

A high-profile company with many productions that have won all the awards and transferred to long runs on Broadway and at major Off Broadway theaters, including *Avenue Q, This Is Our Youth, Ecstasy, Another American Asking and Telling,* and others. Call two weeks in advance for ushering reservations.

NEW YORK THEATRE WORKSHOP (NYTW)
79 East 4th Street (between Second Avenue and Bowery)
(212) 780–9037, ext. 102
www.nytw.org
Ushers per performance: 6

NYTW produces some of the most daring and artistically challenging productions of any Off Broadway theater; it was the original producer of such Broadway hits as *Rent* and *Dirty Blond*. Ushering slots can be reserved anywhere from the day of a performance to three weeks in advance, depending on the popularity of the show. Be sure to get on their ushering mailing list and they will send you reminders for each new show. They also throw in free coffee or tea at the concession stand for ushers.

THE PEARL THEATRE COMPANY
Theatre 80
80 St. Marks Place (between First and Second Avenues)
(212) 598–9802
www.pearltheatre.org
Ushers per performance: 4

One of the few true classical repertory companies remaining in New York. Their seasons concentrate on the works of Shakespeare, Chekhov, Coward, the Greeks, and other Dead European White Men. Their productions are almost never startlingly original, but almost always respectably done. Call one to two weeks in advance for ushering reservations.

PERFORMANCE SPACE 122
150 First Avenue (at East 9th Street)
(212) 477–5829, ext. 304
housemanager@ps122.org
www.ps122.org
Ushers per performance: 2

The longtime home of experimental and cutting-edge theater and dance, P.S. 122 continues to host many well-known and emerging performance artists, including Eric Bogosian, John Leguizamo, and Karen Finley. You never know what you're going to catch there, but it's always daring and innovative. Call or e-mail the week of the performance to book an ushering slot in one of their two theaters.

PLAYHOUSE 91
316 East 91st Street (between First and Second Avenues)
(212) 831–2001

Ushers per performance: 2
The theater was the longtime home of the Jewish Repertory Theater and many other companies and productions over its more-than-thirty-year history. It's now an independent commercial theater and has been home to such productions as *The Syringa Tree, A Bronx Tale,* and others. Stop by the box office from 1:00 to 7:00 P.M. Monday through Friday or call the house manager to reserve an ushering slot. There are usually dates available within two weeks.

PLAYWRIGHTS HORIZONS
416 West 42nd Street (between Ninth and Tenth Avenues)
(212) 564–1235
usher@playwrightshorizons.com
www.playwrightshorizons.org
Ushers per performance: 4
Produces a season of new plays and musicals by well-known and up-and-coming playwrights, many of which transfer to larger Off Broadway or Broadway theaters. Past productions have included *Driving Miss Daisy, The Heidi Chronicles, Once on This Island,* and James Joyce's *The Dead*. They maintain a large list of ushers and send out mailings before each show begins performances. You have to be a real go-getter to get one of these coveted ushering slots. First you need to get on their e-mail list by sending them an e-mail (address above) with the words "Add to list" in the subject line. Then they will send out a mass e-mail telling you (and thousands of others) when they will be accepting reservations. On that day, you had better call first thing in the morning, because they usually fill all of their slots within hours.

RATTLESTICK THEATRE
224 Waverly Place (off Seventh Avenue at 11th Street)
(212) 627–2556
www.rattlestick.org
Ushers per performance: 1
This up-and-coming Off Broadway theater has begun to build a strong name for itself producing contemporary playwrights. Past productions have included *Down South, Whale Music,* and *Killers and Other Family*. Call early in the run to snag an ushering slot. They also offer up a schedule of free play readings; check their Web site for details.

SECOND STAGE THEATRE
307 West 43rd Street (at Eighth Avenue)
(212) 787–8302, ext. 216

jscheifer@secondstagetheatre.com
www.secondstagetheatre.com
Ushers per performance: 6
Hailed in past years by the *New York Times* as "the season's most indispensable theater," Second Stage produces a season chock-full of theater heavyweights like August Wilson, Stephen Sondheim, Edward Albee, and many others. The house manager prefers that requests be e-mailed to him. You should make a reservation a week to a month in advance, depending on the popularity of the show.

THE SIGNATURE THEATRE COMPANY

Peter Norton Space
555 West 42nd Street (between Tenth and Eleventh Avenues)
(212) 244-7529
www.signaturetheatre.org
Ushers per performance: 4
Specializes in highly regarded productions focusing each season on the works of a single American playwright. Past seasons have included Arthur Miller, Edward Albee, Maria Irene Fornes, and Sam Shepard. Call at least two weeks in advance. Free coffee, tea, and hot chocolate for ushers!

SOHO PLAYHOUSE

15 Vandam Street (between Spring and Prince Streets)
(212) 691-1555
Ushers per performance: 1
This theater has been home to such productions as *Killer Joe, Grandma Silvia's Funeral,* and others. Make reservations a few days to a week in advance by calling the box office noon to 7:00 P.M., Tuesday through Saturday.

THEATRE ROW

410 West 42nd Street (between Ninth and Tenth Avenues)
(212) 714-2442
www.theatrerow.org
This newly constructed space is the home of five state-of-the-art Off Broadway theaters—the Acorn, the Beckett, the Clurman, the Kirk, and the Lion. These spaces are used by many of New York's A-list theater companies, many of whom, though not all, use volunteer ushers. To find out if you can volunteer-usher for a particular show, you need to contact the production company for that show. Call the Theatre Row administrative offices (listed above) to get the contact information for the various companies. For best results, you may want to stop by sometime close to showtime and ask about ushering at that specific theater.

Off the Menu

If there's an Off Broadway show that you're interested in seeing and the theater isn't on this list, just ask at the box office if they use volunteer ushers for that show. There are always new venues popping up, and nontraditional performance spaces being used for new shows. Staff are very much used to answering this question. Nine times out of ten, they will say yes and tell you how to go about making a reservation.

UNION SQUARE THEATRE
100 East 17th Street (between Union Square East and Irving Place)
(212) 505–0700
Ushers per performance: 5
A large Off Broadway house that has played host to such shows as *Wit*, *The Laramie Project*, *BatBoy*, and others. Call one to three weeks in advance.

VARIETY ARTS THEATER
110 Third Avenue (between 13th and 14th Streets)
Ushers per performance: As needed
This theater has a regular ushering staff and uses volunteers only on an as-needed basis. To sign up for a date, you need to drop by the theater when the house manager is available. This means near or during a performance. The best time to stop by is about 8:30 or 9:15 P.M. Tuesday through Saturday, and 3:30 or 4:15 P.M. on Saturday and Sunday. Usually hosts high-profile Off Broadway shows such as the Pulitzer Prize–winning *Dinner with Friends*.

THE VINEYARD THEATRE
108 East 15th Street (between Union Square East and Irving Place)
(212) 353–3366, ext. 226 (usher hotline)
housemanager@vineyardtheatre.org
www.vineyardtheatre.org
Ushers per performance: 2
The Vineyard produces and develops new works by many major figures in the American theater. They have brought to life such shows as *Fully Committed*, the Pulitzer Prize–winning *How I Learned to Drive*, and *Three Tall Women*. Make ushering reservations by phone or e-mail one to three weeks in advance.

WOMEN'S PROJECT THEATRE
424 West 55th Street (between Ninth and Tenth Avenues)
Administrative offices: 55 West End Avenue
(212) 765–1706
info@womensproject.org
www.womensproject.org
Ushers per performance: 6

Dedicated to producing and developing the talents of women playwrights, over its more-than-twenty-year history this theater has been among the first to work with such artists as Eve Ensler, Maria Irene Fornes, Anna Deavere Smith, Liz Diamond, Tina Landau, and Joyce Carol Oates, among others. Call the office or e-mail them to get on their ushering list. Two weeks before a performance, you'll receive an e-mail that will tell you how to make reservations for that show. Also look for the free series of readings they hold once a year, usually around November.

THE WOOSTER GROUP
The Performing Garage
33 Wooster Street (between Broome and Grand Streets)
(212) 966–3651
www.thewoostergroup.org
Ushers per performance: 2–6

Founded in the early 1970s by Jim Clayburgh, Willem Dafoe, Spalding Gray, and others, this company remains one of the premier experimental theater groups in the world. Their productions regularly tour internationally, but you can see one for free at the garage where it all started by reserving a slot as a volunteer usher. The ushering slots go fast, so call far in advance to nab one.

YORK THEATRE COMPANY
St. Peter's Church
619 Lexington Avenue (at 54th Street)
(212) 935–5824, ext. 19
www.yorktheatre.org
Ushers per performance: 2

For more than thirty years, York has produced such award-winning musicals as *The Grass Harp, Pacific Overtures, She Loves Me, Company, 110 in the Shade, Sweeney Todd, Carnival,* and *Merrily We Roll Along.* Many of its productions have made the move to Broadway or larger Off Broadway theaters. Call two weeks ahead to make ushering reservations. The theater also presents free staged readings of new musicals on a regular basis. Call or check their Web site for the schedule.

THE ZIPPER THEATER

336 West 37th Street (between Eighth and Ninth Avenues)
(212) 563–0480
www.zippertheater.com
Ushers per performance: 4

This fun and funky theater space located in a converted zipper factory plays host to a variety of no-holds-barred, screw-traditional-theater productions. Call for ushering reservations anywhere from a couple of days to three weeks in advance, depending on the popularity of the show.

CHEAP SEATS

Truth be told, the following listings are not exactly my idea of bargains. I mean, if you have to put out some actual cash for something, what's the point? But the rest of the world thinks these are good deals, so I'd be remiss if I didn't include this information. Here are a few worthy organizations that can get you good seats in loads of Broadway and Off Broadway theaters and concert halls for a minimum of cash.

AUDIENCE EXTRAS (AE)

61 Lexington Avenue, Suite 1A
(212) 686–1966
www.audienceextras.com

THE CATCH $85.00 yearly membership fee, and $30.00 personal reserve fund toward the $3.00 service charge per ticket.

This company's sole purpose is to get living, breathing bodies into the seats of concert halls and theaters around the city. When a production needs a crowd—either because critics will be reviewing the production that night, or because it's early in the run and they want a full house to gauge audience response—producers turn to these guys to "paper the house" (translation: fill the seats). The bulk of the tickets offered are for the big-name and edgier Off Broadway theaters and classical concerts at such places as Lincoln Center. They occasionally also have tickets for Broadway shows, as well as Off Off Broadway. They charge a membership fee, and you are charged a $3.00 service fee per ticket (which is deducted from your "personal reserve fund"); otherwise the tickets are "free."

PLAY BY PLAY

312 West 36th Street (between Seventh and Eighth Avenues)
(212) 868-7052
www.play-by-play.com

 $99.00 yearly membership, and $3.00 service fee per ticket.

Exactly the same service as Audience Extras, with the only difference being that Play by Play sometimes offers tickets to a larger variety of performances and possibly more opportunities for Broadway shows. Just like AE, the bulk of the shows they offer tickets for are Off Broadway and classical concerts, with the occasional Broadway or Off Off Broadway show, but they also regularly offer tickets to stand-up comedy, cabarets, and movie screenings. Once you've paid the yearly membership fee ($99.00), any performance will only cost you $3.00 per ticket.

THEATER EXTRAS

(914) 304-4093 or (212) 802-7277
www.theaterextras.com

 $99.00 annual membership, and $4.00 service charge per ticket.

Also along the same lines as AE and Play by Play, Theater Extras gives you the chance to get great seats for a variety of Broadway, Off Broadway, and Off Off Broadway productions as well as comedy shows, concerts, and the odd magic show. One difference here is Theater Extras also regularly offers tickets to venues in the boroughs, Westchester, and New Jersey. Another big difference is convenience. Theater Extras is a Web-based operation, so you are able to purchase tickets twenty-four hours a day and often a bit more in advance than the other two companies, whose offers vary between day-of-performance tickets and tickets available up to a couple of weeks in advance. The yearly membership will run you $99.00, and there is a $4.00 service charge per "free" ticket reserved.

TKTS BOOTH

Theater Development Fund (TDF)
Duffy Square (47th Street and Broadway)
South Street Seaport; 186 Front Street (at John Street)
(212) 221-0013
www.tdf.org

> **THE CATCH**   Sells tickets for 25 or 50 percent off ticket price plus a $3.00 service charge per ticket.

"We'll get tickets at the booth" has been the cry of many a spontaneous the-atergoer for more than twenty-five years. The TKTS booth sells tickets to Broadway, Off Broadway, music, and dance events the day of the performance at 25 or 50 percent off the ticket price (plus a $3.00 service charge per ticket). They post the available shows outside the booth on boards, which change throughout the day. They accept payments only in cash or traveler's checks. As a rule, you can be sure you won't find tickets available to the newest, hottest show. The lines can be long, particularly on weekends and holidays. The tickets, however, are for some of the best seats in the theaters. Both locations are open seven days a week.

JUST PLAIN FREE THEATER

AMERICAN ACADEMY OF DRAMATIC ARTS
120 Madison Avenue (between 30th and 31st Streets)
(212) 453–5340
www.aada.org

Some of the most legendary stars of stage and screen have trained at this institution, including Lauren Bacall, Spencer Tracy, John Cassavetes, Grace Kelly, Cecil B. DeMille, Danny DeVito, Colleen Dewhurst, Anne Bancroft, Ron Leibman, Jason Robards Jr., Kirk Douglas, and many others. To date academy alumni have received nominations for seventy-two Oscars, fifty-eight Tonys, and 205 Emmys. From September through February the Academy Company—made up of third-year students—presents a season of free productions. Here's a chance to say you saw them when. Click on "Company Plays" on the Web site or call for dates and schedules.

BOOMERANG THEATRE COMPANY
Center Stage/NY
48 West 21st Street, fourth floor (between Fifth and Sixth Avenues)
(212) 501–4069
www.boomerangtheatre.org

This up-and-coming Off Off Broadway company presents a series of readings of new plays. Also be sure to catch their summer season of free Shakespeare in the parks and public spaces around New York City.

52ND STREET PROJECT
Ensemble Studio Theater
549 West 52nd Street (between Tenth and Eleventh Avenues)
(212) 642–5052
www.52project.org

A program through Ensemble Studio Theater that creates short theater pieces by or for the children of Hell's Kitchen in collaboration with professional theater artists. While these may not be Broadway productions, they are surprisingly well put together and offer an evening that is always full of laughter, original music, and a lot of talent (community and professional).

HB PLAYWRIGHTS FOUNDATION
124 Bank Street (between Greenwich and Washington Streets)
(212) 989–7856

Established by acting legends Herbert Berghoff and Uta Hagen in 1965 as an offshoot of their renowned (and low cost!) acting school, the theater presents four productions a year (always free) and has featured many well-established writers, actors, and directors. In recent years the company has given birth to such productions as *Mrs. Klein, Collected Stories,* and others that have moved to larger pay-for-your-ticket venues. The best way to find out about the performances is to call the office during business hours and ask to be added to their mailing list.

JEAN COCTEAU REPERTORY (BOUWERIE LANE THEATRE)
330 Bowery (at 2nd Street)
(212) 677–0060, ext. 16
www.jeancocteaurep.org
Monday evenings at 7:00 P.M.
A series of readings of plays considered "new classics," with symposiums and receptions often following.

THE JUILLIARD SCHOOL
60 Lincoln Center Plaza (Broadway and 65th Street on plaza level)
(212) 769–7406 (Box Office)
(212) 799–5000, ext. 251 (Drama Division)
www.juilliard.edu

You must call to get on the drama division's mailing list to get their calendar of events.

See tomorrow's stars of stage and screen today. This is considered the preeminent conservatory for actors in the country, and they present a full

Standing Room Only

Dying to see that boffo Broadway hit, but you don't have the hundred bucks for the ticket or can't wait the six months until one becomes available? Standing room is what you're looking for. Many, but not all, Broadway theaters sell standing-room tickets. They're available only on the day of the performance and only if the show is completely sold out. It will cost you somewhere between $15 and $25 for the honor of standing to watch the show. The good news is that you'll have a great view: Standing room is directly behind the orchestra seating. And if you get tired, keep your eyes peeled for an empty seat for the second act. Check with the specific box offices for details.

schedule of productions throughout the school year featuring students at every level of development. Often productions are put together by well-known directors—both faculty members and guest artists. All performances in the fall and early spring are free, though tickets are required and go fast. Call to put your name on the drama division's mailing list to get the calendar of free performances. Every spring they remount all of these productions for a Spring Repertory, but they charge for those tickets ($15). To get the free tickets, line up at the box office on the day they become available, usually two weeks before the performances begin; otherwise you'll probably be sold out of the event. You can also line up an hour before the show to try to get in on a standby basis. Performances by the music division are also free, though not those by the dance and opera departments.

NEW DRAMATISTS
424 West 44th Street (between Ninth and Tenth Avenues)
(212) 757–6960
www.newdramatists.org

New Dramatists is an organization devoted to developing playwrights, both up-and-coming and established, along with their material. They conduct an ongoing series of readings and workshops of new plays, musicals, and screenplays staffed with many leading actors and directors from the New York theater scene. Performances take place throughout the week (Monday through Friday) in the late afternoon or evening. All readings are free, and almost all are open to the public. Check the Web site or call for a calendar of events.

THE NEW SCHOOL FOR DRAMA
151 Bank Street (between Washington Street and the West Side Highway)
(212) 229–5859
www.newschool.edu/academic/drama

From the end of January through May, The New School For Drama presents The One Act Festival, with graduating MFA (Masters of Fine Arts) students performing in original one acts written by students in the playwrighting program. All performances are free, but reservations are required.

NEW YORK SHAKESPEARE FESTIVAL/
THE PUBLIC THEATER
425 Lafayette Street (at Astor Place)
(212) 260–2400
www.publictheater.org

From the people who bring you Shakespeare in Central Park every summer come other free theater events throughout the year. Every spring and fall they hold a two-week festival of readings and workshops called New Work Now!; many of the pieces presented here have later ended up on their main stage, including the plays *Stop Kiss, References to Salvador Dali Make Me Hot, Topdog/Underdog,* and others. Click on "Free Events" at their Web site for more details and for other goings-on that pop up throughout the year.

NEW YORK UNIVERSITY GRADUATE ACTING
PROGRAM
721 Broadway (between Waverly and Washington Streets)
111 Second Avenue (between 6th and 7th Streets)
(212) 998–1921
www.gradacting.tisch.nyu.edu

Only second-year productions are free.

One of the most respected graduate acting programs in the country has a distinguished alumnus list that boasts the likes of Billy Crudup, Camryn Manheim, Marcia Gay Harden, Barry Bostwick, Tony Kushner, and many others. See full productions of classics and contemporary plays mounted by the second-year students (they charge for the third-year student productions). Tickets are available one week before performances begin and sell out very quickly for these intimate performance spaces. Check the Web site or call for schedule and details.

RATTLESTICK THEATRE COMPANY
224 Waverly Place (off Seventh Avenue at 11th Street)
(212) 627–2556
www.rattlestick.org

Rattlestick annually offers a three-week festival of readings of new plays and works in progress. Call or check their Web site for schedule and details. Two free readings every Tuesday as part of their Exposure Festival—at 3:00 and 8:00 P.M.

WOMEN'S PROJECT THEATRE
424 West 55th Street (between Ninth and Tenth Avenues)
(212) 765–1706
www.womenswork.org

Every fall they present a two-week festival of "Women's Work," new works by some of the leading women playwrights in the nation. Call or check their Web site for schedule and details. "First Looks" is a free reading series most Mondays at 4:00 P.M.

YORK THEATRE COMPANY
St. Peter's Church
619 Lexington Avenue (at 54th Street)
(212) 935–5824, ext. 19
www.yorktheatre.org

Presents a varied schedule of free staged readings of new musicals at various times throughout the week. Call or check their Web site for schedule and details. Presents free staged readings on new musicals most Monday nights at 7:30 P.M.

FREE WILL(IAM): FREE THEATER IN THE PARKS

SHAKESPEARE IN CENTRAL PARK
New York Shakespeare Festival/The Public Theater
Delacorte Theater
Turtle Pond (midpark at West 81st or East 79th Street)
(212) 539–8750
www.publictheater.org

The granddaddy of all Shakespeare in the Park festivals, now in its sixth decade of free performances in Central Park. They present star-studded productions each summer (at least one of which is always a Shakespeare play). They start handing out the free tickets at 1:00 P.M. each day at the Delacorte in Central Park and from 1:00 to 3:00 P.M. at the Public Theater (425 Lafayette Street between East 4th Street and Astor Place). In recent years they have also started handing out tickets in various locations throughout the five boroughs; call for details. These tickets are always in demand, so plan to spend a while on line. But don't let that deter you: This event attracts a great cross section of people, and waiting on line is often as much fun, if not more, than the show itself. If you don't have the time to wait, take a chance and stop by the Delacorte box office at 7:30 P.M., when they release many reserved tickets.

Here are some other companies that bring the Bard and other works to a neighborhood near you. All the performances are free, but some of these companies are not shy about passing the hat at the end of the night. Call or check their Web sites for shows, times, and specific locations:

BLUNT THEATER COMPANY, La Plaza Cultural Community Garden, 9th Street and Avenue C; (646) 479–8140; www.blunttheater.org.

BOOMERANG THEATRE COMPANY, Prospect Park and other parks; (212) 501–4069; www.boomerangtheatre.org.

CIRCUS AMOK, politically minded circus performances in public parks throughout the five boroughs every June; (718) 486–7432; www.circus amok.org.

CYPRECO THEATER GROUP, classical Greek theater in various parks and libraries throughout the five boroughs; (718) 626–7896.

HUDSON WAREHOUSE, Riverside Park; (212) 560–6579.

INWOOD SHAKESPEARE FESTIVAL, Inwood Hill Park and other parks; (917) 918–0394, www.moosehallisf.org.

KINGS COUNTY SHAKESPEARE COMPANY, various Brooklyn parks; (718) 398–0546; www.kingscountyshakespeare.org.

LITE THEATRE COMPANY, Prospect Park; (212) 414–7773; www.thelite co.org.

NEW YORK CLASSICAL THEATRE, West 103rd Street and Central Park West; (212) 252–4531; www.newyorkclassical.org.

PLAY OUTSIDE, a festival of free outdoor performances throughout the five boroughs by many different companies and performers; www.play outside.org.

SHAKESPEARE IN THE PARK(ING LOT), Ludlow Street (between Delancey and Broome Streets); www.ludlowten.org.

THEATER FOR THE NEW CITY, parks throughout the five boroughs; (212) 254–1109; www.theaterforthenewcity.net.

THEATREWORKS/USA, call for theater location; (212) 627–7373; www. theatreworksusa.org.

"I'll open my case, and I might catch a coin, but all ears may listen for free."

—Steve Forbert
"Grand Central Station,
March 18, 1977"

NEW YORK IS AWASH in free music, from almost any street corner or subway platform to clubs, bars, churches, parks, and concert halls. Any season, any day of the year, you can find the strains of any style of music: classical, rock, jazz, country, folk, experimental, world, ethnic... if you can hum it, you can find it somewhere in New York for free. Particularly during the summer months, you can hardly turn around without being enticed into another amazing free performance at one of the many free concert series all over the city. This being New York, these venues attract top-name artists whom you'd usually have to pay top dollar to see. And I'm not talking about one great show a summer; this goes on week after week, all summer long. One thing to be aware of when attending free shows at many bars and clubs is they do often have a one-, two-, or more-drink minimum, which could add up to a tidy sum. Check out the prices before you order, too; sometimes even a Coke could cost as much as $5.00.

ROCK, POP, FOLK, AND ALTERNATIVE

THE BACK FENCE
155 Bleecker Street (at Thompson Street)
(212) 475-9221
www.thebackfenceonline.com

 They charge admission on Saturday night only.

Straw on the floor, peanuts at the bar, and free classic rock, country, and folk rock six nights a week.

THE BAGGOT INN
82 West 3rd Street (between Thompson and Sullivan Streets)
(212) 477-0622
www.thebaggotinn.com

 No cover or minimum for shows Sunday through Wednesday nights only.

During the week you will find nights of bluegrass jams, acoustic open mike, blues, country, and rock.

THE C-NOTE
157 Avenue C (at 10th Street)
(212) 677-8142
www.thecnote.com

 ONE-DRINK MINIMUM PER ACT signs are posted but not enforced.

This slim bar is all about the music, and the music is all over the place. On any given night you can hear five to seven acts playing any combination of acoustic, rock, folk, jump, jazz, fusion, funk, or Latin. On rare occasions they do charge a cover, but primarily it's free music seven nights a week.

DEMPSEY'S PUB
61 Second Avenue (between 3rd and 4th Streets)
(212) 388-0662
www.thebaggotinn.com/dempseys.html
Grab your penny whistle and uilleann pipes and come on down to Dempsey's

every Tuesday for a traditional Irish music *seisun* (jam session) at 8:00 P.M. Musicians and listeners welcome.

HANK'S SALOON
46 Third Avenue (at Atlantic Avenue)
Brooklyn
(718) 625–8003
www.myspace.com/hankssaloon

Free live country/rock/rockabilly music Tuesday through Sunday nights at this Brooklyn dive. Sunday night, don't miss the free barbecue. No cover, no minimum.

LAKESIDE LOUNGE
162 Avenue B (between 10th and 11th Streets)
(212) 529–8463
www.lakesidelounge.com

A honky-tonk bar with a band in the back room late nights. It's free, but sometimes you get what you pay for. They book some good rock bands who try their damnedest to play above the roar of the crowd. No cover, no minimum.

THE LIVING ROOM
154 Ludlow Street (between Stanton and Rivington Streets)
(212) 533–7235
www.livingroomny.com

 One-drink minimum per act, loosely enforced.

Intimate, welcoming storefront bar/lounge. While it's a bit sparsely furnished for a "Living Room" (only one cozy chair and a lot of plain old restaurant tables and chairs), you'll find that the spirit of the spot lives up to the name. They book an eclectic lineup of acoustic and indie music types and attract a fun and attentive audience. This is a great place to hear music. They never charge a cover.

PADDY REILLY'S MUSIC BAR
519 Second Avenue (at 29th Street)
(212) 686–1210

 Free shows/no minimum Sunday through Thursday nights (except some Tuesdays).

The definitive home of Irish music in New York. You'll find everything from

Irish rock to traditional Irish music *seisun* on the schedule. Musicians are always welcome to join in on the *seisun*.

PARKSIDE LOUNGE

317 East Houston Street (at Attorney Street)
(212) 673–6270
www.parksidelounge.com

 Two-drink minimum that they do try to enforce—but "we're not gonna trow ya out if ya don't drink."

A local bar complete with pool table, pinball games, and a hip jukebox, along with a snazzy back room with live shows every night. You'll find a lot of local rock/alternative/blues bands most nights. They also have a comedy night every Tuesday and a very popular salsa night every Friday; bring your own instrument and join in. Shows are almost always free (except for the two-drink minimum).

POSTCRYPT COFFEEHOUSE

Columbia University
Basement of St. Paul's Chapel
116th Street and Broadway
(212) 854–1953
www.columbia.edu/cu/postcrypt/coffeehouse

This is one of the great hidden treasures of New York City. Since 1964 every Friday and Saturday night during the school year, this small performance space (only about twenty-five seats) has been filled with the sounds of some of the top names in folk and acoustic music. Past performers have included David Bromberg, Jeff Buckley, Shawn Colvin, Ani DiFranco, John Gorka, Patty Larkin, Lisa Loeb, Ellis Paul, Martin Sexton, Tony Trischka, Suzanne Vega, Jerry Jeff Walker, and Dar Williams. No place in the city presents this music in a more pure form. Here acoustic means *acoustic*—no mikes, no nothing. Always brings in a crowd that is serious about hearing the music. They also serve cheap beer and brownies, but best of all, the popcorn is always free.

THE RED LION

151 Bleecker Street (between Thompson Street and Laguardia Place)
(212) 260–9797
www.redlion-nyc.com

 Free shows Sunday through Thursday nights.

A full schedule of rock bands attracts a very young crowd.

JAZZ AND BLUES

ARTHUR'S TAVERN
57 Grove Street (off Seventh Avenue South)
(212) 675–6879
www.arthurstavernnyc.com

 Two-drink minimum per act loosely enforced.

Since 1937 Arthur's Tavern has been serving up a variety of music for every taste: straight-ahead jazz, New Orleans–style jazz, real Chicago blues. On Monday nights for more than thirty-five years, it's been home to the same Dixieland jazz band. Stop by any time of night; there's always something going on. Never a cover.

DETOUR
349 East 13th Street (between First and Second Avenues)
(212) 533–6212
www.jazzatdetour.com

 Two-drink minimum per set.

Seven nights a week the jazz flows freely from the stage of this intimate and cozy East Village bar. You'll hear everything from sweet soul jazz to postbop from a talented crew of local musicians. The music starts at 9:00 P.M. during the week and 9:30 on the weekend.

55 BAR
55 Christopher Street (between Seventh Avenue South and 8th Street)
(212) 929–9883
www.55bar.com

 Early shows on Friday and Saturday nights are always free.

Since 1919 this Prohibition-era dive has been presenting top-of-the-line jazz, funk, and blues. Stop in for the early show any Friday or Saturday night (6:00 to 9:00 P.M.) for a hot set of music with no cover, no minimum, and no attitude. They charge $3.00 to $5.00 for their other performances, but there is always free popcorn.

GROOVE
125 MacDougal Street (at West 3rd Street)
(212) 254–9393
www.clubgroovenyc.com
Live rhythm and blues, funk, and hip-hop. Free admission every night.

PARLOR ENTERTAINMENT
555 Edgecombe Avenue, Studio 3F (between 159th and
160th Streets)
(212) 781–6595
www.parlorentertainment.com

Occasionally you come across one of those events that you feel privileged to
have been a part of. Well, that's exactly what goes on every weekend at Ms.
Marjorie Eliot's North Harlem apartment. Marjorie graciously welcomes you
into her living room, hallway, kitchen, and anyplace else you can find some
space to listen to some of the purest, sweetest, swingin'est jazz you will
hear anywhere and for any price. And here, of course, there isn't any price.
The music begins at 4:00 P.M. with an informal jam session on Saturday and
a polished performance on Sunday. Every week Ms. Eliot brings together an
ensemble of guest musicians and fifty or more of her closest friends for an
afternoon of joyful music. And anyone who attends quickly becomes one of
those dear friends. The atmosphere is so warm and comfortable, and the
music played so intimately, you'll think you're sitting in a friend's house listening to some of your favorite tunes. Which, in fact, you are.

ST. NICK'S PUB
773 Saint Nicholas Avenue (corner of 149th Street)
(212) 283–9728

THE CATCH A posted three-drink minimum, but it is basically never
enforced.

This nondescript Harlem pub is the home of the city's hottest jam session
every Monday night starting at 9:30 P.M. But the swinging doesn't end on
Monday; every night of the week some of the best players around take to the
stage, including many top-name surprise guest appearances by the likes of
Wynton Marsalis, Savioun Glover, Olu Dara, James Carter, and others. There is
a sign on the tables saying they charge a cover and a three-drink minimum,
but they basically never enforce it.

Underground Music

For years the platforms of the New York City subway system have been the place to hear a varied, eclectic mix of music from all parts of the world played by some of the most talented (and sometimes not-so-talented) musicians around, all playing their hearts out for a handout. And for just as long, the police and MTA wished these folks would stop clogging up the subway's platforms and tunnels. They tried everything from ticketing to arresting offenders to get rid of them. It didn't work. The musicians stayed, and the quarters kept being tossed.

Finally, though, someone smart at the MTA convinced the city to give in to the old adage "If you can't beat 'em, join 'em" and organized the MTA Arts for Transit Music Under New York (MUNY) program. So now you'll find jazz bands, folksingers, didgeridoo players, steel drummers, tap dancers, break-dancers, blues singers, salsa, and, of course, the ever-present Ecuadorian pan flute bands playing throughout the MTA system. MUNY holds auditions every spring at Vanderbilt Hall in Grand Central Station (open to the public) and has twenty-three locations where there are more than 150 performances every week. Some of the most popular sites are Grand Central Terminal, Penn Station, Times Square Station, 42nd Street (Sixth and Eighth Avenue stations), Grand Central Shuttle, Columbus Circle Station, Union Square, and Astor Place. Performances take place throughout the day and into the late night. For more information, check out www.mta.info/mta/aft or call (212) 878–7452.

Of course, you'll still find plenty of other musicians littered throughout the system. My personal favorite is singer-songwriter Kathleen Mock (www.mockmusic.com), whose haunting melodies and beautifully resonant voice ring out in stations around the Upper West Side and Williamsburg and Park Slope in Brooklyn. When you're waiting for that late-night train to finally arrive, you'll be glad these folks are there to help you through the long wait.

CLASSICAL MUSIC

BROOKLYN HEIGHTS MUSIC SOCIETY
Zion Lutheran Church (Open Rehearsals)
125 Henry Street (between Clark and Pierrepont Streets)
St. Ann's Church (Performances)
157 Montague Street (between Henry and Clinton Streets)
info@brooklynsymphonyorchestra.org
www.brooklynheightsorchestra.org

This well-respected community orchestra is made up of a mix of amateur, student, retired, semiprofessional, and professional musicians. They present an array of symphony, orchestral, and chamber concerts in libraries, churches, and temples around Brooklyn, as well as a full concert series at St. Ann's Church in Brooklyn Heights. You are also welcome to bring your own bassoon, tuba, or triangle and join in on their open rehearsals every Monday evening at Zion Lutheran Church. Check their Web site for the schedule or e-mail them for more information. Performances and rehearsals are always free, but they will be happy to accept your donation.

BROOKLYN QUEENS CONSERVATORY OF MUSIC
58 Seventh Avenue (at Lincoln Place)
Park Slope, Brooklyn
(718) 622-3300
42-76 Main Street (at Blossom Avenue)
Flushing, Queens
(718) 461-8910
www.bqcm.org

The conservatory is one of the country's oldest community music schools. They offer a full schedule of free concerts that run the gamut from children's recitals to professional-level classical and jazz performances. Sometimes there's a charge for guest performers and the larger concerts, but most shows are free.

CARNEGIE HALL NEIGHBORHOOD CONCERT SERIES
Locations throughout the five boroughs
(212) 903-9670
www.carnegiehall.org

For more than twenty-five years, the distinguished hall has presented more than eighty concerts a year (September through April) in neighborhoods throughout the five boroughs in libraries, churches, and community centers. The series presents a mix of classical, jazz, pop, and folk music; all shows are

How Do You Get to Carnegie Hall?

Forget about practicing—just join Norman Seaman's Concert/Theater Club and he can get you there (and into Lincoln Center, Merkin Hall, and others) for hundreds of concerts a year for free. The Concert/ Theater Club is a mom-and-pop organization that has been filling seats at major concert halls and theaters all around the city for more than fifty years. Primarily offering the best seats in the house to classical performances, the club also offers its members the chance to attend the occasional Broadway production, Off Broadway play, and film screenings. One-year memberships to the club will run you $29.95 for single tickets to all events, $39.95 for two tickets to all events, or $49.95 for four tickets to all events. For more information, call (212) 330–7932 (daily-offering hotline) or (845) 279–8296. To join, send a check to Norman Seaman's Concert/Theater Club, 322 West 52nd Street, Suite 693, New York, NY 10101.

free and open to all. For schedule and location information, call or click on the "Education" menu at their Web site.

DONNELL LIBRARY CENTER
20 West 53rd Street (between Fifth and Sixth Avenues)
(212) 621–0618
www.nypl.org
This library presents an extensive calendar of musical performances throughout the week, including classical, jazz, show tunes, opera, and more. All performances are free.

THE INTERCHURCH CENTER
475 Riverside Drive (between 119th and 120th Streets)
(212) 870–2200
www.interchurch-center.org
This interdenominational center for all faiths offers free concerts every Wednesday at 12:05 P.M., September through May. Performances last about thirty minutes; the programs range from string quartets to woodwind ensembles, traditional African folk music to Celtic songs and dances, medieval to jazz, vocal soloist to choir, piano to organ, emerging artists to established professionals.

THE JUILLIARD SCHOOL
60 Lincoln Center Plaza (Broadway and 65th Street on the plaza level)
(212) 769-7406
www.juilliard.edu

 Free tickets go quickly.

See the leading artists of tomorrow, today. This is the preeminent conser-vatory for classical musicians in the country, and they present a huge array of classical, chamber music, and jazz concerts by students and faculty throughout the year. Most of the performances are free, though some require tickets. To get tickets for these events, stop by the box office on the day they become available; otherwise you may be sold out of the event. You can also line up an hour before the show to try to get in on a standby basis. Venues are throughout Lincoln Center and the Juilliard School and scheduled in the afternoon and evening all week long. Check the Web site or pick up a copy of the performance schedule at the box office. Perform-ances by the drama division are also free, though not those by the dance and opera departments.

MANHATTAN SCHOOL OF MUSIC
120 Claremont Avenue (between 121st Street and Seminary Row)
(212) 749-2802, ext. 4528
www.msmnyc.edu
A full schedule of free classical and jazz concerts by students, faculty, and vis-iting artists, and master classes.

MANNES COLLEGE OF MUSIC
150 West 85th Street (between Columbus and Amsterdam Avenues)
(212) 496-8524
www.mannes.edu
A full schedule of free orchestral, chamber-music, and jazz concerts through-out the school year.

NYU DEPARTMENT OF MUSIC AND PERFORMING ARTS PROFESSIONS
35 West 4th Street, Suite 777 (at Greene Street)
(212) 998-5424
www.nyu.edu/education/music
Students and faculty present a full schedule of classical, chamber, jazz, and musical theater concerts along with their calendar of talks and workshops, all free and open to the public.

TEMPLE EMANU-EL
10 East 66th Street (between Fifth and Madison Avenues)
(212) 744–1400
www.emanuelnyc.org

This largest house of Jewish worship in the world offers eight to ten free classical concerts from October through May. The performances include a young artists series, chamber orchestras, and opera. Call to get on their mailing list.

TRINITY CHURCH
74 Trinity Place (Broadway at Wall Street)
(212) 602–0747
www.trinitywallstreet.org

THE CATCH $2.00 suggested contribution, but nothing required.

The Concerts at One series offers classical, jazz, and popular music performances every Thursday afternoon. You can also catch lunchtime performances at their sister church nearby, St. Paul's Chapel (Broadway and Fulton Street) every Monday at 1:00 P.M. Both of these national landmarks are steeped in American history and worth a look anytime.

OUTDOOR SUMMER CONCERTS

During the summer months New York is the Mecca, Medina, Jerusalem, and Emerald City of free music. Almost any open green space transforms into a concert hall for an amazing array of established stars and cutting-edge performers of practically every genre of music. Many of these venues have become quite popular over the years—which means you should be sure to show up early to claim your space on the lawn or in the stands.

BAM RHYTHM & BLUES FESTIVAL
Metrotech Center (between Flatbush Avenue, Jay, Johnson and Willoughby Streets)
Downtown Brooklyn
(718) 636–4100
www.bam.org
Thursday at noon, June through August.

Brown-bag it over to Brooklyn for this hot festival of legendary stars. Don't be misled by the name of the festival: In the past the festival has lined up a varied roster of top-name performers such as Dr. John, the Robert Cray Band, Los Lobos, Steel Pulse, Burning Spear, and others.

BRYANT PARK
Sixth Avenue between 41st and 42nd Streets
(212) 768–4242
www.bryantpark.org

Known mostly for the hugely popular film series on Monday nights, the park also hosts a great deal of concerts and performances throughout the summer. You will find the likes of the B52s, Carly Simon, the Beach Boys, and other big-name groups performing in the park for the TV show *Good Morning America*. Also, classical, jazz, and Broadway performances in the afternoon and evening. Check the Web site for the extensive schedule.

CELEBRATE BROOKLYN
Prospect Park Bandshell (Prospect Park West and 9th Street)
Park Slope, Brooklyn
(718) 855–7882, ext. 45
www.celebratebrooklyn.org
June through August.

Brooklyn's popular free series presents a star-studded schedule of everything from free films to spoken word and dance performances, rock, jazz, Latin, folk, and world music.

CENTRAL PARK SUMMERSTAGE
Rumsey Playfield
72nd Street, midpark
(212) 360–2777
www.summerstage.org
June through August.

If New York is the Promised Land of free concerts during the summer, this is the Wailing Wall. The schedule runs the entire length of the summer, with performances almost every night of the week and a wildly varied schedule that runs the gamut from opera to hip-hop, from world to teeny-bopper pop. You're likely to find names you're familiar with—like Joan Jett, Randy Newman, David Byrne, or the Indigo Girls—and just as likely to be wowed by performers whose names you never would have come across if not for SummerStage's daring programming. There are also evenings devoted to spoken word and dance. Seating is on a first-come, first-served basis; for some of the more popular shows, the line starts hours before the gates open.

CHELSEA PIERS
Pier 62, Hudson River and 23rd Street
(212) 336–6881
www.chelseapiers.com
Saturday and Sunday, noon–4:00 P.M., June through September.
Every Saturday and Sunday afternoon you will find the free music flowing at
the usually pricey Chelsea Piers. Two different bands are on hand each day to
entertain you with a variety of styles that could be Latin, jazz, Dixieland,
bluegrass or rock. No big names here, just some fun free tunes.

COOL MUSIC FOR WARM SUMMER DAYS
1 Battery Park Plaza (between Pearl and Bridge Streets);
Wednesday at 12:30 P.M.

345 Park Avenue (between 51st and 52nd Streets);
Thursday at 12:30 P.M.

(212) 407–2429
www.rudin.com
Local musicians of every sort (Dixieland, folk, rock, classical, and more)
entertain the lunchtime crowd every Wednesday (downtown) and Thursday
(uptown).

EL MUSEO DEL BARRIO
1230 Fifth Avenue (at 104th Street)
(212) 831–7272
www.elmuseo.org
Thursday at 6:00 P.M., June through August.
Every Thursday evening the museum turns on the heat (and the volume!) with
an exhilarating Latin concert series. Spotlighting both local favorites and international stars performing in a surprising variety of styles within the Latin music
world, including hip-hop, Cuban surf, rock, reggae, bachata, and of course
salsa.

FREE CONCERTS IN PARKS
Neighborhood parks throughout Brooklyn, the Bronx, and Manhattan
(212) 360–8290
www.cityparksfoundation.org
July and August.
The name says it all. The free concerts (in parks) are a mix of well-known
oldies rock and roll, rhythm and blues, funk, and Latin groups. Call or check
the Web site for locations and schedule.

HARLEM MEER PERFORMANCE FESTIVAL
Charles A. Dana Discovery Center
Central Park (110th Street and Central Park North)
(212) 860–1370
www.centralparknyc.org
Sunday at 4:00 P.M., June through August.
Upper Central Park makes a beautiful backdrop for this free concert series showcasing established and emerging jazz, Latin, dance, and gospel artists.

HARLEM WEEK/HARLEM JAZZ AND MUSIC FESTIVAL
Throughout Harlem and Manhattan
(212) 862–8477
www.harlemdiscover.com
August.
What started out as a one-day event has grown into a monthlong celebration of African-American life in America. The festival offers many concerts throughout the month in different locations around Harlem and Manhattan, as well as films, lectures, sporting events, street fairs, and more. Most events are free. Check the Web site for this year's schedule.

JAZZMOBILE
154 West 127th Street (between Lenox and Seventh Avenues)
(212) 866–4900 or (212) 866–3616 (concert hotline)
www.jazzmobile.org
Various locations around the five boroughs.
Since 1964, Jazzmobile has been bringing the music to the people by presenting a lineup of world-class musicians in parks, libraries, schools, and street corners all around New York and the surrounding areas. They also offer free Saturday workshops and master classes for students ages seven and up at PS 197 in Harlem, with such artists as Max Roach, Branford Marsalis, and Donald Byrd. Check the Web site for details.

MARTIN LUTHER KING JR. CONCERT SERIES
Wingate Field (across the street from Kings County Hospital)
Winthrop Street (between Brooklyn and Kingston Avenues)
(718) 469–1912
www.brooklynconcerts.com
Monday, July and August.
Stars of gospel, soul, funk, and jazz perform. Performers have included Mighty Clouds of Joy, Teena Marie, Stephanie Mills, the O'Jays, Chaka Khan, Hezekiah Walker, and the Gap Band.

The Best of the Fests

During the summer months the entirety of downtown Manhattan can be summed up by three words and one punctuation mark: It's a festival! From the Hudson River, around Battery Park, up to the South Street Seaport, and everywhere in between, there are literally hundreds and hundreds of free concerts, performances, and events scheduled from June to September as a part of these downtown fests. While many of the specific venues and concert series are listed in this chapter, the scope of these festivals is ever expanding. You owe it to yourself and your ever-contracting entertainment budget to check out their Web sites or nab a copy of their festival guides.

DOWNTOWN NYC RIVER TO RIVER FESTIVAL, *www.rivertorivernyc.org*
HUDSON RIVER FESTIVAL, *www.hudsonriverfestival.com*
SEAPORT MUSIC FESTIVAL, *www.seaportmusicfestival.com*

MET IN THE PARKS
Parks throughout the five boroughs
(212) 362–6000
www.metopera.org
June.
For three weeks in June, the world-renowned Metropolitan Opera Company sheds the pomp and pretense of the opera hall and presents concert performances to the masses in Central Park and other parks throughout the five boroughs. Check the Web site for schedule and locations.

MUSIC AT CASTLE CLINTON
Battery Park
(212) 835–2789
www.downtownny.com
July 4 and Thursday evenings in July and early August.
The season opens with a large open-air concert in Battery Park on the Fourth of July weekend, drawing thousands of listeners; then the shows move into the smaller space at Castle Clinton. Tickets are required (free, but limited) for the Castle Clinton shows and given out on a first-come, first-served basis at 5:00 P.M. on the day of the show. Past performers have included Crash Test Dummies, Taj Mahal, Mark Cohen, Billy Bragg, Emmylou Harris, Shawn Colvin, and Junior Brown.

NAUMBURG ORCHESTRAL CONCERTS

Naumburg Bandshell, Central Park (midpark at 72nd Street)
info@naumburgconcerts.org
www.naumburgconcerts.org
Tuesday evenings, late June to August.
This may not be the biggest or most well known outdoor concert series, but having presented free concerts in Central Park since 1905, it is the oldest continuous series of such concerts anywhere in the country. The series regularly includes performances by the New York Chamber Symphony, Empire Brass, and others. Check their Web site for a schedule of concerts.

NEW YORK PHILHARMONIC

Concerts in the Parks
(212) 875–5709
www.newyorkphilharmonic.org
July.
For more than thirty-five years, the Philharmonic has brought millions of people into the parks for what they call "Priceless Music Absolutely Free." With guest musicians and conductors, they present two programs of classical and popular music in city parks throughout the five boroughs and always cap the evening off with a spectacular fireworks display.

RIVER & BLUES

Battery Park City Parks
Robert F. Wagner Jr. Park (at Battery Place)
(212) 267–9700
www.bpcparks.org
Thursday evenings, July and August.
Bring a picnic dinner and enjoy the spectacular sunset views of the lower Hudson while you enjoy these jazz, blues, funk, and fusion performances. Past performers have included Hiram Bullock, Glen Velez, and Howard Fishman.

SEASIDE SUMMER CONCERT SERIES

Asser Levy Park (Sea Breeze and Ocean Avenues)
Brighton Beach, Brooklyn
(718) 469–1912
www.brooklynconcerts.com
Thursday evenings, July and August.
Travel out to the heart of Brooklyn and travel back in time to this series that features many of the biggest names in music and comedy from the 1950s, 1960s, 1970s, and 1980s (golden oldies, disco, rock, and stand-up comedy).

In past years they have featured appearances by Gladys Knight, Liza Minnelli, Michael Bolton, Jay Black and the Americans, Todd Rundgren, Pat Benatar, Kenny Rogers, the Temptations, David Brenner, the Village People, and others.

SOUTH STREET SEAPORT
Pier 17 (at Fulton and South Streets)
(212) SEAPORT (732–7678)
www.southstreetseaport.com
Tuesday through Sunday at noon and 5:30 P.M., May through September.
Starting with a huge Cinco de Mayo Festival and running throughout the spring and summer, the South Street Seaport presents lunchtime and after-work concerts in every style of music, from country, folk, and rock to gospel, jazz, and Latin. The performers often include well-known acts as well as up-and-coming artists. Many summer weekends are also filled with full-day music, sports, and other festivals. Any day you can count on running across your fair share of jugglers, mimes, magicians, and other buskers to keep you entertained. Monday is the only day they don't schedule any official programs. Call or check the Web site for up-to-date information.

SUMMER IN THE SQUARE
Union Square (14th to 17th Streets between Park Avenue and University Place)
(212) 460–1208
www.unionsquarenyc.org
Wednesday at 12:30 P.M., June through August.
Stop by the park for a midday, midweek jolt of music. Every week brings something completely different, including jazz, classical, blues, Brazilian, theater, and more. Make a day of it with storytelling at 5:00 P.M. and dance performances at 6:00 P.M.

MUGGER: "Don't make a move. This is a stick-up. Your money or your life! . . . Look, bud, I said your money or your life!"

JACK BENNY: "I'm thinking it over."

FILM: CHEAP SHOTS

NOW THAT WORLD WIDE CINEMAS is a distant memory (what most cheap New Yorkers used to lovingly refer to as "the $3.00 theater") and prices are more than $10.00 a ticket, there has never been a greater need to find places to see movies without spending the moolah. If you've ever been among the throngs of people camped out at Bryant Park on a summer Monday evening, you know what I mean. Well, Bryant Park is only the beginning of the cheap cinema offerings throughout the city. From outdoor screenings under the stars during the summer to bars, libraries, and even theaters throughout the year, here is your list of where to get your fix of free flicks.

FREE MOVIES BY THE WEEK
(YEAR-ROUND)

TIME	MONDAY	TUESDAY	WEDNESDAY	THURSDAY	FRIDAY	SATURDAY	SUNDAY
MULTIPLE SCREENINGS: Call for schedule		French Institute (with membership)					
1:30 P.M.	Brighton Beach Library	Saratoga					
2:00 P.M.			St. Agnes Library		58th Street Library	Van Nest Library / Sony Wonder (twice a month)	
2:15 P.M.							
2:30 P.M.			Donnell Library				
2:45 P.M.							
3:00 P.M.					Yorkville Library (twice a month)		
3:15 P.M.							
3:30 P.M.							
3:45 P.M.							
4:00 P.M.					MoMA (after 4:00 P.M.)		
4:15 P.M.							
4:30 P.M.							
4:45 P.M.							
5:00 P.M.				Chatham Square Library (third Thursday)			
5:15 P.M.							
5:30 P.M.			New Amsterdam Library (first of the month)				
5:45 P.M.							
6:00 P.M.	Jefferson Market Library			Sony Wonder (every other week)	Central Library (twice a month)		
6:15 P.M.			Instituto Cervantes				
6:30 P.M.		Kips Bay Library (once a month)			Deutsches Haus (selected weeks)		
7:00 P.M.		Central Library (twice a month)					
7:15 P.M.							
7:30 P.M.							
7:45 P.M.							
8:00 P.M.				Czech Center (every other week)			
8:15 P.M.							
8:30 P.M.							
8:45 P.M.							
9:00 P.M.							
9:15 P.M.							
9:30 P.M.							
9:45 P.M.							
10:00 P.M.	RiFiFi						

FREE MOVIES BY THE WEEK
(SUMMER)

TIME	MONDAY	TUESDAY	WEDNESDAY	THURSDAY	FRIDAY	SATURDAY	SUNDAY
6:30 P.M.	Monday Movie Series						
7:00 P.M.			St. Johns				
7:30 P.M.					Celebrate Brooklyn		
NIGHTFALL	Bryant Park		Movies under the Stars River Flicks Socrates Riverside Park South	Movies with a View	Open Cine River Flicks		

FREE FLICKS

ANTHOLOGY FILM ARCHIVE
32 Second Avenue (at 2nd Street)
(212) 505–5181
www.anthologyfilmarchives.org

 You must be an Anthology member.

For those of you on the lookout for something other than what you will find at your local multiplex, Anthology is definitely the place for you. This world-renowned institution specializes in collecting, preserving, and exhibiting American independent, experimental, and avant-garde films and video, as well as some classics from Hollywood and European filmmakers. If you are willing to shell out the $50 yearly membership fee, you are entitled to attend all of their Essential Cinema screenings, which happen at least once a week, for free. Without the membership you would pay $8.00 for each screening. The membership also gets you into any of their other screenings for $5.00.

BRYANT PARK SUMMER FILM FESTIVAL
West 40th to West 41st Streets (between Fifth and Sixth Avenues)
(212) 512–5700
www.bryantpark.org
Monday at nightfall, June through August.
This is the granddaddy of all free film screenings in New York. It has become incredibly popular, and as a result you need to get there mighty early if you have any hope of claiming a piece of the greenery for your own. They start

letting people onto the lawn at 5:00 P.M. Since HBO foots the bill for this event, you can be sure you'll get a preview of something coming soon to a friendly cable network near you. There is always a cartoon before the feature, and then you can join the crowd dancing to the HBO trailer just before the film begins (don't ask me why). The features on the huge screen range from cinema classics *(Doctor Zhivago, Rear Window, An American in Paris)* to kitschy favorites *(Viva Las Vegas, The Wild One)*.

CASA ITALIANA ZERILLI-MARIMÒ
24 West 12th Street (between 5th and 6th Avenues)
(212) 998-8739
www.nyu.edu/pages/casaitaliana
This NYU institution hosts four to five free screenings of classic and contemporary Italian films throughout the school year. The films are just a small part of their full schedule of exhibitions, performances, and talks on all things Italian. All events are free and open to the public.

CELEBRATE BROOKLYN
Prospect Park Bandshell (Prospect Park West and 9th Street)
Park Slope, Brooklyn
(718) 855-7882, ext. 45
www.celebratebrooklyn.org
Most Fridays at 7:30 P.M., July and August.
Brooklyn's popular free series presents everything from free films to spoken-word and dance performances, rock, jazz, Latin, folk, and world music. Classic and silent films are often accompanied by live contemporary music and performers.

CZECH CENTER
1109 Madison Avenue (at 83rd Street)
(212) 288-0830
www.czechcenter.com
Thursday at 8:00 P.M., every other week throughout the year.
Shows new and old films from the Czech Republic with English subtitles.

DEUTSCHES HAUS
42 Washington Mews (near University Place)
(212) 998-8660
www.nyu.edu/deutscheshaus
Selected Fridays at 6:30 P.M., and other times.
This cultural center for all things German regularly holds free film screenings. Recent series have focused on film versions of Kafka's novels, gay films in

early German cinema, and the films of Marlene Dietrich, as well as contemporary films from Germany. Most screenings are held on Friday evenings, but there are others scattered throughout the week on their schedule. Often films are accompanied by lectures and live performances. Call or check the Web site for schedule and details.

FRENCH INSTITUTE/ALLIANCE FRANÇAISE
Florence Gould Hall
55 East 59th Street (between Madison and Park Avenues)
(212) 355–6160
www.fiaf.org
Tuesday afternoons and evenings.

 You must be a French Institute member.

While not exactly free, for fans of French films this is a pretty worthwhile deal. If you're a member of the French Institute ($75.00 for a single or $115.00 for a family), you can attend the weekly Cine Club screenings every Tuesday for free (otherwise it costs $8.00 each week). This usually consists of a double feature, often of recent popular favorites as well as classics and lesser-known films. All films are shown in French with English subtitles.

INSTITUTO CERVANTES
211–15 East 49th Street (between Second and Third Avenues)
(212) 308–7720
www.cervantes.org
Wednesday at 6:15 P.M.
For lovers of Spanish and Latin American films or English-language films that deal with those parts of the world, there is no better destination than these two weekly film series put together by the Cervantes Institute. They also offer free panel discussions, lectures, and a great library (see page 189). For more information on other activities, call or check their Web site.

IRIS & B. GERALD CANTOR FILM CENTER AT NYU
36 East 8th Street (between Broadway and University Place)
(212) 998–4100
Every week during the school year, the center holds many screenings of international films, Hollywood hits, and student films. Some events are limited to NYU students; others are free and open to the public. Call or drop by for a schedule.

Who Wants to Be a Moviemaker?

Do you ever find yourself walking out of a movie thinking I could do better than that? Or do you just know you could be the next Scorsese, if you knew where to start? Well, here's your chance to put your money (or should I say time?) where your mouth is. By volunteering your time at schools and facilities like Film/Video Arts (462 Broadway, at Grand Street; 212–941–8787) or Downtown Community Television Center (87 Lafayette Street, between White and Walker Streets; 212–966–4510), you are able to take classes and use their equipment and facilities free of charge. Both ask for a commitment of approximately sixteen hours a week doing administrative or production work in exchange for the free ride. For more information, see the chapter titled "Education: Cents-Less Smarts."

MONDAY MOVIE SERIES

All Saints Parish Hall
707 Washington Street (at 7th Street)
Hoboken, New Jersey
summermovies@aol.com
www.allsaintshoboken.com
Monday at 6:30 P.M., July and August.
Just on the other side of the Hudson, you can escape the heat of the city with this series of classic Hollywood films shown in the air-conditioned Parish Hall. They even throw in free seltzer and popcorn.

MOVIES UNDER THE STARS

Pier A Park (1st Street and Frank Sinatra Drive)
Hoboken, New Jersey
(201) 420–2207
www.hobokennj.org
Wednesday at 8:00 or 8:30 P.M., June through August.
For the cost of a ride on the PATH train ($1.50), hop over to Hoboken, where they show many recent hits and blockbusters in this summer series.

MOVIES WITH A VIEW

Empire-Fulton State Park (between the Brooklyn and
Manhattan Bridges)
(718) 802–0603
www.brooklynbridgepark.org
Thursday nights, July and August.

In the shadow of the majestic Brooklyn Bridge, this film series offers up Hollywood and independent films, many of which have been shot in, are about, or are made by people from Brooklyn. The evening always starts off with a live DJ spinning some tunes to set the mood, and they also provide free valet parking for your bicycle.

MUSEUM OF MODERN ART (MoMA)

11 West 53rd Street (between Fifth and Sixth Avenues)
(212) 708–9480
www.moma.org
Free Friday, 4:00–8:00 P.M.

The museum has two movie theaters that are free with admission to the museum—and on Friday afternoons and evenings, that's free, too (well, technically it's "pay what you wish," but . . .). They show classic and contemporary independent and art films. Call for the latest schedule and details.

OCULARIS

Galapagos Art and Performance Space
70 North 6th Street (between Wythe and Kent Streets)
Williamsburg, Brooklyn
(718) 388–8713
www.ocularis.net

Ocularis runs a number of art film series in Williamsburg, Long Island City, and Astoria throughout the year. The screenings are in conjunction with institutions like P.S. 1 Contemporary Art Center, the Asia Society, the African Film Festival, and others. They show documentaries, experimental and avant-garde films, and contemporary and emerging-artist flicks, as well as features from around the world (in other words, you are not going to see *Terminator 3* here). Screenings are often accompanied by live music and dance. Some films are free, others are not; check the Web site for a detailed schedule.

OPEN CINE

De Salvio Playground (at Mulberry and Spring Streets)
(212) 431–5795
www.storefrontnews.org
Friday nights, July and August, at nightfall.

This is absolutely the Anti–Bryant Park. A splat of white paint on the far end of a basketball court wall serves very well as a screen (that is, once the basketball games subside). A small crowd gathers every Friday night to view films with a gritty, urban feel to them. Some are well-known *(Mean Streets, Taxi Driver)*, some not so well-known, and some foreign. The evening always starts with a couple of choice silent shorts with a soundtrack of car horns and neighborhood voices. This is a pure New York experience not to be missed.

RIFIFI

332 11th Street (between First and Second Avenues)
(212) 677–1027
www.rififinyc.com
Monday at 10:00 P.M.

One-drink minimum (but beer is always cheap!).

The blood and guts flow every Monday night along with Pabst Blue Ribbon. It is always a fun and lively crowd in this comfy coffeehouse-esqe bar/screening room. Each week they schedule such bloody good classics as Hellraiser, Halloween, Evil Dead, Dawn of The Dead, and all of their many sequels. They also have great free comedy shows almost every other night of the week.

RIVER FLICKS

Tribeca Pier, Hudson River Park
(call or check Web site for exact location)

Pier 54, Hudson River and 14th Street
(212) 732–7467
www.hudsonriverpark.org

Wednesday, dusk at Pier 54 (PG-13 and R-rated films).
Friday, dusk at a Tribeca Pier (family-friendly films).
July and August.

Every Friday night grab the kids and take them down to Hudson River Park for some of the best family films ever put to celluloid. Whether it is animated features like *Shark Tales* or *Shrek,* live-action comedies like *Back to the Future* or *Daddy Day Care,* or classics like *Willy Wonka and the Chocolate Factory* (an annual event!) the whole family is sure to have a great time. (Due to renovations, the exact location is unknown as of press time, call for details.) Or you can get a sitter for the little ones every Wednesday night and make your way up to Pier 54 to catch some adult films. All right, don't get crazy, these are all films rated PG-13 or R, like *Fast Times at Ridgemont*

Everyone's a Critic

Here's your chance to let Hollywood know what you think of their films. Many major film studios run private screenings of soon-to-be-released films. They're hoping to gauge response, figure out how to market the movie, learn what changes might be needed, or simply see if the movie's any good. There's no way to necessarily get on a list to see these previews, because they want a random sampling of people, but they are constantly going on and there are ways to increase your chances of getting an invitation.

You'll often find people handing out screening passes in front of multiplexes around New York (particularly Loews Lincoln Square–Broadway between 67th and 68th Streets) and Tower Records (66th Street and Broadway location). If you see someone handing out passes, don't be afraid to approach and ask for one. These folks are paid by the number of people they can get to show up at the screenings. If you promise to show up, they want you. They are usually (though not always) looking for people between the ages of seventeen and thirty-four, but they don't check IDs. And they won't let anyone involved in the entertainment industry into the screenings. If that's you, when they ask what you do for a living, remember to embrace your inner accountant.

High, Clerks, and *The Big Lebowski.* Whenever you decide to go, the films are all free, and even the popcorn is on the house.

RIVERSIDE PARK SOUTH
Pier 1 (Hudson River between 70th Street)
(212) 408–0219
www.riversideparkfund.org
Wednesday evenings at dusk, July and August.
As the development of the Hudson River waterside continues to spread uptown, the free opportunities are following. The newest addition to the riverside, and your weekly calendar of free events, is this newly developed park between 65th and 72nd Streets. Grab a blanket and picnic under the stars while you catch a fun selection of cinema classics and Hollywood blockbusters such as *Chicago, Who's Afraid of Virginia Woolf?, Dirty Rotten Scoundrels,* and *Fiddler on the Roof.* The park also hosts a full schedule of other free events every week, including yoga and Pilates classes, concerts, lots of kids events, and free kayaking.

ST. JOHN'S IN THE VILLAGE

224 Waverly Place (at West 11th Street, 1 block west
of Seventh Avenue)
(212) 243–6192
www.stjvny.org
Wednesday at 7:00 P.M. (every week during the summer).
During the summer this friendly West Village church welcomes all for this film
festival that features only films shot on location in New York. All of the films
portray the city in a variety of historical eras and genres. And, best of all, the
popcorn is free-flowing.

SOCRATES SCULPTURE PARK'S OUTDOOR CINEMA

32–01 Vernon Boulevard (at Broadway)
Long Island City, Queens
(718) 956–1819
www.socratessculpturepark.org
Wednesday at 7:00 P.M., July and August.
Since the borough of Queens is the most culturally diverse place on the face
of the planet, with communities from almost every country in the world, you
can say this festival is both a local and an international one. Each week the
series chooses a film that represents a community in Queens (Greek, Cuban,
Korean, Brazilian, Indian, etc.). They fill out the evening with live music and
dance performances from the country and have local restaurants provide the
regional cuisine. The performances and film are free, but you will have to
pay for the food. Films have included *Zorba the Greek, Buena Vista Social
Company, Central Station,* and *House Party.*

SONY WONDER TECHNOLOGY LAB

550 Madison Avenue (at 56th Street)
(212) 833–7858
www.sonywondertechlab.com
Saturday at 2:00 P.M. (twice a month).
They screen recent and some less recent Hollywood favorites *(The Wedding
Planner, Hitch, House of Flying Daggers, Muppets from Space)* on their amazing high-definition screen. They accept reservations the week of the film and
give out any remaining tickets at 1:45 P.M. One Thursday a month they also
offer a free screening geared toward kids age six and younger *(Elmo, Sesame
Street,* etc.) followed by fun kid-friendly workshops. Check their Web site or
call for the schedule of screenings. Get there early and enjoy the four floors
of interactive activities—everything's free.

BETTER THAN THE BOOK

PUBLIC LIBRARIES
www.nypl.org/branch/events/
www.brooklynpubliclibrary.org
Many public libraries throughout Manhattan, Brooklyn, and the Bronx show regularly scheduled films every week. These films could include black-and-white classics from the 1930s and 1940s, documentaries, foreign films, and recent features. Here's a list of the branches with screenings on a regular basis; call or check the Web site to confirm schedules.

MANHATTAN BRANCHES

CHATHAM SQUARE LIBRARY, 33 East Broadway (between Catherine and Market Streets), (212) 964-6598; the third Thursday of the month at 5:00 P.M.

DONNELL LIBRARY CENTER, 20 West 53rd Street (between Fifth and Sixth Avenues); (212) 621-0618; Wednesday at 2:30 P.M.

58TH STREET LIBRARY, 127 East 58th Street (between Lexington and Park Avenues); (212) 759-7358; Friday at 2:00 P.M.

JEFFERSON MARKET LIBRARY, 425 Sixth Avenue (at 10th Street); (212) 243-4334; Monday at 6:00 P.M.

KIPS BAY LIBRARY, 446 Third Avenue (at East 31st Street); (212) 683-2520; Tuesday at 6:30 P.M. (once a month).

NEW AMSTERDAM LIBRARY, 9 Murray Street (between Broadway and Church Street); (212) 732-8186; the first Wednesday of every month at 5:30 P.M.

ST. AGNES LIBRARY, 444 Amsterdam Avenue (between 80th and 81st Streets); (212) 877-4380; Wednesday at 2:00 P.M.

YORKVILLE LIBRARY, 222 East 79th Street (between Second and Third Avenues); (212) 744-5824; Friday at 3:00 P.M. (twice a month).

BROOKLYN BRANCHES

BRIGHTON BEACH, Brighton First Road (near Brighton Beach Avenue); (718) 946-2917; Monday at 1:30 P.M.

BROWER PARK, St. Marks Avenue near Nostrand Avenue; (718) 773–7208, call for details.

CENTRAL LIBRARY, Grand Army Plaza (Flatbush Avenue and Eastern Parkway); (718) 230–2100; Friday at 6:00 P.M. (feature films), Tuesday at 7:00 P.M., twice a month (documentaries), and other times; call for schedule.

SARATOGA, Thomas S. Boyland Street at Macon Street; (718) 573–5224; Tuesday at 1:30 P.M.

BRONX BRANCHES

BAYCHESTER LIBRARY, 2049 Asch Loop North; (718) 379–6700; call for details.

VAN NEST LIBRARY, 2147 Barnes Avenue (at Lydig Avenue); (718) 829–5864; Saturday at 2:00 P.M.

ALIEN: "On this cable system, we receive over one million channels from the farthest reaches of the galaxy."

BART: "Do you get HBO?"

ALIEN: "No, that would cost extra."

—The Simpsons

TELEVISION TAPINGS: PUBLIC ACCESS

*A*FTER HOLLYWOOD, NEW YORK is home to the most small-screen shows. While Los Angeles is the place to be if you want to see tapings of sitcoms, the kinds of programs that are based in New York have a mix of everything, including talk shows, game shows, variety shows, comedies, and courtroom shows. It's possible to get tickets to many of these shows the week of the taping, but many of the more popular shows have long waiting lists and require you to request tickets from a couple of months to up to a year in advance. All television tapings are free, but be warned that some do require a substantial commitment of time. The upside is that there's usually a very funny comedian working the crowd trying to keep you entertained while you sit around waiting for the official fun to begin.

The audience is an important part of the show, so they want to keep you lively for when they need you to hoot, holler, and applaud wildly. And one of the best ways they have found to keep you interested is through bribery. Often these shows offer giveaways for the audience. You could receive anything from key chains and T-shirts to Broadway tickets, CDs, and books.

THE COLBERT REPORT
513 West 54th Street (between Tenth and Eleventh Avenues)
(212) 586-2477
audience@thecolbertreport.org
www.comedycentral.com/shows/colbert_report

Tape days: Monday through Friday at 7:30 P.M. The Daily Show's Stephen Colbert tackles the issues of the day, and hurts them. E-mail or call for advanced tickets. You can also show up at the studio at 7:00 any night to try for standby tickets.

THE DAILY DOWNLOAD
1110 Penn Plaza (32nd Street and Seventh Avenue)
(212) 324-3461
www.fuse.tv

Tape days: Monday through Friday at 4:30 P.M. Fuse's daily countdown of their audience's favorite videos, The Daily Download, is a loud, fun, raucous good time with tons of audience giveaways (DVDs, CDs, T-shirts) and often great live performances from top artists like Foo Fighters, Green Day, Gwen Stefani, and Kanye West. Give them a call a few days to a week ahead of time for tickets.

THE DAILY SHOW WITH JON STEWART
733 Eleventh Avenue (between 51st and 52nd Streets)
(212) 586-2477
www.comedycentral.com

Tape days: Monday through Thursday from 5:30–7:30 P.M. (arrive by 4:00). Emmy-winning news satire/comedy talk show. Call a month ahead for tickets. You must be at least age eighteen. No day-of standby tickets, but you can call on Friday from 11:00 to 11:30 A.M. to see if there are any cancellations for the next week's shows.

EMERIL LIVE
(212) 401-2422
www.foodnetwork.com

"Bam!" It's a cooking show with a live band and celebrity guests. They tape shows at various times throughout the year and only give tickets away through a lottery system. The Food Network runs the ticket lottery once a year or so. Check out their Web site or call periodically, or sign up for their newsletter to find out when to send in an entry.

GOOD MORNING AMERICA
West 44th Street and Broadway
(212) 456–7384
www.abcnews.go.com/GMA
Tape days: Monday through Friday 7:00–9:00 A.M. Hang out with Diane Sawyer and the GMA gang in their Times Square studio as they talk about world events, chat with celebrities, and tell you the best way to clean your dust bunnies. Send for tickets through the Web site about a month in advance. Plan to arrive at 6:00 A.M.; the show is on the air from 7:00 to 9:00. You can also always join the crowd on the street outside the studio.

HOPE & FAITH
Silvercup Studios East, 34–02 Starr Avenue (at 34th Street)
Long Island City, Queens
(718) 906–3287
www.tvtickets.com
Tape days: Most Fridays from 6:00 to 9:30 P.M. See Kelly Ripa and Faith Ford yuck it up in New York's only real live sitcom. Your best bet is to get tickets through the Web site; they do not have standby line for last-minute tickets. They also offer a free shuttle to the studio from the Hunt's Point subway stop (7 train) or free audience parking.

ISAAC
501 West 36th Street (between Tenth and Eleventh Avenues)
(917) 934–5200
isaactickets@eentertainment.com
Tape days: Tuesday through Friday at noon and 3:00 P.M. (arrive one hour before). Fashion maven and master of fabulousness Isaac Mizrahi hosts this new daily talk show for Style Network, with lots of celebrity guests, makeovers, and, most importantly, audience giveaways! Call or e-mail a few days to a few weeks ahead of time to make a reservation.

JUDGE HATCHETT
National Studios
460 West 42nd Street (between Ninth and Tenth Avenues)
(866) 283–4362 or (212) 352–3322
www.judgehatchett.com
The court is in session Tuesday, Wednesday, and Thursday at 10:30 A.M. and 3:00 P.M.

LATE NIGHT WITH CONAN O'BRIEN
NBC Studio
30 Rockefeller Plaza (49th Street, between Fifth and Sixth Avenues)
(212) 664–3056
www.nbc.com/conan

Tape days: Tuesday through Friday, 5:30–6:30 P.M. Join Conan for his late-night wiseass interviews. Call the ticket request line for reservations two to three months in advance. Standby tickets are given out at 9:00 A.M. at the NBC Studio lobby on a first-come, first-served basis. Standby tickets do not guarantee you'll get into the show; it will depend on how many people with reserved tickets fail to show up at the taping later that day.

THE LATE SHOW WITH DAVID LETTERMAN
The Ed Sullivan Theater
1697 Broadway (between 54th and 55th Streets)
New York, NY 10019
(212) 975–1003 (general info)
(212) 247–6497 (standby tickets)
www.cbs.com/latenight/lateshow

Tape days: Monday through Thursday at 5:30 P.M. (4:15 arrival time), and again on Thursday at 7:00 P.M. (5:00 arrival time). It's the top ten list, viewer mail, Stupid Pet Tricks, Paul, Dave, and you, all together in a very chilly studio (bring a sweater!). For advance tickets, fill out an application at their Web site, or in person at the theater (Monday through Friday 9:30 A.M. to 12:30 P.M. or Saturday and Sunday 10:00 A.M. to 6:00 P.M.) They will call you if they have tickets available for the day you requested, but be prepared to answer a David Letterman trivia question when they call (Who runs the Hello Deli? Name a recent Top Ten category? Who is Dave's announcer?) or you are out of luck. Send for tickets at least two months in advance. To get standby tickets on the day of the taping, call the standby phone line at 11:00 A.M. You have to be pretty lucky and persistent to nab one of these rare tickets, but give it a shot; there isn't an in-person standby line.

LIVE WITH REGIS AND KELLY
7 Lincoln Square (at 67th Street and Columbus Avenue)
(212) 456–3054
www.tvplex.go.com/buenavista/regisandkelly

Tape days: Monday through Friday at 9:00 A.M. (arrive at 8:00). Regis tries not to lose it, Kelly tries to understand it, and Gelman tries to keep it all together on this morning chat show. For advance tickets, send a postcard with your name, address, phone number, the date for which you would like tickets, and the number of tickets requested (limit four per person). Send ticket requests to Live Tickets, Ansonia Station, P.O. Box 230777, New York, NY 10023. Requests can take up to a year to be filled. To try for standby tickets on the day of taping, arrive at the studio as early as 7:00 A.M.; tickets are given out on a first-come, first-served basis.

MARTHA
221 West 26th Street (between Seventh and Eighth Avenues)
(917) 438–5999
www.marthastewart.com/martha
Tape days: Tuesday at 10:00 A.M., Wednesday and Thursday at 10:00 A.M. and 2:00 P.M. Martha loosens up the apron strings on her morning talk show, which includes lots of celebrity guests, audience participation, and, of course, a few tips on everything from homemade apple pies to handmade xylophones. The tickets can be hard to come by, and they can be had only through the Web site. Check it often for when new dates are available. For standby tickets the day of, get there two hours before showtime and bring your knitting to work on while you wait on line.

THE MAURY SHOW
New York's Hotel Pennsylvania
401 Seventh Avenue (between 32nd and 33rd Streets)
(212) 547–8421
www.mauryshow.com
Tape days: Wednesday, Thursday, and Friday at 8:30 A.M. (arrive by 8:15 A.M.). Audience-participation talk show. Call for tickets any time up until the day of taping. If you don't have tickets, they say you can always come to the studio the day of the taping; they'll probably be able to get you in.

THE MONTEL WILLIAMS SHOW
433 West 53rd Street (between Ninth and Tenth Avenues)
(212) 989–8101
www.montelshow.com
Tape days: Wednesday and Thursday at 10:00 A.M., 1:00 P.M., and 4:00 P.M. Audience-participation talk show. Call for tickets any time up until the day of taping, or fill out a request form on their Web site.

THE PEOPLE'S COURT
401 Fifth Avenue, eighth floor (at 37th Street, between Fifth and Madison Avenues)
(888) 780–8587
tickets@peoplescourt.com

www.peoplescourt.com

Tape days: Tuesday and Wednesday at 10:00 A.M. and 2:00 P.M. (be prepared to stay for three hours). Courtroom reality show. Call or e-mail for tickets any time up until the day of taping.

SATURDAY NIGHT LIVE

NBC Studio

30 Rockefeller Plaza (49th Street, between Fifth and Sixth Avenues)

(212) 664–3056

www.nbc.com/snl

Tape days: Saturday, September through June. The original late-night comedy sketch show, with popular guest stars and top-of-the-charts musical guests. They run a lottery every August to give away tickets for the upcoming year of shows. Check the Web site for details. You may have better luck getting standby tickets, which are distributed every Saturday at 7:00 A.M. at the NBC Studio lobby on a first-come, first-served basis. Standby tickets do not guarantee you'll get into the show; it will depend on how many people with reserved tickets fail to show up later for the dress rehearsal at 8:00 P.M. or the live show at 11:30.

T.R.L.

45th Street and Broadway

(212) 398–8549

TRLcasting@mtvstaff.com

www.mtv.com/onair/trl

Tape days: Monday through Friday at 5:00 P.M. You pick the hits, and they play the videos. Call or e-mail for tickets three months ahead of time. To be a member of the studio audience, you must be at least sixteen years old and no older than twenty-four. For standby tickets on the day of the show, line up at the 44th Street entrance at about 3:30 P.M. If you don't make it into the studio, join the throngs of screaming fans outside on Broadway between 44th and 45th Streets, Monday through Friday at 5:00 P.M.

THE VIEW

320 West 66th Street (off West End Avenue)

New York, NY 10023

(212) 456–0900

www.abc.go.com/daytime/theview

Tape days: Monday through Friday at 11:00 A.M. (plan to arrive by 9:30 A.M.). Barbara and the gals talk about everything from terrorism to bra sizes. Send a postcard with your name, address, phone number, and number of tickets requested, or fill out a request form at the Web site. Tickets will be sent for dates about four to six months from the date they are received. They often have room for you the day of the show, however: Stop by the studio no later than 8:30 A.M. to stand in line. These tickets are distributed on a first-come, first-served basis. You must be at least 18 years old to attend.

WHO WANTS TO BE A MILLIONAIRE
30 West 67th Street (at Columbus Avenue)
(212) 479–7755
www.millionairetv.com

Tape days: Tuesday and Wednesday at 2:00 and 4:00 P.M. and Thursday at 3:00 and 5:00 P.M. Meredith Vieira is the host with the most (money, that is). Call or fill out their ticket request form at their Web site. And when you attend a taping, you can also audition to get into the "hot seat" yourself. You must be at least eighteen to attend.

> "I've been asked to say a couple of words about my husband, Fang. How about 'short' and 'cheap'?"
> —Phyllis Diller

COMEDY: CHEAP JOKES

I COULD SAY THAT the price of comedy shows in New York is no laughing matter, but that would be too obvious, so I'll just say the cost of laughing in the city is no joke (sorry, couldn't resist). Suffice it to say, yucks cost bucks (okay, I'm done). But you can have the last laugh by stopping in at one of these free comedy nights. Many feature newcomers taking their first shots at stand-up or are opportunities for more established comics or improv troupes to try out new material—or more likely a combination of the two. The schedules do change from time to time, so be sure to call to confirm information before showing up.

COMEDY BY THE WEEK

TIME	MONDAY	TUESDAY	WEDNESDAY	THURSDAY	FRIDAY	SATURDAY	SUNDAY
4:00 P.M.	New York Comedy Club						
4:30 P.M.							
5:00 P.M.							
5:30 P.M.							
6:00 P.M.				New York Comedy Club			
6:30 P.M.							
7:00 P.M.							RiFiFi
7:30 P.M.							
8:00 P.M.	RiFiFi	RiFiFi	RiFiFi	RiFiFi			
8:30 P.M.	Xando						
9:00 P.M.							
9:30 P.M.							Upright Citizens Brigade
10:00 P.M.		Galapagos					
10:30 P.M.							
11:00 P.M.			Upright Citizens Brigade				
11:30 P.M.						No Name (every other week)	

GALAPAGOS

70 North 6th Street (between Kent and Wythe Streets)
Williamsburg, Brooklyn
(718) 782–5188
www.galapagosartspace.com
Tuesday at 10:00 P.M.

This alternative-arts mecca is the home of a host of unexpected and daring performances every week, ranging from their monthly Amateur Burlesque contest (with real cash prizes!) and evenings of erotic readings to experimental improv and films and straight-up stand-up comedy. Every Tuesday night, the unexpected thing about their ongoing free stand-up comedy night is that top-ranked comedians and notable up-and-comers will haul it out to Brooklyn to take part. They also have many other free shows every week; check their Web site for the schedule.

NEW YORK COMEDY CLUB

241 East 24th Street (between Second and Third Avenues)
(212) 696–5233
www.newyorkcomedyclub.com

Monday at 4:00 P.M. and Thursday at 6:00 P.M.

 "We couldn't possibly charge you to watch the open mike."

Once a week this stand-up club opens its microphone to anyone who has $5.00 and thinks he's the next Seinfeld. You never know what you're going to see during this show. It might be painful, it might be sad, it might be offensive, and it might even occasionally be funny, but if you want to try your luck, watching is free: There's no charge, and no drink minimum (though you may need a couple of shots of something to make it through).

NO NAME AND A BAG O' CHIPS
Common Basis Theatre
750 Eighth Avenue (between 46th and 47th Streets)
(212) 928–1950
www.nonamenyc.com
Every other Saturday at 11:30 P.M.
You never know exactly what to expect at this biweekly variety show. Sure, there is always some stand-up and sketch comedy, maybe a singer/songwriter type, the odd magician or two, and even an actor working up a new dramatic monologue, but the big question is will your Bag o' Chips be plain or Bar-B-Que flavored.

PERFORMANCE SPACE NBC (PSNBC)
www.nbc.com/psnbc
Various locations and days.
NBC (the TV network) puts together performances and showcases of writers, comics, and actors who they are considering eventually signing on to be the next big thing on the small screen. The performances are held throughout the year but on an irregular basis, and they are almost always free (there may be a few bucks charged on occasion). Check out their Web site to find out about upcoming performances.

RIFIFI
332 11th Street (between First and Second Avenues)
(212) 677–1027
www.rififinyc.com
Sunday at 7:00 P.M. and Monday, Tuesday, Thursday, and Friday at 8:00 P.M.

 One-drink minimum (but beer is always cheap!).

Time Out for Laughs

Far be it from me to ever recommend laying down some cash for anything, but if you are in the market for free comedy, you may want to fork over a few bucks for a copy of Time Out New York. *In addition to those ongoing free shows listed in this chapter, there are always tons of other shows popping up all over the place. These free shows change venues more often than stand-up comics get heckled, so for the most up-to-date listings for every-thing around town,* Time Out *can't be beat. Their listings include comedy, theater, film, music, clubs, museums, and much more. They also make a special note of those events that are free. A typical week is likely to have up to 300 free events. Check out their Web site for free access to some but not nearly all of their listings (www.timeoutny.com). The cheapest of you will take a notebook with you and peruse the listings at any of New York's major bookstores; but if you are ready to take the plunge, pick up a copy at any newsstand around the city.*

Almost any night of the week the comedy is served up cheap along with the Pabst Blue Ribbon at the easygoing coffeehouse-like bar/performance space. The shows run the gamut from stand-up and sketch comedy to live game shows and political comedy. Also, Monday nights are always a scream if you hang out after the comedy for the weekly free horror movie.

UPRIGHT CITIZENS BRIGADE
   161 West 22nd Street (between Sixth and Seventh Avenues)
   (212) 366–9176
   www.ucbtheater.com
Sunday at 9:30 P.M. and Wednesday at 11:00 P.M.
UCB is one of New York's leading comedy improv troupes and the only one that gives it away for free. They host two freewheeling performances every week. Wednesday night is School Night, a late-night set of stand-up comedy hosted by Justin Purnell with guest appearances by some of the city's best comedians (www.ucbschoolnight.com). On Sunday nights, don't miss Asssscat 3000 for improvisation at its purest, with guest performers from such shows as *Saturday Night Live, Late Night with Conan O'Brien, The Daily Show with Jon*

Stewart, and others. They don't take reservations for these shows, so get there a couple of hours early to grab tickets. They always have a full house for these shows, and the evening is well worth the effort.

"Dancing: The highest
intelligence in the
freest body."

—Isadora Duncan

DANCE: FREE EXPRESSION

AYBE IT'S BECAUSE New Yorkers are always on their feet—racing along the sidewalks, crammed together in the subways, or trudging up a five-story walk-up—but it seems that everyone in New York dances in one way or another. Or perhaps it's the palpable energy of the city that draws dancers from every corner of the planet. Whatever the reason, New York is like a dance itself, and its clubs, public spaces, and studios abound with opportunities for you to strut your stuff without unstuffing your bank account. If you prefer to watch, New York is home to some of the world's leading dance companies and conservatories, so the talent on display at no cost is unrivaled anyplace in the world.

WATCHING IT

CELEBRATE BROOKLYN
Prospect Park Bandshell (Prospect Park West and 9th Street)
Park Slope, Brooklyn
(718) 855–7882, ext. 45
www.brooklynx.org/celebrate
June through August.
Brooklyn's popular free series regularly commissions new works by local and internationally recognized dance companies and presents dance concerts throughout the summer schedule. Their calendar also includes free films, readings, and music of every genre.

CENTRAL PARK SUMMERSTAGE
Midpark (enter at East or West 72nd Street)
(212) 360–2777
www.summerstage.org
June through August.
A complete schedule of free performances throughout the summer, from big names to the cutting edge in music, opera, dance, spoken word, and more. This is a very popular venue; claiming a spot on line early is recommended. Dance performances most Friday evenings.

DANCING IN THE STREETS
545 Eighth Avenue, Suite 8SE (between 37th and 38th Streets)
(212) 625–3505
www.dancinginthestreets.org
Commissions and presents all forms of dance and movement performances throughout the city. All productions are site-specific performances in various parks, open spaces, and indoor spaces. Most performances are free.

THE JOYCE THEATER
175 Eighth Avenue (at 19th Street)
(646) 792–8355
www.joyce.org

 Work as a volunteer usher to see the performances for free.

The leading theater for dance companies, the Joyce plays host to practically every major company from around the country and around the world. Call to set up dates to be a volunteer usher and see the show for free. They begin taking reservations two weeks in advance.

THE KITCHEN
512 West 19th Street (between Tenth and Eleventh Avenues)
(212) 255–5793
usher@thekitchen.org
www.thekitchen.org

 Work as a volunteer usher to see the performances for free.

Although its location has moved farther uptown in recent years, The Kitchen remains firmly downtown in ethos. For the last thirty years, it has been home to such nontraditional, uncategorizable performers as Philip Glass, Laurie Anderson, Bill T. Jones and Arnie Zane, Eric Bogosian, David Byrne with the Talking Heads, Meredith Monk, Brian Eno, John Lurie, Robert Mapplethorpe, Cindy Sherman, and many others. Performances strive to combine music, dance, video, spoken word, and any other forms an artist feels like playing with at the moment. E-mail about two weeks in advance to reserve a spot as a volunteer usher.

LINCOLN CENTER OUT OF DOORS FESTIVAL
65th Street and Broadway
(212) 875–5766
www.lincolncenter.org
Throughout August.
This eclectic performance, music, and dance festival every August features leading modern, ethnic, and cutting-edge dance companies, as well as music from around the world in almost every genre and a great selection of children's performances.

MOVEMENT RESEARCH
Dance Theater Workshop
219 West 19th Street (between Seventh and Eighth Avenues)
(212) 539–2611
www.movementresearch.org
Sunday at 8:00 P.M., September through June.
Presents free modern, improvisational, adventurous dance performances every Sunday night at 8:00 P.M., September through June, by leading downtown movement artists.

NEW YORK UNIVERSITY
Tisch School of the Arts—Graduate Dance School
111 Second Avenue, fifth floor (between Sixth and Seventh Streets)
(212) 998–1982
www.dance.tisch.nyu.edu
October through May.
The graduate dance department offers free contemporary dance performances throughout the school year, often with notable guest choreographers.

DOING IT

CHELSEA MARKET
75 Ninth Avenue (between 15th and 16th Streets)
www.chelseamarket.com

Soho Dance Studio
(212) 226–6767
www.sohodancestudio.com

Triangulo School of Argentine Tango
(212) 633–6445
www.tangonyc.com
Saturday, 2:30 to 4:00 P.M. (salsa) and 4:00 to 7:00 P.M. (tango).
What was once the birthplace of that most American of icons, the Oreo cookie, is transformed into a truly international atmosphere every Saturday afternoon. This gourmet marketplace plays host to a free salsa class from the Soho Dance Studio, followed by a free milonga (tango salon) provided by the Triangulo School of Argentine Tango. When you need to take a break from the dancing, stop in and grab a few free samples at many of the gourmet shops in the market.

CONSULATE GENERAL OF ARGENTINA IN NEW YORK
12 West 56th Street (between Fifth and Sixth Avenues)
(212) 603–0400
www.consarny.com
Tuesday and Wednesday at noon.
If you want to learn how to tango, who better to teach you than the country of Argentina itself. The Consulate General of Argentina holds two free ongoing classes every week on Tuesday and Wednesday for anyone interested in learning how to tango (and if that makes you want to take a trip to Argentina, they don't mind that either).

DANCE TANGO
Central Park midpark at 66th Street (at the Shakespeare statue);
Saturday 6:00–8:30 P.M.

South Street Seaport, Pier 16 (between the Ambrose and Peking
ships); Sunday 7:00–10:00 P.M.
(212) 726–1111
www.dancetango.com
May through September.
Put a rose in your mouth and head down to Central Park (Saturday) or South
Street Seaport (Sunday) for free tango lessons and dancing to live and
recorded music under the stars.

DANCING ON THE PLAZA
Charles A. Dana Discovery Center, Central Park
110th Street and Central Park North
(212) 860–1370
www.centralparknyc.org
Thursday at 6:00 P.M., August.
The Harlem Meer makes a stunning backdrop as you dance beneath the stars
at this free summer dance series. Each week it's a new style of live music to
dance to: swing, salsa, rock and roll, disco, or ballroom. Free lessons begin
at 6:00 P.M., live bands at 7:00 P.M.

MIDSUMMER NIGHT SWING AT LINCOLN CENTER
65th Street and Broadway
(212) 875–5766
www.lincolncenter.org
Late June through July.
Yes, you too can be a dancer at Lincoln Center. Beginning in late June and
running through July, the plaza at this famed performance center turns into
the best dance floor in New York City. Every night they present top names
from every sort of dance music, including American regional, Latin,
Caribbean, African, ballroom, rhythm and blues, and, of course, swing! You
can pay your way onto the official dance floor ($12), which is usually pretty
overcrowded, but the savvier folks spread out on the vast plaza to Savoy
shuffle to their heart's content. Dance lessons begin at 6:30 P.M., dancing
at 8:00 P.M.

MOONDANCE

Hudson River Park
(212) 533–Park (7275)
www.hudsonriverpark.org
Sunday evenings, July and August.

Swing, tango, and cha-cha away every Sunday night under the stars with live music from New York's hottest bands. Free lessons begin at 6:30 p.m., and the dancing keeps going until 10:00. Due to renovations to the Tribeca section of the park, MoonDance has been temporarily relocated, but at press time the specific location was unknown. Call or check their Web site for the exact location.

PARKSIDE LOUNGE

317 East Houston Street (corner of Attorney, between
Avenues B and C)
(212) 673–6270
www.parksidelounge.com
Friday night, 10:00 P.M.–3:00 A.M.

 Two-drink minimum that they do try to enforce—but "we're not gonna throw ya out if ya don't drink."

A local bar complete with pool table, pinball games, and a hip jukebox, along with a snazzy back room with live shows every night. Join local musicians and neighbors in a celebration of the salsa beat every Friday night. While not officially a dance club (due to those stingy cabaret laws), people have been known to shake a little something to the infectious rhythms, and I'm not just talking about maracas.

SANDRA CAMERON DANCE CENTER

199 Lafayette Street (between Broome and Kenmore Streets)
(212) 674–0505
www.sandracameron.com
The last Friday of every month.

This popular dance studio offers classes to the masses in swing, salsa, ballroom, and tango. Stop in for one of the monthly guest nights and get a free introductory swing and salsa class, some hot dance performances, and open swing, salsa, and ballroom dance sessions. There's even free wine and cheese!

SO YOU WANT TO BE A DANCER: WORK-STUDY DANCE CLASSES

New York is the place to be if you hope to join those tapping feet on 42ND Street—but it's not a cheap dream to pursue. Group dance classes can cost as much as $15 per hour. But fear not, there are ways for you to make it to the Great White Way without spending such a great green amount. Many of the leading dance studios around New York offer scholarships, internships, or work-study options in exchange for free classes, or to greatly reduce the cost of classes.

BROADWAY DANCE CENTER
221 West 57th Street (between Broadway and Eighth Avenue)
(212) 582–9304
www.broadwaydancecenter.com

 Reduced rate of $5.00 per class in exchange for work-study hours.

Classes in jazz, ballet, tap, modern, tumbling, and aerobics with leading teachers from Broadway and around the world. They run an extensive work-study program that's open to dancers at any level. Students work in various positions around the studio (front desk, cafe, office, boutique, or cleaning crew). For each work-study hour worked, you earn one class at a discounted rate of $5.00 instead of the regular rate of $18.00 per class. No audition is required, but you must apply, interview, and make a four-to-six-month commitment to a work-study schedule.

MOVEMENT RESEARCH
Dance Theater Workshop
219 West 19th Street (between Seventh and Eighth Avenues)
(212) 598–0551
(212) 539–2611 (hotline)
www.movementresearch.org

Movement Research classes are more likely to win you a chance to work on an Off Off Broadway performance art piece than a part in a Broadway musical. If that's your type of dance, this is absolutely the place for you. They offer a full schedule of classes and workshops in contact improvisation and modern and postmodern techniques, as well as other classes that defy simple definition but combine all kinds of movement influences from around the world. Work-study students are expected to work about ten hours a week in exchange for unlimited free classes. Hours and assignments are flexible and could include registering students for morning or weekend classes, working on the tech crew during performances, running light errands, or distributing flyers. Call to schedule an interview; no audition required.

PERIDANCE
132 Fourth Avenue, second floor (between 12th and 13th Streets)
(212) 505–0886
www.peridance.com

Offers classes in ballet, jazz, tap, yoga, hip-hop, and an emphasis on all forms of modern. They have cleaning work-study positions. Clean a studio (8:00 to 11:00 P.M. any Monday through Friday) and get a free class. Stop by to fill out an application; no audition required.

STEPS ON BROADWAY
2121 Broadway (between 74th and 75th Streets)
(212) 874–2410
www.stepsnyc.com

THE CATCH $15 registration fee required.

Classes in all styles and levels. They accept all levels of dancers into the work-study program, but you must be committed to training and be willing to work eight to ten hours a week. Work-study students work at the registration desk or in their administrative offices, clean studios, or help prepare for performances. Depending on your specific job, you will be able to take all the classes you want either for free or $3.00 each (regularly $14.50 per class). Call to set up an interview.

THE WEST SIDE DANCE PROJECT
357 West 36th Street (between Eighth and Ninth Avenues)
(212) 563–6781
www.westsidedanceproject.com

This small dance studio offers classes in jazz, ballet, and tap. They have auditions a couple of times a year for their scholarship program. You don't necessarily need to be a "dancer" to win one of these positions. They look for people who are pursuing careers in the musical theater and are hoping to improve their dance skills. Scholarship winners are required to work one three-hour shift at the front desk a week and must take at least five hours of dance classes a week.

"Money disappears
like magic."
—Arabic Proverb

YOU MIGHT THINK THE closest you can get to seeing a free magic show in New York is watching how quickly people's money disappears when they play three-card monte, but you'd be wrong. There is a thriving world of magic in this city, and even with nothing up your sleeve, you can be entertained by many of the finest magicians in the world without spending a single quarter (not even that one you have hidden behind your ear). Just stop into any of the handful of magician supply shops around the city to be dazzled at the magic counter, or visit during one of their weekly free performances.

HALLOWEEN ADVENTURE
104 Fourth Avenue (at 11th Street)
(212) 673–4546
www.halloweenadventure.com

Just walking around this store, playing with all the unusual novelty items and gags, and trying on all the wild costumes, masks, and hats could be enough entertainment for a day. Down in the basement they have just added a new theater where they plan to offer a full schedule of magic shows throughout the year (though probably not in October, the busy season). Call the store for information. You can always stop by the magic department and pull something out of their hats.

SOCIETY OF AMERICAN MAGICIANS
Soldiers', Sailors', Marines', and Airmens' Club
283 Lexington Avenue (between 36th and 37th Streets)
www.geocities.com/samparentassembly
First Friday of the month at 8:00 P.M.

This is the oldest and most prestigious magicians society in the world. Their monthly meeting brings together an array of talent from those trying to break into the business to masters of the art. And wherever there are magicians, there is magic. Once they take care of their secret magician business, they often open up the meetings to the public with free magic shows. Check their Web site for schedule and information.

Old Dogs and New Tricks

How do you make a burrito disappear? Stop by the downstairs dining room at Maui Tacos (330 Fifth Avenue, between 32nd and 33rd Streets; 212–868–9722) any Saturday afternoon from 1:00 to 4:30 P.M. Since 1938 a group of professional and amateur magicians has been gathering (only recently at Maui Tacos) to perfect new tricks, exchange ideas, sample some exotic salsas, take full advantage of the free refills on the sodas, and try to slip something past their hardest audience—each other. There is no formal show here, just a chance to see some amazing artists working on their craft in an informal, one-on-one setting. And the tacos are pretty tasty too. Over the years, the group has migrated to various eateries. If you don't find them at Maui Tacos, call the folks at Tannen's. They should know where to find them.

TANNEN'S MAGIC STUDIO

45 West 34th Street, Room 608 (between Fifth and Sixth Avenues)
(212) 929–4500
www.tannens.com

Well, they won't tell you how they're done, but everyone behind the counter at Tannen's is a bona fide magician and can show you any trick in the house. And there are thousands of tricks in the place. Of course, the only way to find out the secrets behind the magic is to buy the tricks, but they will demonstrate any one of them for free. There are no shows at this store, but just spend some time around the counter and you're sure to catch a trick or two.

LIVING IN NEW YORK

"The remarkable thing about my mother is that for thirty years she served us nothing but leftovers. The original meal has never been found."

—Calvin Trillin

FOOD: ON THE HOUSE

FAST FOOD, GOURMET FOOD, exotic food, health food, breads, cakes, wings, hors d'oeuvres, hot dogs, canapés, sushi, Italian, Mexican, Chinese, food, food, food. Anything you desire, it's in New York, and it's better than anywhere else in the world. But for free? Yes indeed. Wander through the many gourmet markets and selected specialty stores around the city and you'll find a delightful (and filling) selection of samples to chow down on. Make your way to any number of bars and restaurants that set out some grand and some not-so-grand spreads during happy hours. And if you must spend money, you can shop at some fancy joints for pennies, if you know when to go.

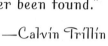

HAPPY HOURS

Many bars, pubs, and restaurants around the city offer some kind of free food during happy hours. What you'll find at these places runs the gamut from basic bar food to sumptuous buffets. For the most part you are expected to buy a drink to partake of the eats, but there are usually all kinds of discounts on the drinks as well during happy hours. And hey, if you don't drink or don't feel like footing the bill for a martini, no one says you can't just order a club soda. Be sure to leave the bartender a nice tip though. Yes, in New York, even Cheap Bastards should remember to tip. While I have included here only those places that have a long history of offering free eats, policies do change from time to time.

EAST SIDE

ASHTON'S
208 East 50th Street (at Third Avenue)
(212) 688–8625
There's always something substantial to chow down on during happy hour at this friendly Irish pub. Monday through Friday, 5:00 to 7:00 P.M.

MCCORMACK'S PUBLIC HOUSE
365 Third Avenue (between 26th and 27th Streets)
(212) 683–0911
An Irish pub with free food available from 5:00 to 7:00 P.M. On Thursday and Friday they usually offer appetizers like skins or wings (though one night they put out some kind of black sausage thing—mmm-mm). Also, they broadcast international rugby games.

NEVADA SMITHS
74 Third Avenue (between 11th and 12th Streets)
(212) 982–2591
www.nevadasmiths.net
Local Irish pub and soccer haven that offers up a buffet of wings and sandwiches every Friday afternoon starting at 5:30 P.M.

PIG 'N WHISTLE ON 3RD
922 Third Avenue (between 55th and 56th Streets)
(212) 688–4646

This low-key Irish pub sets out a small buffet of a couple of tasty selections like chicken fingers, mini pizzas, poppers, or wings. Monday through Friday, 5:30 to 7:30 P.M.

RODEO BAR
375 Third Avenue (at 27th Street)
(212) 683–6500
www.rodeobar.com

A fun and casual Tex-Mex bar/restaurant with barrels full of freshly roasted peanuts all around. At happy hours (Monday through Friday, 4:00 to 7:00 P.M.) they supply a small buffet of munchies (wings, nachos, potato skins, and the like). On Monday nights kids eat free, and every night they have live rockabilly or country music and never charge a cover. Yee-ha!

ROLF'S
281 Third Avenue (at 22nd Street)
(212) 477–4750

This German restaurant sets out free finger sandwiches at the bar at 6:00 P.M. until they're gone seven nights a week. Be sure to check out the over-the-top Christmas decorations.

RYAN'S DAUGHTER
350 East 85th Street (between First and Second Avenues)
(212) 682–2613

This neighborhood Irish pub sets out a great sandwich spread every Thursday, Friday, and Saturday about 6:00 P.M.

T. G. WHITNEY'S
244 East 53rd Street (between Second and Third Avenues)
(212) 888–5772
www.tgwhitneys.com

Free wings, vegetables, and dip, Thursday and Friday, 5:00 to 7:00 P.M.

TRACY J'S WATERING HOLE
106 East 19th Street (between Park Avenue and Irving Place)
(212) 674–5783
www.tracyjs.com

This small bar packs a big gastronomic wallop by setting out an extensive free buffet every Monday through Friday for the after-work crowd. But you better be quick, the grub is only out from 5:30 to 6:30, and it goes fast.

YODO RESTAURANT OF JAPAN
13 East 47th Street (between Fifth and Madison Avenues)
(212) 751–8775
Need I say anything more than *"free sushi"* . . . talk about a raw deal! This Japanese restaurant rolls out the goods during its happy hour every Monday through Friday, 5:30 to 8:00 P.M.

WEST SIDE

CHANNEL 4
58 West 48th Street (between Fifth and Sixth Avenues)
(212) 819–0095
ww.channel4barnyc.com
This stylish Irish bar and restaurant sets out a nice spread of appetizers—wings, spring rolls, quesadillas—Monday through Friday from 5:00 to 7:00 P.M.

D. J. REYNOLDS
351 West 57th Street (between Eighth and Ninth Avenues)
(212) 245–2912
Try your luck at this quiet and friendly Irish pub. Every Thursday and Friday from 5:00 to 8:00 P.M., they set out something different. It might be a hearty snack of wings or chicken nuggets, or you could end up with a substantial meal of steak or chicken marsala over pasta.

KENNEDY'S
327 West 57th Street (between Eighth and Ninth Avenues)
(212) 759–4242
This Irish pub puts out a bit of bar food—wings or meatballs—Monday through Friday, 4:30 to 7:00 P.M. or until it's gone. Good for a nibble, but it probably won't fill you up.

LANGAN'S
150 West 47th Street (between Sixth and Seventh Avenues)
(212) 869–5482
This makes a great pretheater stop. Monday through Friday, 5:00 to 8:00 P.M., you'll find chips and salsa at the bar and a small buffet of bar food, which could include wings, mozzarella sticks, meatballs, or other tasty munchies.

O'FLAHERTY'S ALE HOUSE

334 West 46th Street (between Eighth and Ninth Avenues)
(212) 581–9366 or (212) 246–8928

This theater-district Irish pub satisfies its starving-actor clientele with free shepherd's pie or pasta Sunday through Wednesday nights at about 10:30 P.M. Don't worry—you don't have to recite any Shakespeare to partake. They also have free live music seven nights a week (acoustic, rock, and Irish).

O'REILLY'S TOWNHOUSE

21 West 35th Street (between Fifth and Sixth Avenues)
(212) 502–5246

This lively Irish pub with a busy after-work crowd sets out a free buffet of shepherd's pie, pasta, or wings Monday through Friday from 5:00 P.M. "till it's gone."

PETER'S RESTAURANT

182 Columbus Avenue (between 68th and 69th Streets)
(212) 877–4747

This comfortable upscale restaurant treats its upper West Side customers to a sampling of its Asian-influenced American menu at their bar Monday through Friday, from 5:00 to 8:00 P.M.

PIG 'N WHISTLE

165 West 47th Street (between Sixth and Seventh Avenues)
(212) 302–0112

Just down the block from Langan's, this makes a great pretheater stop as well. Monday through Friday, 5:00 to 8:00 P.M., chow down on chips and salsa at the bar and a buffet of appetizers.

RUDY'S BAR AND GRILL

627 Ninth Avenue (at West 44th Street)
(212) 974–9169

Look for the Big Pig outside to find the place and "pig out" on the free hot dogs. This is a real neighborhood joint. The franks are always available (1:00 to 10:00 P.M.), but don't try asking for one without ordering a drink first.

THE SUN ROOM

123 West 57th Street (between Sixth and Seventh Avenues)
(212) 664–1589

The saying goes, God works in mysterious ways. Well, one mystery I have no desire to see solved is the Sun Room. Sponsored by the Calvary Baptist

Sing for Your Supper

Here are a couple of places to stop by and lend a hand or join in on some chanting and get yourself a full meal.

FOOD NOT BOMBS NYC, *Tompkins Square Park; (212) 254–3697; www.abcnorio.org. The artists collective/punk rock club ABC No Rio serves up free vegetarian meals in Tompkins Square Park every Friday, Sunday, and Monday at about 3:30 P.M. This meal is generally meant for the homeless, but they always need volunteers to help in food preparation—and, of course, they'll feed you too. Stop by ABC No Rio at about 1:00 P.M. to help cook (156 Rivington Street, between Clinton and Suffolk Streets).*

SRI SRI RADHA GOVINDA MANIR, *305 Schermerhorn Street (between Nevins and Bond Streets), Brooklyn; (718) 855–6714; www.radhagovinda.net. This is the main New York Hare Krishna temple; it's very large and well attended. They offer free vegetarian feasts on Wednesday and Sunday nights at about 8:00. All are welcome, and there's no need to shave your head.*

Church, this is by all outward appearances your everyday Starbucks-style coffeehouse, complete with cozy couches, reading material, and, of course, coffee and snacks. Now, while you may not be able to get your Caramel Macchiato here, you will save enough money to fill your own coffers because everything in the shop is completely free. *Okay,* you are thinking, *what's the catch? Do I have to listen to a sermon while I sip my coffee?* No, you do not. Born out of the aftermath of September 11, 2001, the cafe strives simply to be a "refuge from the noise." There is no proselytizing going on here, and everyone is welcome to stop in and get a drink, have a nibble, and relax. Of course, if you do have some crisis of faith that a strong cup of joe won't solve, they will be happy to talk it over with you. Otherwise, no catches. Just free coffee, tea, cookies, muffins, and more every Monday through Friday from 11:00 A.M. to 4:00 P.M.

DOWNTOWN, EAST AND WEST VILLAGE

BLIND TIGER ALE HOUSE
518 Hudson Street (at West 10th Street)
(212) 675–3848
www.blindtigeralehouse.com

This friendly West Village ale house not only knows its beers (more than twenty-six microbrews on tap), but it also knows how to please its customers: Give them friendly service, play some great music, but not too loud, and most importantly, give them free food! Every Monday night after 6:00 P.M., it's free beer-steamed foot-long hot dogs with all the fixin's; every Wednesday evening there is a beer-and-cheese tasting (only the cheese is free); and every Saturday and Sunday from 1:00 to 4:00 P.M., stop by for their free bagel brunch.

THE CAJUN
129 Eighth Avenue (between 16th and 17th Streets)
(212) 691–6174
www.jazzatthecajun.com

This Chelsea stalwart has been the New York home for traditional jazz and Dixieland music for more than twenty years. Along with the free music seven nights a week, they set out a swell buffet of traditional bar food every Monday through Friday during happy hour (5:00 to 7:00 P.M.).

CUCINA DI PESCE
87 East 4th Street (between Second and Third Avenues)
(212) 260–6800

This Italian restaurant sets out free mussels at the bar every day beginning at about 5:00 P.M.

11TH STREET BAR
510 East 11th Street (between Avenues A and B)
(212) 982–3929

Free wings on Friday, Saturday, and Sunday 4:00 to 7:00 P.M.

THE THIRSTY SCHOLAR
155 Second Avenue (between 9th and 10th Streets)
(212) 777–6514

They set out a free load of wings, rings, shepherd's pie, or whatever the kitchen happens to have available from about 6:00 P.M. until whenever it's gone. Monday through Friday, 6:00 to 8:00-ish P.M.

TY'S BAR
114 Christopher Street (between Bleecker and Hudson Streets)
(212) 741-9641
On the second Tuesday of every month, get yourself a hearty meal and shake the hand of some of New York's bravest (and gayest) as this gay saloon plays host to the monthly gathering of the gay firemen and EMS organization, Fire-FLAG/EMS. All are welcome. The buffet opens at about 8:30 P.M.

BROOKLYN

HANK'S SALOON
46 Third Avenue (at Atlantic Avenue)
Brooklyn
(718) 625-8003
www.hankstavern.com
Free live country/rock/rockabilly music Wednesday through Sunday nights at this hard-core Brooklyn dive. On Sunday night don't miss the free barbecue. You never know what they'll be serving up; some weeks it could be a mighty fine spread, others it might be hockey-puck hamburgers and shriveled hot dogs. No cover, no minimum.

FREE SAMPLES: A SAMPLING

New York City is overrun with gourmet markets, farmers' markets, and specialty stores that charge an arm and a leg for anything from a leg of lamb to over-priced olives from around the world. These markets, however, are also gold mines of free samples. You can get a taste of almost anything, from gourmet breads, cakes, and cookies to olive oils, cheeses, and exotic fruits.

AGATA & VALENTINA
1505 First Avenue (at 79th Street)
(212) 452-0690
One of New York's premier gourmet markets, they often set out a wide variety of samples of everything from smoothies and cheeses to bread and sometimes even pizzas. But when, oh, when will they set out some tasty tidbits from their incredible-looking desserts and pastries? You will find the best selection of samples on the weekends.

AJI ICHIBAN

37 Mott Street (between Pell and Mosco Streets);
(212) 233–7650

167 Hester Street (between Mott and Elizabeth Streets);
(212) 925–1133

153A Center Street (between Canal and Walker Streets);
(212) 625–1879

23 East Broadway (between Catherine and Market Streets);
(212) 571–3755

188 Lafayette Street (between Broome and Grand Streets);
(212) 219–4010
www.ajiichiban-usa.com

This Chinese candy store offers some truly unusual, intensely flavorful deli-cacies. You'll find signs all over the store encouraging you to try such unusual fare as the dried curry squid, mini roasted crabs, and preserved chili olives. There are tamer selections of chocolates, biscuits, and gummy candies as well.

BAKERY SOUTINE

104 West 70th Street (between Columbus Avenue and Broadway)
(212) 496–1450
www.soutine.com

A lovely neighborhood bakery that always sets out something sweet to nibble on.

BALTHAZAR BOULANGERIE

80 Spring Street (between Crosby Street and Broadway)
(212) 965–1785
www.balthazarbakery.com

 It's not easy to get away without buying something.

Considered one of the best bakeries in the city (and one of the most expensive), Balthazar always offers something to snack on at the register. It's a very small place, so it isn't easy to get away without buying something so you don't look like a Cheap Bastard. If you're willing to brave the stares from behind the counter and from those on line, dive right in—their treats are delicious.

CHELSEA MARKET

75 Ninth Avenue (between 15th and 16th Streets)
(212) 243–6005
www.chelseamarket.com

The former home of the Nabisco Company and the birthplace of the Oreo cookie has been transformed into a sumptuous marketplace of gourmet shops. Sample breads, brownies, gourmet butters, cookies, and fruit. Selections are particularly abundant on weekends, when you can also sample some fine wines (Friday and Saturday) and even take free dance classes on Saturday. They even supply free high-speed Internet access for those of you who have a laptop equipped for the wireless Web.

ELI'S

1411 Third Avenue (at 80th Street); (212) 717–8100

431 East 91st Street (between York and First Avenues); (212) 987–0885
www.elizabar.com

Stop by these dreamy gourmet markets often to gorge yourself on the generous samples in their bakeries and to ogle at the tantalizing displays. But be warned: While the fresh food is awfully inviting, the prices are ridiculously steep.

GODIVA CHOCOLATIER

www.godiva.com

DOWNTOWN LOCATIONS

33 Maiden Lane (at Nassau Street); (212) 809–8990

21 Fulton Street (at Front Street, South Street Seaport);
(212) 571–6965

World Financial Center (at the West Side Highway); (212) 346–7720

MIDTOWN LOCATIONS

86 Grand Central Terminal (at 42nd Street and Lexington Avenue);
(212) 808–0276

52 West 50th Street (between Fifth and Sixth Avenues);
(212) 399–1875

701 Fifth Avenue (between 54th and 55th Streets);
(212) 593–2845

560 Lexington Avenue (at 50th Street); (212) 980–9810

Cosí and Toasty

Walk into any of the many Cosi restaurants popping up around New York for a toasty treat. At their sandwich counter you will find a bowl full of ends from the delicious seasoned breads they make for their heaping sandwiches. These hunks of bread are free for the taking, and if you ask nicely, the folks behind the counter will even throw in a side of some tangy dipping sauce. There are more than thirty Cosi locations in New York and more opening up all the time. You are sure to stumble upon one in daily travels, or you can go to their Web site, www.getcosi.com, for an up-to-date list of their locations.

200 Park Avenue (at 42nd Street); (212) 697–9150

1460 Broadway (at 41st Street); (212) 840–6758

UPTOWN LOCATIONS

2325 Broadway (at 84th Street); (212) 579–3197

245 Columbus Avenue (between 71st and 72nd Streets); (212) 787–5804

793 Madison Avenue (at 67th Street); (212) 249–9444

Gourmet chocolates at gourmet prices, but on selected days they have some sweets out for sampling, as well as offering free cups of their high-class coffee or hot chocolate. Stop into any location and pick up a copy of their catalog, where they publish what they'll be giving away and when every month.

GOURMET GARAGE

453 Broome Street (at Mercer Street); (212) 941–5850

117 Seventh Avenue South (at Christopher Street); (212) 414–5910

2567 Broadway (between 96th and 97th Streets); (212) 663–0656

301 East 64th Street (between First and Second Avenues); (212) 535–6271

1245 Park Avenue (at 96th Street); (212) 348–5850
www.gourmetgarage.com

Sample from the olive bar, cheeses, and other gourmet treats from time to time.

GREENMARKET FARMERS MARKET
Union Square, 17th Street and Broadway
(212) 788–7476
www.cenyc.org

New York has many official farmers' markets (forty throughout the five boroughs), which attract a wide variety of upstate and Long Island farmers to
the city to sell their wares. The hands-down best market for samples of everything from heirloom tomatoes and organic apples, beans, and peppers to
fresh bread, cakes, and jams is the Union Square market, held every Monday,
Wednesday, Friday, and Saturday. Call or check the Web site for information
on other markets around the city.

JEFFERSON MARKET
450 Sixth Avenue (between 10th and 11th Streets)
(212) 533–3377

Good bakery, cheese, and deli samples.

MURRAY'S CHEESE SHOP
257 Bleecker Street (at Cornelia, between Sixth and Seventh
Avenues); (212) 243–3289

Grand Central Station, 73 Grand Central Terminal (43rd Street at
Lexington Avenue); (212) 922–1540
www.murrayscheese.com

Murray's is considered to be one of the finest cheese shops in the world, and
you are welcome to sample any cheese in the world at either one of their
shops. They often have samples out for you to dip into, but feel free to ask
for a bit of anything they have. Their helpful and extraordinarily knowledgeable staff will happily slice off for you a bit of whatever you request. At the
Grand Central location, they hold organized cheese tastings every Thursday
afternoon from 4:00 to 7:00 P.M. Stop by any week to meet cheese makers
from all over the world and sample their goods.

THE PENINSULA HOTEL
700 Fifth Avenue (at 55th Street)
(212) 956–2888
www.peninsula.com

This indulgent hotel keeps you healthy and happy with its giveaways. To the
left of the front desk, you will always find an inviting bowl of Red Delicious
and Granny Smith apples, and to the right a big jar of Lindt chocolate truf-
fles beckons.

POMMES FRITES

123 Second Avenue (between 7th and 8th Streets)
(212) 674–1234
www.pommesfrites.ws

Specializing in "authentic Belgian fries," they offer free samples that consist of about six large fries and your choice of two gourmet dipping sauces. No pressure to buy. A great little snack.

RENAISSANCE NEW YORK HOTEL

714 Seventh Avenue (between 47th and 48th Streets)
(212) 765–7676
www.renaissancehotels.com

Bowls of apples are available in the second-floor lobby, along with some nice comfy chairs. A good place to duck into when you have some time to kill.

TODARO BROS.

555 Second Avenue (between 30th and 31st Streets)
(212) 532–0633
www.todarobros.com

A gourmet market with samples of cheeses, olive oils, bread, and more.

TWO LITTLE RED HENS

1652 Second Avenue (between 85th and 86th Streets)
(212) 452–0476

1112 Eighth Avenue (at 11th Street); Park Slope, Brooklyn
(718) 499–8108

Like a little bit of country in the city, this adorable bakery serves up a delicious selection of cakes, cookies, and pastries, and they always have a generous selection of treats out for your sampling pleasure.

UNION MARKET

754–756 Union Street (at Sixth Avenue)
Park Slope, Brooklyn
(718) 230–5152
www.unionmarket.com

This gourmet market in the heart of Park Slope sets out some tasty samples in their deli, and you can always grab an olive or marinated mushroom or two at their olive bar.

VINTAGE NEW YORK

482 Broome Street (at Wooster Street); (212) 226–9463

2492 Broadway (between 92nd and 93rd Streets); (212) 721–9999
www.vintagenewyork.com

You might expect to find this listing in the wine-tasting section, but they charge for tastes of their New York wines (five one-ounce tastes for $1.00). Don't let that stop you from visiting the store. Go for the delicious cheese and sinful chocolate truffles they always have out for the taking.

VOSAGE HAUTE-CHOCOLAT

132 Spring Street (between Wooster and Greene Streets)
(212) 625–2929
www.vosagechocolate.com

You will always find some delicious and exotic chocolates set out on the counter of this wonderfully original chocolate store. The combinations of sweet and spice that they put together somehow manage to melt in your mouth and explode with flavor at the same time.

WHOLE FOODS MARKET

250 Seventh Avenue (at 24th Street)
(212) 924–5969

4 Union Square South (at Fourth Avenue and 14th Street)
(212) 673–5388

10 Columbus Circle (between 58th and 60th Streets)
(212) 823–9600
www.wholefoodsmarket.com

These health food megamarkets are often, though not always, great destinations to fill up on samples of everything from delicious organic fruits and vegetables to fresh baked goods and exotic teas and coffees. Your best bet is to stop by on the weekend or during lunch hour, but you will almost always find something to nibble on somewhere in the store.

W HOTELS

201 Park Avenue (Union Square at 17th Street); (212) 253–9119

541 Lexington Avenue (at 49th Street); (212) 755–1200

130 East 39th Street (between Lexington and Park Avenues);
(212) 685–1100

120 East 39th Street (between Lexington and Park Avenues);
(212) 686–1600

1567 Broadway (at 47th Street); (212) 930–7400
www.whotels.com

These elegant and funky hotels have amazing lobbies with board games, books, couches, comfy chairs, and overflowing bowls of delicious green apples for you to munch away on.

WILLIAMS-SONOMA

10 Columbus Circle (between 58th and 60th Streets)
(212) 832–9750
www.williams-sonoma.com

The New York flagship location for this purveyor of all things cooking is equipped with a huge kitchen itself. The staff is almost always dishing up something tasty to try. They also hold a regular schedule of cooking classes and demos by many of New York's top chefs. While you do officially have to pay to take part in the classes (and eat the results), you are able to stand in the back and observe for free.

EAT LATE, EAT CHEAP!

Hey, eating late may not be very good for the size of your waist, but it can do wonders for the size of your wallet. If you must spend money—and, of course, I generally do frown on that—then drop by one of these places to eat for half price (after the specified times). These shops, restaurants, gourmet markets, and health food stores all have a policy of cutting their prices at the end of the day to get rid of that day's fresh sandwiches, salads, and other assorted taste delights.

AMISH MARKET

731 Ninth Avenue (between 49th and 50th Streets)
(212) 245–2360
www.amishfinefoods.com

This market slices the prices on their precut sandwiches at 6:00 P.M. daily. The store closes at 10:00 P.M. They don't exactly advertise this, so make sure they don't try to charge you the full price when you get to the register. They also have great olive bars for sampling and occasionally cheeses and desserts for you to taste.

BREAD MARKET & CAFÉ

485 Fifth Avenue (between 41st and 42nd Streets)
(212) 370–7356
Grab a handful of delicious half-priced sandwiches, wraps, and salads available every day from 5:00 to 6:00 P.M.

CAFÉ ANGELIQUE

68 Bleecker Street (between Broadway and Laffayette Street)
(212) 475–3500
www.cafeangelique.com
Delightful little Parisian bakery and cafe slashes the prices in half every night on their sandwiches and pastries from 7:00 till they close at 8:00 P.M.

THE CITY BAKERY

3 West 18th Street (between Fifth and Sixth Avenues)
(212) 366–1414
www.citybakerycatering.com
This gourmet cafe and bakery turns out some of the city's most scrumptious pastries—the problem is a single one of them can easily run you $5.00. But if you stop by after 3:30 in the afternoon, you might just be lucky enough to snag a whole box of treats (four to six per box) for the ludicrously low price of $5.00. They don't offer these every day, just when they have a surplus of sweet delights. They often run two-for-one specials late in the day on their artistic tarts. Also, if you are a chocoholic and have never tried their hot chocolate, it is worth spending the money to try it once. The cup is rich enough to warrant its rich price tag—$3.75 with the homemade marshmallow.

FASHION SOUP

124 West 41st Street (between Sixth Avenue and Broadway)
(212) 704–0909
www.fashionsoup.com
As the Campbell's soup commercial goes, "Soup is good food." But these soups are nothing like those watered-down cans of cream of mushroom your mom used to stockpile. These are hearty, tasty, thick, and chunky bowls of soups that fill you up like a meal. Every day there's a new selection of soups and stews with delicious twists on favorites (tomato soup with fennel and artichoke, corn chowder with chicken) or ingenious blends (cream of carrot with ginger, vegetarian mulligatawny). Half-price soups are offered from 3:30 P.M. to closing (about 5:30).

THE GIANT BAGEL SHOP

120 University Place (at East 13th Street)
(212) 243–2775

New York University students (and anyone else) can stock up at this local bagel shop/deli when the price on their salad bar drops to just $2.99 a pound every day after 3:00 P.M.

INTEGRAL YOGA NATURAL FOODS

229 West 13th Street (between Seventh and Eighth Avenues)
(212) 243–2642
www.integralyoganaturalfoods.com

A natural food store with an extensive salad bar including all kinds of beans, vegetables, tofu creations, and other green and brown edibles. They sell off generous platters of leftovers from the day at greatly reduced prices ($2.25 for a small and $4.25 for a large) starting at 6:00 P.M. Monday to Friday and at 5:30 on weekends.

NEWS CAFE

107 University Place (between 12th and 13th Streets)
(212) 353–1246

A newsstand/sandwich shop that slashes the prices on its tasty sandwiches, wraps, salads, and baked goods at 7:00 every night. Feel free to sit and read the newspapers and magazines from around the world while eating your cheap dinner (try not to get any dressing on the papers, though). Closes at 10:00 P.M. every night.

TARTARE

653 Ninth Avenue (between 45th and 46th Streets)
(212) 333–5300
www.tartare.com

This welcoming gourmet take-out shop drops the prices to half off on its supply of prepared sandwiches every day after 4:00 P.M.

TODARO BROS.

555 Second Avenue (between 30th and 31st Streets)
(212) 532–0633
www.todarobros.com

At this gourmet market they sell off their leftover fresh sandwiches for half price from 8:00 to 10:00 P.M. every night.

WILD OATS COMMUNITY MARKET

2421 Broadway (corner of 89th Street)
(212) 874–4000
www.wildoats.com

A health food store that offers 50 percent off at the salad bar after 8:00 P.M.; they close down the salad bar at about 10:00 or 10:30 P.M.

ZABAR'S

2245 Broadway (between 80th and 81st Streets)
(212) 496–1234 or (800) 697–6301
www.zabars.com

At this world-famous marketplace for gourmet cheeses, deli, coffee, baked goods, and more, they often cut the prices on prepared sandwiches, depending on how much is still left at the end of the day. They make the decision at about 6:00 P.M. They close at 7:30 P.M. Monday through Friday and 8:00 P.M. on Saturday.

"I like best the wine
drunk at the cost
of others."

—Bergen Evans

OT ONLY DO the wine shops of New York offer you a chance to try some of the finest wines and spirits from around the world, but you can also end up learning a heck of a lot about the fruits of the vine. You'll find two types of wine-tasting situations at stores around the city. One is the local shop that uncorks a bottle or two for customers to try (and hopes you'll buy). The other, more desirable situation is when a vintner or wine distributor brings out an entire line of wines for the public to sample. You get to try more wines, the staff are usually very knowledgeable and eager to teach you about the wines without pushing you to buy anything, and you can usually depend on them bringing something tasty along "to cleanse the palate" between wines. All this can be true about the local shop, but you're just as likely to find a guy with a bottle saying, "Here, try some of this stuff, I hear it's good." Most shops offer a discount on whatever is being tasted that day, so if you're inspired to lay down some cash, this will lighten the blow.

EAST SIDE

AMBASSADOR WINES & SPIRITS
1020 Second Avenue (at 54th Street)
(212) 421–5078
This local shop holds tastings Tuesday through Saturday, 4:00 to 8:00 P.M.

BEEKMAN LIQUORS
500 Lexington Avenue (between 47th and 48th Streets)
(212) 759–5857
www.beekmanliquors.com
This sophisticated local shop hosts a full schedule of tastings throughout the week. In addition to the many varieties of wine offered, they often pour various spirits as well. Their events are most consistently held on Thursday and Friday evenings from 4:00 to 7:00 P.M., but check their Web site for many additional chances to imbibe on other evenings.

BEST CELLARS
1291 Lexington Avenue (between 86th and 87th Streets)
(212) 426–4200
www.bestcellars.com
This is a great no-nonsense yet know-it-all place to go to check out some great-tasting wines. The very knowledgeable staff serve up some delightful, inexpensive wines on weekday evenings (5:00 to 8:00); on Saturday (2:00 to 4:00 P.M.) they usually pair the wine with food prepared by local chefs.

CORK & BOTTLE
1158 First Avenue (between 63rd and 64th Streets)
(212) 838–5300
Friday, 5:00 to 7:00 P.M.

CRUSH WINE CO.
153 East 57th Street (between Lexington and Third Avenues)
(212) 980–9463
www.crushwineco.com
Crush may very well be the Holy Grail of wine shops in New York City for anyone interested in tastings. They give you what you want—loads of high quality wines to taste—when you want it—any time! Step into the comforts of the tasting room at this sleek and modern shop, and you will always find a diverse selection of six bottles opened and ready for you to gulp down. And it doesn't stop there; they also play host to a variety of larger tastings and

WINE TASTINGS BY THE WEEK

SHOP	MONDAY	TUESDAY	WEDNESDAY	THURSDAY	FRIDAY	SATURDAY
Acker Merrall & Condit Co.						2:00–5:00 P.M.
Ambassador Wine & Spirits		4:00–8:00 P.M.	4:00–8:00 P.M.	4:00–8:00 P.M.	4:00–8:00 P.M.	4:00–8:00 P.M.
Astor Wines & Spirits				5:00–8:00 P.M.	5:00–8:00 P.M.	3:00–6:00 P.M.
Beekman Liquors				4:00–7:00 P.M.	4:00–7:00 P.M.	
Best Cellars	5:00–8:00 P.M.	5:00–8:00 P.M.	5:00–8:00 P.M.	5:00–8:00 P.M.	5:00–8:00 P.M.	2:00–4:00 P.M.
Bierkraft		7:00–8:00 P.M.				
Burgundy Wine Co.	5:00–7:00 P.M.	5:00–7:00 P.M.	5:00–7:00 P.M.	5:00–7:00 P.M.	5:00–7:00 P.M.	11:00 A.M.–7:00 P.M.
Candlelight Wines						1:00–5:00 P.M.
Chelsea Wine Vault					4:00–7:00 P.M.	1:00–5:00 P.M.
Cork & Bottle					5:00–7:00 P.M.	
Crush Wine Company	10:00 A.M.–9:00 P.M.	10:00 A.M.–9:00 P.M.	10:00 A.M.–9:00 P.M.	10:00 A.M.–9:00 P.M.	10:00 A.M.–9:00 P.M.	10:00 A.M.–9:00 P.M.
86th Street Corner Wine				4:00–8:00 P.M.	4:00–8:00 P.M.	4:00–8:00 P.M.
86th Street Wine & Liquor						5:00–8:00 P.M.
Elizabeth & Vine						5:00–8:00 P.M.
Erlich Wine and Spirits				5:00–8:00 P.M.	5:00–8:00 P.M.	5:00–8:00 P.M.
Gramercy Park Wines & Spirits					5:00–8:00 P.M.	
International Wines & Spirits					4:00–7:00 P.M.	4:00–7:00 P.M.
Mister Wright Liquors				4:00–7:00 P.M.	4:00–7:00 P.M.	4:00–7:00 P.M.
Morell & Company						2:00–5:00 P.M.
Ninth Avenue Vintner					5:00–8:00 P.M.	5:00–8:00 P.M.
Park East Wines & Spirits						4:00–7:00 P.M.
Sea Grape Wine & Spirits				5:30–8:30 P.M.		
67 Wines & Spirits		4:00–7:00 P.M.	4:00–7:00 P.M.	4:00–7:00 P.M.	4:00–7:00 P.M.	4:00–7:00 P.M.
Spirits of Columbus						4:00–7:00 P.M.
Union Square Wine & Spirits				4:00–7:00 P.M.	4:00–7:00 P.M.	2:00–5:00 P.M.
Vintage New York						5:00–7:00 P.M. (DOWNTOWN) 2:00–4:00 P.M. (UPTOWN)
Washington Square Wines						4:00–7:00 P.M.
Windsor Court				5:00–8:00 P.M. (Sept.–May)	5:00–8:00 P.M. (Sept.–May)	5:00–8:00 P.M. (Sept.–May)

events (some of which are not free), when they crack open even more bottles by specific vineyards or varietals and often include generous spreads of cheese and gourmet food. Check their Web site for a schedule of classes and events.

86TH STREET WINE & LIQUOR
306 East 86th Street (at Second Avenue)
(212) 396–3535
www.86wine.com
Saturday, 5:00 to 8:00 P.M.

EHRLICH WINES & SPIRITS
222 Amsterdam Avenue (at 70th Street)
(212) 877–6090
www.ehrlichwines.com
A small corner shop that opens a bottle or two for sampling Thursday, Friday, and Saturday from 5:00 to 8:00 P.M.

GRAMERCY PARK WINES & SPIRITS
121 East 23rd Street (between Park and Lexington Avenues)
(212) 505–0550
www.gramercywine.com
Friday, 5:00 to 8:00 P.M.

MISTER WRIGHT LIQUORS
1593 Third Avenue (between 89th and 90th Streets)
(212) 722–4564
This large store cracks open a few bottles for tasting on Thursday, Friday, and Saturday from 4:00 to 7:00 P.M. It could be anything from cheap (or shall I say *inexpensive*?) to fine wines.

PARK EAST WINES & SPIRITS
1657 York Avenue (at 87th Street)
(212) 534–2093
Saturday, 4:00 to 7:00 P.M.

UNION SQUARE WINE & SPIRITS
33 Union Square West (between 16th and 17th Streets)
(212) 675–8100
www.unionsquarewines.com
This posh shop is always pouring something wonderful and unusual for you to try. Every week (Thursday and Friday, 4:00 to 7:00 P.M.; Saturday, 2:00 to 5:00 P.M.) they play host to a number of distributors, vintners,

Brooklyn Brew

If your tastes are more Michelob then merlot, you will definitely want to hop over the bridge to the borough that once was the home to as many as forty-eight breweries. While many of these are gone, the thirst for beer is still strong in Brooklyn. Bierkraft is a Park Slope gourmet market with a vast selection of beers from every corner of the world (more than 650 brands) and they are not afraid to give it away. Every Tuesday night at 7:00, anyone can stop in for their semiformal beer tastings. No tuxedos required, but a real interest in the art and craft of beer making is. This is a sit-down affair in which a master brewer will lead you through a tasting of five or so handpicked beer and food pairings. You can also stop by anytime to try their house brew of the day. The staff master brewer is known for his batches of unfamiliar beers that can be anything from a Belgian triple to an English mild. Bierkraft is located at 191 Fifth Avenue (between Sacket and Union Streets); (718) 230-7600; www.bierkraft.com.

The Brooklyn Brewery in Williamsburg has brought the fine art of mass-produced beer to Brooklyn and every Saturday it is on display for all to see. The brewery offers free tours and samples of their brews. For more information, see pages 214–15.

And Williamsburg's thriving art galleries, a decidedly more downscale scene than its richer Manhattan counterpart, hands out free bottles of beer at its openings. For a selection of Williamsburg's galleries, see pages 243–45.

and sommeliers from around the city and the world who pour their selections for you to sample in the lavish upstairs salon. From time to time they also collaborate with local restaurants to provide food to match the wines.

WINDSOR COURT WINE SHOP
474 Third Avenue (between 32nd and 33rd Streets)
(212) 779-4422

This local shop pours some wines every Thursday, Friday, and Saturday, 5:00 to 8:00 P.M., September through May.

ACKER MERRALL & CONDIT CO.

160 West 72nd Street (between Columbus Avenue and Broadway)
(212) 875–1700 (store)
(212) 875–0222 (wine workshop)
www.ackerstore.com

America's oldest and finest wine shop (if they don't say so themselves) is a great place to head any Saturday from 2:00 to 5:00 P.M. to sample some of their "finest" wines. This is a great chance to learn a few things from their knowledgeable staff or visiting vintners. They also run **The Wine Workshop**, which holds a full schedule of seminars and classes on the finer points of wine. They charge a pretty penny for these workshops, but they do use volunteers as pourers in the classes, which allows you to attend them for free. Call The Wine Workshop to add your name to the list, and they will call you when they have an opening (see page 152–53 for more information).

BACCHUS

2056 Broadway (at 71st Street)
(212) 875–1200
www.bacchusnyc.com

They don't offer free tastings on a regular basis, but when they do, they do it right. They like to make a real party out of the events; depending on the region the wines are from, they will include the music and dancing of the country as well. Great extras like free dance lessons are also often included. Check out their Web site for the schedule.

CANDLELIGHT WINES

2315 Broadway (between 83rd and 84th Streets)
(212) 877–7085

A small local store that opens up a couple of bottles and sets out some cheese and crackers on Saturday, 1:00 to 5:00 P.M.

CHELSEA WINE VAULT

75 Ninth Avenue (between 15th and 16th Streets)
(212) 462–4244
www.chelseawinevault.com

A great wine find located in the Chelsea Market. They offer two days of tastings every week. Stop by any Friday from 4:00 to 7:00 P.M. for a free evening of wine and food tastings. This is a very social, cocktail-hour type of atmosphere. On Saturday afternoon from 1:00 to 5:00 P.M., they crack open a few bottles for a much less formal take-a-swig-as-you-buy-a-bottle ambience. Don't miss their once-a-year Open House Anniversary celebration. This is a wonderful event that happens on a Saturday in early November: You'll find more than fifty wines for sampling, free catered hors d'oeuvres, and free introductory wine classes.

86TH STREET CORNER WINE & LIQUOR COMPANY
536 Columbus Avenue (at 86th Street)
(212) 496–1769
Thursday, Friday, Saturday, 4:00 to 8:00 P.M.

INTERNATIONAL WINES & SPIRITS
2903 Broadway (at 113th Street)
(212) 280–1850
Friday and Saturday, 4:00 to 7:00 P.M.

MORRELL & COMPANY WINE & SPIRITS MERCHANTS
1 Rockefeller Plaza (at 49th Street, between Fifth and Sixth Avenues)
(212) 688–9370
www.morrellwine.com
This fancy (and expensive) wine store brings in distributors to hawk their line of wines every Saturday, 2:00 to 5:00 P.M.

NINTH AVENUE VINTNER
669 Ninth Avenue (between 46th and 47th Streets)
(212) 664–WINE (9463) or (877) 664–9463
A friendly community shop that brings in vintners to show off their wines most Fridays and Saturdays, 5:00 to 8:00 P.M.

67 WINES & SPIRITS
179 Columbus Avenue (at 68th Street)
(212) 724–6767
www.67wine.com
A fine store for fine wines and every bit of wine paraphernalia you could ever imagine. Make your way up to the second-floor kitchen area and get an education in wines by sampling vintages of different countries, regions, types, and styles Tuesday through Saturday, 4:00 to 7:00 P.M. They often have cooking demonstrations or at least something tasty to nibble along with the wines. Check their Web site for a listing of weekly events.

Corkscrew U

Don't know your Asti Spumonti from your elderberry wine? Take a class. There are many courses offered throughout the city that will let you expand your choice of wines beyond twist-off or cork. Most of these are one-day seminars on wines from specific regions of the world, but some are in-depth courses exploring every aspect of the wine, from seeds to sipping. And you can take the classes for free by volunteering to be a "pourer" for these classes. Basically all that's involved is showing up for the class an hour or so early, setting out the glasses and class materials for the paying students, pouring the wines that are used in the classes, and staying a little while after the class ends to load the glasses in the dishwasher. While the class is on, you're able to fully participate and taste all the wines used. See the chapter titled "Education: Cents-Less Smarts" for more details on classes at the New School Culinary Arts Program and The Wine Workshop.

SPIRITS OF COLUMBUS
730 Columbus Avenue (between 95th and 96th Streets)
(212) 865–7070

This local shop offers tastes from a few inexpensive bottles Saturday, 4:00 to 7:00 P.M. They sometimes sample a selection of kosher wines on Friday.

VINTAGE NEW YORK
Uptown, 2492 Broadway (between 92nd and 93rd Streets);
(212) 721–9999

Downtown, 482 Broome Street (between Wooster and Greene Streets);
(212) 226–9463
www.vintagenewyork.com

Every other Saturday from 2:00 to 4:00 P.M. at the downtown store and from 5:00 to 7:00 P.M. at the uptown store, it is your chance to "Meet Your (Wine) Maker." This series of events features New York State vintners and their fine wines. At all other times, this store charges for its samples, but you can also always stop in to sample some delicious New York cheese and chocolates. Check their Web site for the schedule of events.

ASTOR WINES & SPIRITS
12 Astor Place (8th Street, between Lafayette Street and Broadway)
(212) 674–7500
www.astoruncorked.com

New York's largest wine store offers tastings grouped by region or type, giving you the opportunity to try everything from Dom Perignon to the wines of New Zealand and South Africa; from moderately priced to fine wines. The friendly staff offer samples in a no-pressure-to-buy atmosphere. Be sure to cleanse your palate with the gourmet breads and cheeses that often accompany the wines. Thursday and Friday, 5:00 to 8:00 P.M.; Saturday, 3:00 to 6:00 P.M. Check the Web site for a calendar of events.

ELIZABETH & VINE
253 Elizabeth Street (between Houston and Prince Streets)
(212) 941–7943

This tiny shop offers samples from a few bottles along with cheese and crackers. Saturday, 5:00 to 8:00 P.M.

BURGUNDY WINE COMPANY
143 West 26th Street (between Sixth and Seventh Avenues)
(212) 691–9092
www.burgundywinecompany.com

The folks at this specialty shop like their Burgundy, and they also like to share it. You can stop in any day they are open and you will have a chance to sample a bottle or two of their favorite wines. They crack open a bottle for you to sip every night from 5:00 to 7:00 P.M. and on Saturday from 11:00 A.M. to 7:00 P.M. They make a point of making Wednesday evenings a particularly good night to stop in, mostly because they want a good excuse to goof off from work. They always have at least three bottles open, some cheese, and often some live jazz to get you in the mood.

SEA GRAPE WINE & SPIRITS
512 Hudson Street (between Christopher and West 10th Streets)
(212) 463–7688
www.seagrapewines.com

Thursday, 5:30 to 8:30 P.M.

WASHINGTON SQUARE WINES
545 LaGuardia Place (between Bleecker and West 3rd Streets)
(212) 477–4395
A local shop that holds a tasting most Saturdays, 4:00 to 7:00 P.M.

"You'd be surprised
how much it costs
to look this cheap."
—Dolly Parton

HAIR, BEAUTY, AND MASSAGE: FREE-STYLE

JUST BECAUSE YOUR bank account is running low doesn't mean you can't look and feel like a million bucks. In fact, looking good and feeling good can look and feel a whole lot better the less you pay to get that way. And in New York anything you need or want done can be had for nothing or very little: haircuts, coloring, highlights, facials, makeovers, manicures, and massage. The most common places to look for free or cheap services are salons with training programs, beauty and barbering schools, and manufacturers testing new products.

PRODUCT TESTING CENTERS

Here's your chance to be the first on your block to try out the newest products that some of the leading hair care manufacturers are developing. These companies are in the final stages of testing these items and want your opinion. Fear not: These creams, colors, mousses, and gels have all gone through a battery of tests already and are safe for you to use. In other words, you won't end up with a head full of green hair (unless, of course, that's what you want). You should know, though, that they won't be able to customize colors for your hair. You will be able to choose your colors, but they must be selected from the standard set of colors prepared for the shelves of any local store.

CLAIROL PRODUCT EVALUATION SALON
345 Park Avenue, lobby (between 51st and 52nd Streets)
(646) 885–4200 or (646) 885–4201

The services they offer and the products they test include hair coloring, highlights, relaxers, conditioners, styling mousses, and gels. All services are free and performed by licensed and skilled stylists. You must stop by first to apply—Monday through Thursday from 9:00 A.M. to noon or 1:00 to 4:00 P.M. All men and women age eighteen or older may participate. The services they provide at any given time depend on the products being tested. The most common and consistent service offered is hair coloring. Once you're accepted onto the models' panel, you're welcome to come back in once a month for treatments.

L'ORÉAL TECHNICAL CENTER
575 Fifth Avenue, second floor (at 47th Street)
(212) 984–4008

 Women must have shoulder-length or shorter hair (but not too short).

This is the product evaluation salon for all L'Oréal coloring and hair care products. Stop by Monday through Thursday 10:00 A.M. to 4:00 P.M. for an evaluation and patch test. If they accept you into the program, they will color your hair every four weeks. They occasionally use men as well (long hair not necessary), but primarily seek women.

Don't Be THAT Cheap!

While these may be students, and you may be getting your hair done for free or at a very low price, this is still New York, so don't forget to tip! The fact is, as students these stylists probably aren't being paid. They may even be paying to do this work for you. A Cheap Bastard can still be a nice bastard.

HAIR SALONS

These are some of the most exclusive (and expensive) salons in the city, and they all have training programs for fully licensed hairstylists who are receiving further instruction in specific styles or techniques. This makes it a low-risk situation: You can feel reasonably confident you won't end up with an accidental Mohawk at these salons. The only catch is that you are sometimes required to spend two to three hours at the salon when you are modeling for a class. Many of the salons that offer free services can be picky about whom they use as models; women are generally used more than men, and longer hair gets you an appointment quicker than shorter hair. All the salons listed below offer free cuts and/or colorings.

ARTE SALON
294 Elizabeth Street (between Houston and Bleecker Streets)
(212) 941–5932
www.artesalon.com

This no-nonsense salon offers free cuts (colorings cost $35) by their assistants. Call to leave your phone number and an assistant will call you back to set up an appointment for an upcoming Tuesday or Wednesday class.

BUMBLE & BUMBLE
146 East 56th Street (between Lexington and Madison Avenues)
415 West 13th Street, sixth floor (between Greenwich and Washington Streets)
(917) 606–5091 (hair model information)
(212) 521–6500 (appointments with apprentices)

(888) 528–6253
www.bumbleandbumble.com

 For free cuts and styling, models must have long enough hair to have at least 2 to 3 inches cut off.

This salon has a large training program. To get a free cut or style, you'll need to be chosen as a model for one of their seminars (they hold about twenty-five a year). Modeling calls are held on Monday evening from 5:30 to 6:30 P.M. the week before a seminar. If you're chosen as a cut model, you sign up for a slot at 11:00 A.M. or 2:00 P.M. If you're chosen as a styling model, you'll need to be available the entire day, but you'll receive free products as a thank-you. Call to find out when they are holding their next interviews. If you aren't chosen as a model, you can still schedule a low-price cut or color from a staff apprentice for $10 to $20 on Monday from 10:00 A.M. to 4:00 P.M.

CROPS FOR GIRLS
154 Orchard Street (between Stanton and Rivington Streets)
(212) 677–2772
www.cropsforgirls.com

 To get a free cut, you have to go from long hair to very short or let Michael do whatever he wants with your hair.

This salon specializes in short haircuts for women. It may be funky, it may be conservative; you never know what it may end up being. But you know it will be very short and Michael Giovan, the owner, will cut it himself. Call to make an appointment. If you are not quite willing to let Michael have his way with your hair, you can always pay for a cut and have it your way since his rates are darn reasonable (especially the $20 student discount!). Women only.

FACE STATION
855 Lexington Avenue (between 64th and 65th Streets)
(212) 249–8866
www.facestation.com
This bustling Upper Eastside salon offers free cuts and colors by their assistants most weekdays from 10:00 A.M. to 7:00 P.M. Give them a call a few days ahead to schedule an appointment.

Fancy Places at Not-So-Fancy Prices

These salons all run training programs and charge reduced rates for stylish cuts given by their students. These appointments are generally easier to get than the free ones:

AVEDA INSTITUTE, 233 Spring Street (at Sixth Avenue); (212) 807–1492; Tuesday through Saturday from 9:00 A.M. to 7:15 P.M.; cuts $18; coloring and facials also available, but pricey.

CUTLER SALON, 115 East 57th Street (between Park and Lexington Avenues), (212) 308–3838; 465 West Broadway (between Prince and Houston Streets), (212) 674–2210; Tuesday, Wednesday, and Thursday; $10. They hold trainings twice a year, where they offer free cuts to hair models. Check their Web site for times (www.cutlersalon.com).

MINARDI BEAUTY FOCUS, 29 East 61st Street, Fifth Floor (between Fifth and Madison Avenues); (212) 308–1711; Tuesday morning; $25 cut and style (also use models for coloring classes some Monday nights—free coloring, but you must stay for the entire five-hour class).

MIWA ALEX HAIR SALON, 24 East 22nd Street (between Broadway and Park Avenue); (212) 228–4422; Tuesday mornings; $25.

PAUL LABRECQUE SALON, 171 East 65th Street (at Third Avenue); (212) 595–0099; Monday; $25 for cuts; coloring and highlights also available, but pricey.

THE REDKEN EXCHANGE, 565 Fifth Avenue (between 46th and 47th Streets); (212) 984–4703; www.redkensalon.com. Stop by Thursday at noon for a consultation, and they'll schedule you for a color and/or cut by an professional learning new techniques. It could take two weeks to a month to get an appointment. $15 for services. Occasionally offer free services to test new products.

SALON ISHI, 70 East 55th Street (between Madison and Park Avenues); (212) 888–4744; Wednesday evenings; $15 for cuts or color.

SCOTT J. SALONS & SPAS, 242 East 86th Street (between Second and Third Avenues), every Wednesday morning; 257 Columbus Avenue (at 72nd Street), some Wednesday mornings; (212) 769–0107; $10 cuts/$20 color.

SHIGE KOSUDA SALON, 141 East 55th Street (between Lexington and Third Avenues); (212) 759–2397; Tuesday and Wednesday; $10.

VIDAL SASSOON, 90 Fifth Avenue (between 14th and 15th Streets), (212) 229–2200; 730 Fifth Avenue (at 56th Street), (212) 535–9200; show up at 6:00 P.M. on Wednesday for a consultation, and they will schedule an appointment for you the following week; $20–$40 (depending on how far into the program the student is).

YOUNGHEE SALON, 64 North Moore Street (between Greenwich and Hudson); (212) 334–3770; www.youngheesalon.com; Monday, Tuesday, Wednesday; $10.

JEFFREY STEIN SALON

685 Third Avenue (at 43rd Street); (212) 557–0005

1336 Third Avenue (at 76th Street); (212) 772–7717

Jeffrey Stein has seven salons around the city, but these two offer free cuts for hair models on Wednesday mornings (43rd Street) and on Tuesday (76th Street). They offer cuts to men and women, depending on what skills and styles they're working on. Call one to two weeks in advance to set up an appointment.

MATRIX GLOBAL ACADEMY

435 Hudson Street (between Leroy and Morton Streets)
(917) 606–9500
www.matrix.com/globalacademy

This huge and stylish salon is a training facility owned and operated by Matrix, the supplier of endless products to every salon from Super Cuts to the super high-end salons. The academy trains licensed and experienced hair stylists in the latest products, techniques, and styles. They use models during their training events, giving you a chance to get free coloring services (they will also trim and style your hair as well). To be a model, you need to stop by and fill out a short application, and they will take a picture of you. They will call you when they can schedule an appointment for you.

OSCAR BOND SALON SPA

42 Wooster Street (between Grand and Broome Streets)
(212) 334–3777
www.oscarbondsalon.com

Slick Soho style is served up at this salon. Stop by Monday through Thursday from 10:00 A.M. to 4:00 P.M. and let them know you are interested in being a hair model. They will give your hair the once-over and let you know if they have a class coming up that they can use you in. If they use you in the class, all the services are free.

PARLOR

102 Avenue B (between 6th and 7th Streets)
(212) 673–5520

A funky and low-key East Village salon that holds classes on Tuesday and Thursday mornings. Free cuts and colors for hair models, but you must be willing to stay for the whole class (two to three hours). Call or stop by to give them your name for an appointment.

RICCARDO MAGGIORE SALON
18 West 56th Street, second floor (between Fifth and Sixth Avenues)
(212) 586–6482
www.riccardomaggiore.com
Class models get free cuts and/or coloring during the Tuesday classes. Call to put your name on the list.

SALON DE QUARTIER
1032 Second Avenue (between 54th and 55th Streets)
(212) 688–5460

206 Smith Street (between Butler and Baltic Streets)
Cobble Hill, Brooklyn
(718) 246–7244
www.salondequartier.com
High-energy salon offers free cuts by assistants whenever they hold classes (about once a month at the Brooklyn location and every now and then at the Manhattan salon). Call or stop by to leave your name, and they will call you when they are scheduling appointments.

SALON ZIBA
200 West 57th Street (between Broadway and Seventh Avenue)
(212) 767–0577
www.salonziba.com
They hold separate cut and color trainings once a month. Call to put your name on the list, and they will call you when they need a model for the classes, which are generally held on weekday mornings. The appointments for cuts are free and include wash, cut, style, and blow-dry, but they do charge $10 for the color appointments ($15 for highlights), which do not include a blow-dry. Also, they are very strict about appointment times. Be there on time or you are out of luck.

TONY & GUY HAIRDRESSING ACADEMY (TIGI)
673 Madison Avenue, second floor (at 61st Street)
(212) 702–9771 or (800) 256–8585
Hair stylists come from all over the country to take part in the classes and continuing education at this hotshot salon. Thursday, Friday, and Saturday services can cost you up to $300, but if you are able to nab an appointment during their class hours Sunday through Wednesday, not only is your service free, but they will even throw in three free products. Stop by on Friday at 6:00 P.M. for a consultation, and they will set up an appointment for you in

the next week or two if they can use you in one of the classes. All appointment times are in the morning. They are looking for men and women who are willing to make a "noticeable change" in their styles or colors, so no "a little off the top" here. Once you are registered with them, you can call back for more appointments every month or so. These stylists are all experienced professionals, so you can pretty much depend on quality services here.

BEAUTY SCHOOLS

These schools are training folks to sit for their state licensing exams, so the amount of experience and skill fluctuates greatly from student to student. You do take on some risk of a coif catastrophe when you put your head in their hands. In fact, they usually have you sign a release to this effect before you get your haircut. The students are supervised, but the level of supervision varies from place to place. The better you describe what you'd like done, the happier you'll be with your results.

AMERICAN BARBER SCHOOL
   252 West 29th Street (between Seventh and Eighth Avenues)
   (212) 290–2289

 A low fee is charged for work done by students.

They offer haircuts for $4.00, but you might get lucky and find their "flyer guy" handing out flyers for even cheaper cuts at 29th Street and Eighth Avenue. Stop by any time Monday through Friday from 9:00 A.M. to 7:00 P.M. for a cut.

ATLAS BARBER SCHOOL
   34 Third Avenue (between 9th and 10th Streets); (212) 475–1360

   80 East 10th Street (between Third and Fourth Avenues);
   (212) 475–5699

 They charge a fee for services performed by students.

This must be the minor-league farm system for Astor Place Haircutters (world renowned for their quick clipper cuts at $12 a snip). If you're in the market for one of those maybe neat, maybe funky, anything-you-can-do-with-a-clipper-in-ten-minutes-cuts, this is the place for you. It's $5.00 at the Third

Avenue location, but if you walk around the block to 10th Street it's only $4.00. Why is it cheaper around the corner? Cheaper rent.

AVEDA INSTITUTE
233 Spring Street (between Sixth Avenue and Varick Street)
(212) 807–1492
www.aveda.com

 They charge a fee for services performed by students.

This upscale beauty school offers hair, facial, and spa services by students using Aveda's organic products. Prices are a bit steeper than at other beauty schools, but still pretty cheap by New York standards (haircut $18; coloring $25 to $60). You can also be a model for Aveda classes and receive services for free. Call (212) 367–0339 for details. It is best to try to book appointments four to six weeks in advance.

CHRISTIAN NAIL SCHOOL
27 West 34th Street, third floor (between Fifth and Sixth Avenues)
(212) 643–1022
www.nailschool.com

 They charge a low fee for services provided by students.

This nail school offers $7.00 manicures and $10.00 pedicures by their students. They take walk-in clients Monday through Saturday between 1:00 and 2:00 P.M., but you should always call before you show up to make sure they are taking appointments that day. Also, if you are particular about your nail color, you might want to think about bringing your own bottle of polish. The students provide their own supplies and you never know exactly what you will end up with.

CHRISTINE VALMY INTERNATIONAL SCHOOL FOR ESTHETICS
437 Fifth Avenue, second floor (between 38th and 39th Streets)
(212) 779-7800
www.christinevalmy.com

 They charge fees for services provided by students.

Many of the students who train here go on to work at some of the most exclusive (and expensive) spas in New York, but while they are in school it won't cost you much to let them poke and prod at your face. A one-hour facial will run you $27.

LEARNING INSTITUTE FOR BEAUTY SCIENCES
22 West 34th Street (between Fifth and Sixth Avenues);
(212) 967–1717

38–15 Broadway (at Steinway Street), Astoria, Queens;
(718) 726–8383

2384 86th Street (at Twenty-fourth Avenue), Bay Ridge, Brooklyn;
(718) 373–2400
www.libsbeautyschool.com

THE CATCH They charge a low fee for services performed by students.

Okay, this place isn't too swanky, and the cuts won't be cutting edge, but if you're in the market for a basic cut, style, color, or manicure, it certainly is cheap. Their most consistent clientele are old ladies and recently released convicts, which makes for a very interesting waiting room! The fees are $6.00 for a shampoo and cut, manicure $4.00, and lip, chin, or eyebrow wax $4.00. All work is performed by students.

MASSAGE

QUINTESSENCE REIKI
Spring Wellness
636 Broadway (at Bleecker Street)
(917) 570–8013 or (212) 388–9817
reikimaster.michael@gmail.com

This is not your Uncle Ike's idea of a massage. Reiki works with the energy of the universe (rei) and the body's energy (chi); the practitioners only lightly touch you during a session. The results can be surprisingly relaxing, calming, and healing. Lead by Reiki master Michael Stoltz, Quintessence holds free "Healing Circles" the first and third Wednesday of each month from 7:00 to 9:00 P.M., which consists of a guided meditation, a short hands-on session (so-to-speak) lasting between ten to twenty minutes, and a question-and-answer discussion about the practice.

THE SWEDISH INSTITUTE FOR MASSAGE THERAPY
226 West 26th Street (between Seventh and Eighth Avenues)
(212) 924–5900
www.swedishinstitute.com

They charge low fees for massage therapy performed by students.

If you want a free massage, you'll have to start dating a massage therapist, and even then it's not a sure thing (we've all seen the *Seinfeld* episode). So when you need some good cheap hands-on massage, check out the P. H. Ling Clinic at the Swedish Institute. They have two options for low-cost massage. The Stress Reduction Clinic is open to all (but slots fill up quickly) and offers a package of six relaxing and refreshing massages for $150. You register for a series of six one-hour massages, and each week you will receive either a Swedish or Shiatsu session (based on therapist availability). No preferences for modality are taken; you take what you're given from week to week. The Therapeutic Massage Clinic is available to those who have a prescription from a doctor or chiropractor for treatment on a specific injury or condition. You must register for a package of twelve one-hour massages for $250. This series consists of twelve consecutive weekly sessions. Each patient will receive both Eastern (Shiatsu) and Western (Swedish, sports massage, or the like) treatments throughout the twelve weeks. The work is performed by students in their final semester and supervised by faculty. Both clinics are offered three times a year and are very popular; applying for a slot as early as possible is advised.

MAKEUP

IL MAKIAGE MAKE-UP CLUB
107 East 60th Street (between Lexington and Park Avenues)
(212) 371–0551
www.il-makiage.com

Be a model for one of their afternoon makeup classes and you not only get a makeover for nothing but also up to $25 worth of makeup for free. The classes are held Sunday through Wednesday.

NYBS CREATIVE ARTS
7 West 45th Street, second floor (between Fifth and Sixth Avenues)
(212) 245–6371
www.nybsca.com

This makeup school with a primarily Japanese student body is always looking for models for class (of any ethnicity). You may even get paid for your time.

Rugs, a Blender, and a Makeover

Whenever you're in need of some professional beauty assistance, stop by any makeup counter at the finer department stores and have a pro do the work for you. Try the counters at the following stores:

MACY'S, *151 West 34th Street (at Sixth Avenue); (212) 695–4400.*

BERGDORF GOODMAN, *754 Fifth Avenue (at 58th Street); (212) 753–7300.*

SAKS FIFTH AVENUE, *611 Fifth Avenue (at 50th Street); (212) 753–4000.*

LORD & TAYLOR, *424 Fifth Avenue (at 38th Street); (212) 391–3344.*

BLOOMINGDALE'S, *1000 Third Avenue (between 59th and 60th Streets); (212) 705–2000.*

All of the above offer free makeovers using their oh-so-pricey products. Of course, the hope is that you will then buy a load of $43 mascara, $59 lipsticks, and $94 skin-cleansing citrus retonifier—but that's up to you.

Call to set up an interview. Classes held in the afternoon, Monday through Friday.

"The best is the cheapest."
—Benjamin Franklin

YES, APARTMENTS IN New York are just as ridiculously expensive as you've heard they are. With studio apartments the size of a closet going for more than $1,000 a month considered to be a steal—if you can find one—the price of four walls and a bed has really made living in Manhattan almost impossible. But even while the rents were continuing to skyrocket, I managed to find myself a spacious studio apartment in a desirable neighborhood for the unbelievable rent of $560 a month (and it just went up from $521). You might think I'm lucky, but I contend that all it takes for anyone to get such a deal is lots of patience and perseverance. There are thousands of apartments like this all around the five boroughs (and, yes, plenty in Manhattan) through the Mitchell-Lama and 80/20 programs. And these places can be yours without any exorbitant broker's fee, "key fee," or huge deposit.

All that's generally required to move in is the first month's rent and one month's rent as security. The secret is getting your name on as many waiting lists as you can for older buildings, and putting in as many applications as you can for new developments. This won't solve your apartment needs in the short term, though. Unfortunately, it can take between one and ten years for your name to come up (I waited three years), but don't let that stop you from putting your name on lists. Even if you're going through the I-don't-even-know-if-I'll-still-be-in-New-York-in-three-years syndrome, put your name on the lists. If you're still here, and you probably will be, you'll be happy you did. If you aren't, they'll just call the next lucky Cheap Bastard.

LOW-RENT, NO-FEE APARTMENTS

NEW YORK CITY HOUSING DEVELOPMENT CORPORATION

110 William Street (between John and Fulton Streets)
(212) 227–5500 (administrative office)
(212) 863–5610 (affordable housing hotline)
www.nychdc.org

 Each building has various maximum income eligibility restrictions.

Everywhere you look in the city, there is a new building going up, and chances are that building is part of some program through the Housing Development Corporation (HDC) that makes it possible for us Cheap Bastards to get into some of the hottest real estate on the planet. The HDC has any number of programs to get you into these buildings, with such fun names as LAMP, New HOP, Mixed Income, 80/20, Taxable 80/20, New HOP 80/20, and CO-OPS (yes, you can even buy a co-op!), and they seem to be coming up with new programs (and catchy names) every day. But all the programs operate under the same basic premise: The HDC gives the developers certain tax breaks and low-interest loans if they make a portion of the apartments in the swanky new building available to low- and middle-income people (at low- and middle-level rents!). Each building and program has its own income restrictions (some of them up to as much as $157,000 for a family of four), and there are heaps of paperwork and interviews that you need to go

At Your Service

Can't afford any New York City rents? Can't afford to raise a family in New York? Well then, how about raising a family and living in a penthouse duplex on Central Park West? Yes, it can be done. Get a position as a live-in nanny, butler, cook, or personal assistant to the upper crust of New York society and live way beyond your means.

The most common live-in job (particularly for women) is as a nanny. Besides room and board, nannies are paid between $400 and $800 a week for their child care duties and some light housekeeping responsibilities (though some families try to push that part of the job description to the limit). Agencies and families are looking for at least a one-year commitment and some experience. The best way to look for a nanny position is through word of mouth, but there's no shortage of agencies to place you as well. Any reputable agency will not charge you a fee; any fees are paid by the families. Here are a few good places to start your search:

PROFESSIONAL NANNIES INSTITUTE, *501 Fifth Avenue, Suite 908; (212) 692–9510; www.profnannies.com.*

A CHOICE NANNY, *850 Seventh Avenue, Suite 305; (212) 246–5437; www.achoicenanny.com.*

NANNIES PLUS, *(845) 469–5130 or (800) 752–0078; www.nanniesplus.com.*

THE NANNY AUTHORITY, *(973) 466–2669; www.nannyauthority.com.*

NY NANNY CENTER, *787 Seventh Avenue, Ninth Floor; (212) 786–6090; www.nynanny.com.*

FAMILY EXTENSIONS, *(203) 966–9944 or (800) 932–2736; www.familyextensions.com.*

WWW.NANNYJOBS.COM.

If taking care of somebody else's kids isn't your idea of a good time, there are many other live-in positions you can apply for. The rich and famous need you to do everything from cook for them to clean for them, teach their children, keep track of their personal calendars, and attend to their private aircraft. If your calling is to be a majordomo, valet, chauffeur, or housekeeper, try these agencies:

LIFESTYLE RESOURCES, *23 West 36th Street, Suite 4B (between Fifth and Sixth Avenues); (212) 947–9792; www.sterlinglifestyle.com.*

DOMESTIC PLACEMENT NETWORK, *(805) 640–3608 or (877) 206–5262; www.dpnonline.com.*

BEST DOMESTIC SERVICES OF NEW YORK CITY, *10 East 39th Street, Suite 1118; (212) 683–3060; www.bestdomestic.com.*

through. The good news is, once you are in, you are in. You do not need to maintain a low income to remain in the apartments. They list all of the buildings currently accepting applications and those who will soon be accepting applications on their Web site. The competition can be pretty stiff for these apartments, so it is a good idea to apply to a number of buildings at one time. The time between application and move-in date can be anywhere from a few months to a few years.

HOUSING PARTNERSHIP DEVELOPMENT CORPORATION
450 Seventh Avenue, Suite 2401 (between 34th and 35th Streets)
(646) 217–3370
www.housingpartnership.com

THE CATCH Must meet income requirements and limitations to qualify.

This is a chance to own a new home or condo in neighborhoods around the city with small down payments (as low as 5 percent) and many tax exemptions and incentives—and maybe even no closing costs. The mission of the NYCP's New Homes/Neighborhood Builders program is to increase home-ownership opportunities for moderate-income families who are priced out of the conventional real estate market. If you qualify, you can become the owner of a brand-new condo, single-family, or multifamily home. These homes or buildings are built from the ground up by reputable architects and contractors, come complete with many amenities, and are heavily subsidized by the city. There are developments in all five boroughs in such neighborhoods as Fort Green, Harlem, Coney Island, Bedford Stuyvesant, Williamsburg, Crown Heights, Hunts Point, and others. Check out the Web site for a list of current projects.

MITCHELL-LAMA HOUSING COMPANIES

CITY-SPONSORED DEVELOPMENTS

Department of Housing Preservation and Development
100 Gold Street (between Frankfurt and Spruce Streets,
near the Brooklyn Bridge)
(212) 863–6500 (city-sponsored Mitchell-Lama)
(212) 863–5610 (affordable housing hotline)
www.nyc.gov

STATE-SPONSORED DEVELOPMENTS

NYS Department of Housing and Community Renewal (DHCR)
25 Beaver Street (between Broad and New Streets)
(212) 480–7343
www.dhcr.state.ny.us/ohm/ohm.htm

Applicants must meet income requirements, and waiting lists can be long.

There are 132 city-sponsored buildings and 269 state-sponsored buildings in the Mitchell-Lama program (many in the five boroughs), with a total of more than 110,000 units throughout the system. This program was created in the 1950s to provide affordable housing for low- and moderate-income families. The apartments in these buildings are larger than the average shoe boxes most New Yorkers call home, there are no broker's fees, and the rents are amazingly low. Get the lists of buildings with open waiting lists through the Web sites or call. You must apply to each building separately; there is no centralized waiting list. The waits could be anywhere from one to ten years, so apply early and to many buildings. The income requirements vary, depending on the building and the size of your household. Once you have an apartment, though, you are not required to maintain a low income level. You will need to submit your income tax forms to the building management each year, which adjusts your rent yearly according to state-mandated levels. Once you have exceeded a certain prescribed level of income, you'll be required to pay "market value"—still ridiculously cheap. Market value rents (the maximum you will pay) range from studio apartments for $521 to three-bedroom apartments with a terrace for $997 (these do vary somewhat from building to building).

"Children are poor
man's riches."

—English proverb

NEW YORK IS an amazing place for kids, and not just for those who can afford to go to the Manhattan Day School. Yes, at times it may seem like there are so many places to go, sights to see, things to do— and ways to drop a load of cash—that New York doesn't feel very kid-friendly for a parent's wallet. Fear not. There are classes, movies, fun and games, readings, even health insurance, and tons of other fun and useful things for kids without Mom and Dad having to stop at the ATM. During the week, you can fill out any day's schedule with the endless free after-school programs. And on weekends there is never a shortage of creative fun for the whole family in the major parks, museums, and other institutions throughout the city.

Dial-a-Teacher

Can't find the capital of Uzbekistan? Stumped by the square root of the hypotenuse? Or just want to check that you spelled Crispus Attucks correctly? Then call up a teacher and get some help. The Dial-a-Teacher program, run by the United Federation of Teachers, has been helping out baffled students and parents for more than twenty years by fielding more than 2,000 calls a week. A staff of forty-five teachers fluent in Spanish, French, Haitian Creole, Italian, Greek, Hebrew, Chinese, and, yes, English stand at the ready to help you with your homework in any subject Monday through Thursday, 4:00 to 7:00 P.M., throughout the school year.

These folks won't just give you the answers to your questions; since these are all qualified teachers you're talking to, they will strive to reteach the ideas behind the questions, making sure you understand the answers. And if you have already finished your homework, they will be happy to check your work with you. Dial-a-Teacher also offers a battery of workshops for parents during the day or in the evening designed to make parents more aware of what their children are learning and teach them how to help their children more effectively at home.

Dial-a-Teacher can arrange to hold workshops at local schools or at their Manhattan headquarters. If you attend workshops at the Dial-a-Teacher offices, they will send a bus to pick you up, take you home, and even serve you breakfast and lunch! And yes, all help and workshops are free of charge. For homework assistance, call (212) 777–3380. To find out more about workshops, call (212) 598–9205 or click on "parents" at the Web site www.uft.org.

AFTER-SCHOOL PROGRAMS

BEACON SCHOOLS
80 locations throughout the five boroughs
The NYC Department of Youth and Community Development
156 William Street (between Ann and Beekman Streets)
(212) 788–6754
www.nyc.gov/dycd

Don't ever say New York City didn't give you anything! The eighty Beacon School programs are a gift to every student and parent in New York City.

Spread throughout every school district in the five boroughs, the programs offer extensive after-school, evening, and weekend programs that are basically free day camp for students of all ages. Each program's activities vary, but they all generally include time for homework help and tutoring as well as lots of fun structured activities. Activities might include arts and crafts, sports, drama, music, dance, music, photography, martial arts, and computer classes as well as vocational training and health classes. Some classes and activities are offered to adults as well. Registration is required for all programs, but everything is free, even the snacks! To find the locations in your neighborhood, check the Web site.

NEW YORK CITY RECREATION CENTERS
42 locations throughout the five boroughs
(See Appendix D for locations)
(212) 360–8222 or (718) 699–4219 (general information)
www.nycgovparks.org
At every one of New York City's Public Recreation Centers, you will find a variety of after-school programs (Monday through Friday, 3:00 to 6:00 P.M.) for children ages six to fourteen. The programs at each location vary depending on the center's facilities and staffing, but all strive to incorporate the "Straight A's: Athletics, Arts, and Academics." The schedules could include swim programs, sports instruction, computer classes, Internet access, homework help, arts and crafts, and classes in literacy, performing arts, visual arts, and much more. For schedules and more information, check with the local recreation centers.

ARTS AND CRAFTS

THE ART SHACK
Hudson River Park (call or check Web site for exact location)
(212) 732–7467
www.hudsonriverpark.org
Spend a great afternoon on the pier creating all types of projects (painting, drawing, sculpting . . .) with fun teachers and fresh air. All materials are supplied. Weather permitting, Saturday and Sunday, noon to 5:00 P.M., June through August. Due to renovations the Art Shack has relocated. The new location was unknown at press time; call or check the Web site for details.

CHORISTERS

St. John's In The Village
224 Waverly Place (between Perry and West 11th Streets)
(212) 243–6192
www.stjvny.org

Every Monday afternoon children of all religions and backgrounds gather together in the parish hall of St. John's In The Village to take part in this free music and voice-training program. The curriculum of this very serious program focuses on reading music, sight singing, ear training, and musicianship while learning the music of a wide variety of classical styles and periods (no contemporary or children's music here). Auditions are required, and once you are accepted into the program you must commit to a full schedule of classes (every Monday afternoon) and performances (one Sunday a month). While this is a church-run program, it is not a religious program at all.

COOPER-HEWITT, NATIONAL DESIGN MUSEUM

2 East 91st Street (at Fifth Avenue)
(212) 849–8390
www.si.edu/ndm

THE CATCH You must be a New York City high school student.

Through a program called Design Directions, high school students interested in any aspect of design (fashion, industrial, graphic, media, film, interior, architecture, urban planning, and so forth) connect with the vast professional resources in New York City. Programs include daylong workshops, after-school programs, design studio visits, and precollege preparation (college visits; application and portfolio workshops). All classes are free and open to all on a first-come, first-served basis.

FOOLS CO. INC.'S NEW YORK SCHOOL FOR PERFORMING ARTS

Various locations around Manhattan
(212) 307–6000
foolsco@nyc.rr.com
www.foolsco.org

THE CATCH You must be between sixteen and twenty-one years old.

For almost twenty years Jill Russell has been training young adults in all aspects of the performing arts through the Artsworker Apprentice program; free weekly workshops in performance, movement, masks, puppetry, voice and diction, and more, open to all with the desire to learn. No audition or previous experience is needed, but preregistration is required. Call or e-mail for more information.

JAZZMOBILE
PS 197
135th Street and Fifth Avenue
(212) 866–4900 (administrative office); (212) 866–3616 (hotline)
www.jazzmobile.org

 A one-time $80 registration fee is required.

Since 1969 Jazzmobile has been offering free Saturday music workshops and master classes for students age seven and older at PS 197 in Harlem with such musicians as Max Roach, Branford Marsalis, and Donald Byrd. Students need to have at least some basic music knowledge to participate, and they must register and have their skill evaluated to determine if they fit into the beginning, intermediate, or advanced classes. The classes run from November through March, and a one-time registration fee of $80 is required. In summer they also bring a lineup of world-class musicians to the parks, libraries, schools, and street corners of New York City and the surrounding areas. Check the Web site for details.

THE MUSEUM OF MODERN ART (MoMA)
Education Department
11 West 53rd Street (between Fifth and Sixth Avenues)
(212) 708–9828 (high school programs)
(212) 708–9807 (family programs)
www.moma.org

MoMA is an absolute wonderland of free arts activities for everyone from toddlers to teens. The museum offers lively tours and special activities specifically targeted at this young audience (ages four through fourteen), as well as films, discussions with artists, and workshops. All of these family activities are scheduled on the weekends and include free admission to the museum for up to two adults and three children. Many of the programs offer; tickets on a first-come, first-served basis at the museum the day of the event, others do require preregistration. For high schoolers, the museum offers a number of eight-week and sixteen-week courses every year, which might include drawing, printmaking, or curatorial and museum work. Every Friday night starting at 4:45 P.M., high school students are invited to chow down on some free pizza and watch a great selection of classic, contemporary, and experimental films. Preregistration is required for the courses, but you can just show up for the movies. Check out the Web site for details.

NEW YORK UNIVERSITY PROGRAM IN EDUCATIONAL THEATRE

Press Annex, 82 Washington Square East, Room 23 (at Washington Place)
(212) 998–5868
www.nyu.edu/education/music/edtheatre

 $110 materials fee.

Thirteen- to eighteen-year-old budding thespians take part in a free five-week intensive summer program called "Looking for Shakespeare." Throughout the session, students will work with a host of theater professionals to shape an original play based on the Bard's themes but taken directly from the participants' own lives. While working on the play, the performers receive coaching in playwrighting, improvisation, acting, voice, and movement, culminating in a fully staged production for the public. Participants must interview and audition for the program, but no experience is necessary, just enthusiasm and energy.

PROSPECT PARK AUDUBON CENTER

Lincoln Road and Central Drive in Prospect Park
(718) 287–3400
www.prospectparkaudubon.org

Nestled in the wilds of Brooklyn's sprawling Prospect Park, the Audubon Center offers a full roster of free activities for all nature-loving kids, from toddlers to teens. Wednesday afternoons kids ages nine through thirteen can drop by and join the Green Team to learn about the natural wonders of the park and how to help conserve them. Friday afternoons the Nestlings (ages three through five) have a fun afternoon full of storytelling, music, and crafts. And on the weekends you will always find special programs as well as regular crafts classes and bird-watching and nature tours for kids of all ages. Some programs require registrations, but all are free. Call or check out the Web site for schedule and information.

THE PUBLIC THEATER'S SHAKESPEARE LAB JR.

425 Lafayette Street (between East 4th Street and Astor Place)
(212) 539–8621
www.publictheater.org

One of New York's preeminent and leading purveyors of the Bard's work opens its doors to students for an intensive week of workshops and theater training. Students work on Shakespeare with professional actors, learn about the backstage workings of a professional theater, attend a performance at the Delacorte Theater in Central Park, and get a chance to perform themselves. The workshops are open to students entering the tenth grade and above. No audition is required, but you must register. Workshops run for one week throughout the month of August and are filled on a first-come, first-served basis.

THE WOOSTER GROUP
The Performing Garage
33 Wooster Street (between Broome and Grand Streets)
(212) 966–9796
www.thewoostergroup.org

 You must be a twelve- to seventeen-year-old New York City student.

This edgy, experimental theater company offers a free three-week summer institute every August. Students get experience working alongside professional artists like company members Willem Dafoe and Kate Valk, as well as developing performance skills and creating original work. No prior experience is required; call for an application.

FILMS

MUSEUM OF MODERN ART (MoMA)
11 West 53rd Street (between Fifth and Sixth Avenues)
(212) 708–9828 (Friday Night at the Movies
for High School Students)
(212) 708–9805 (family films on Saturday morning
for four- to ten-year-olds)
www.moma.org

The education department at MoMA presents Friday Night at the Movies for High School Students, a series of six classic and contemporary films in the spring and fall. Each series consists of films grouped under an intriguing theme (for instance, The Irresistible Villain: *Dr. Jekyll and Mr. Hyde, Psycho,* and *The Usual Suspects*) and is followed by talks with the film department curators of the museum. Hey, they even throw in free pizza and soda. Saturday at noon the family events department invites you to bring the little kiddies (ages four to ten years old) down to the museum for a free lineup of short films. And on Sunday at 11:30 A.M., it's the tweens turn (ages eleven to fourteen years old) to catch a flick. No tickets required for the Friday-night films. Tickets are distributed for the other screenings on the day of the event on a first-come, first-served basis and include free admission to the museum for two adults and up to three children.

RIVER FLICKS
Hudson River Park (call or check Web site for specific location)
(212) 732–7467
www.hudsonriverpark.org

Great family-friendly films (all rated G or PG) screen on the pier every Friday at about 8:00 P.M. (or when it gets dark) in July and August. In past seasons films have included *Mary Poppins, Little Shop of Horrors, Willy Wonka and the Chocolate Factory, Harry Potter,* and *Chicken Run.* They set up some chairs on the pier for your comfort, and there's also plenty of room for you to bring a blanket and picnic under the stars while you watch. Of course, no movie is complete without the popcorn—and it's free, too. Due to renovations to the Tribeca section of the park, River Flicks has been temporarily relocated, but the specific location was unknown at press time. Call or check their Web site for the exact location.

FILMS AT PUBLIC LIBRARIES

Many public libraries throughout the city have regularly scheduled films and videos for children between the ages of three and ten every week. These programs usually run anywhere from thirty minutes to a couple of hours and consist of a few short films that could include vintage Disney cartoons, films of children's books, and rare children's classics as well as occasional feature-length films. For more details, check out the library Web sites: www.nypl.org (for the Bronx, Staten Island, and Manhattan); www.brooklynpubliclibrary.org; or www.queenslibrary.org. Below is a list of the branches with screenings for children every week. These schedules do change from time to time. Be sure to call the branch to confirm schedules.

MANHATTAN BRANCHES

AGUILAR LIBRARY, 174 East 110th Street (between Third and Lexington Avenues); (212) 534–2930; Tuesday at 4:00 P.M.

BLOOMINGDALE BRANCH, 150 West 100th Street (between Columbus Avenue and Broadway); (212) 222–8030; Monday at 10:30 A.M.

Busting Blockbuster

Forget about spending almost $5.00 to rent videos at Blockbuster or any local video store. Most local libraries have a large collection of children's videos and DVDs. Disney, cartoons, educational and full-length features, classics, and new releases—you'll find plenty on the shelves to please all tastes. You can borrow tapes for a week (three days in Queens). Watch out for the late fees, though: $1.00 per day at the NYPL, $2.00 per day in Brooklyn, and a whopping $3.00 per day in Queens.

COLUMBUS LIBRARY, 742 Tenth Avenue (between 50th and 51st Streets); (212) 586–5098; Friday at 3:30 P.M.

JEFFERSON MARKET LIBRARY, 425 Avenue of the Americas (at 10th Street); (212) 243–4334; Tuesday at 3:30 P.M.

96TH STREET LIBRARY, 112 East 96th Street (between Park and Lexington Avenues); (212) 289–0908; Wednesday at 10:30 A.M.

125TH STREET BRANCH, 224 East 125th Street (between Second and Third Avenues); (212) 534–5050; Wednesday at 4:00 P.M.

ST. AGNES LIBRARY, 444 Amsterdam Avenue (between 81st and 82nd Streets); (212) 877–4380; Thursday at 4:00 P.M.

YORKVILLE BRANCH LIBRARY, 222 East 79th Street (between Lexington and Third Avenues); (212) 744–5824; Wednesday at 4:00 P.M.

BRONX BRANCHES

FORDHAM LIBRARY CENTER, 2556 Bainbridge Avenue (at Fordham Road); (718) 579–4244; Wednesday at 3:30 P.M.

GRAND CONCOURSE LIBRARY, 155 East 173rd Street (at Selwyn Avenue); (718) 583–6611; Friday at 3:30 P.M.

HUNTS POINT LIBRARY, 877 Southern Boulevard (between Barano and Tiffany Streets); (718) 617–0338; Friday at 4:00 P.M.

MELROSE LIBRARY, 910 Morris Avenue (at East 162nd Street); (718) 588–0110; Friday at 4:00 P.M.

MORRISANIA LIBRARY, 610 East 169th Street (at Franklin Avenue); (718) 589–9268; Thursday at 3:30 P.M.

MOSHOLU BRANCH, 285 East 205th Street (and Perry Avenue); (718) 882–8239; Friday at 3:30 P.M.

PELHAM BAY BRANCH, 3060 Middletown Road (at Jarvis Street); (718) 792–6744; Wednesday at 3:30 P.M.

SOUNDVIEW BRANCH, 660 Soundview Avenue (between Seward and Randall Avenues); (718) 589–0880; Wednesday at 4:00 P.M.

VAN NEST LIBRARY, 2147 Barnes Avenue (between Parkway South and Lydig Avenue); (718) 829–5864; Monday at 3:30 P.M.

WEST CHESTER SQUARE LIBRARY, 2521 Glebe Avenue (at St. Peter's Avenue); (718) 863–0436; Friday at 3:30 P.M.

BROOKLYN BRANCHES

BAY RIDGE, Ridge Boulevard at 73rd Street; (718) 748–5709; call for schedule.

BROWER PARK, St. Marks Avenue near Nostrand Avenue; (718) 773–7208; call for schedule.

CENTRAL LIBRARY, Grand Army Plaza (at Flatbush Avenue and Eastern Parkway); (718) 230–2100; Friday at 3:30 P.M., films for teens (with refreshments!); Saturday at 11:00 A.M., films for the whole family.

CONEY ISLAND, Mermaid Avenue near West 19th Street; (718) 265–3880; call for schedule.

FLATBUSH, Linden Boulevard near Flatbush Avenue; (718) 865–0813; call for schedule.

KINGS BAY, Nostrand Avenue near Avenue W; (718) 368–1709; call for schedule.

MARCY, Dekalb Avenue near Nostrand Avenue; (718) 935–0032; call for schedule.

NEW LOTS LIBRARY, New Lots Avenue and Barbey Street; (718) 649–0311; call for schedule.

CENTRAL LIBRARY, 89–11 Merrick Boulevard (between Eighty-ninth and Ninetieth Avenues); (718) 990–0700; Wednesday at 10:30 A.M. (summer only).

FLUSHING LIBRARY, 41–17 Main Street; (718) 661–1200; Friday at 10:30 A.M. (summer only).

QUEENS VILLAGE, 94–11 217th Street (between Jamaica and Hillside Avenues); (718) 776–6800; Friday at 3:30 P.M.

SPORTS AND GAMES

BATTERY PARK CITY PARKS
Rockefeller Park House (Hudson River and Chambers Street)
(212) 267–9700
www.bpcparks.org or www.hudsonriverfestival.com

The schedule is chock-full of regularly scheduled activities for kids from toddlers to teens (and plenty for adults as well!). Starting in May and running through October, their weekly schedule includes everything from soccer, in-line-skating lessons, and gardening to drawing classes, concerts, and family dances. Check their detailed Web sites for schedule and locations.

BIG CITY FISHING
Pier 25 (Hudson River at North Moore Street)

Pier 45 (Hudson River at Christopher Street)

Pier 95 (Hudson River at 56th Street)
(212) 533–PARK (7275)
www.hudsonriverpark.org

New York City and fishing? Not two things you would think go together. Well, the Hudson River is the cleanest it has been for almost a hundred years and the fish are abundant, so come on down and cast a line. The fishing is open to all, but mostly it's children that do the casting. If you're big enough to hold a rod, you're welcome to participate in this catch-and-release fishing. All equipment, bait, and instructions are provided free of charge. Weekends from Memorial Day through Labor Day and weekdays in July and August.

THE CENTER FOR ANTI-VIOLENCE EDUCATION

421 Fifth Avenue, second floor (between 7th and 8th Streets)
Park Slope, Brooklyn
(718) 788–1775
www.cae-bklyn.org

THE CATCH   Free for fourteen- to nineteen-year-old girls only.

Sign up for a free self-defense course or an after-school karate class for teen girls. The self-defense course lasts for five weeks and is offered five times a year; the karate class is taught throughout the school year. The form of karate they teach (Goju) uses a lot of spiritual and meditative exercises (along with the usual kicks, chops, and *hii-yaas!*) to build the girls' inner strength as well as outer. They also offer low-cost/sliding-scale classes for younger children (girls and boys) and adults.

THE CHARLES A. DANA DISCOVERY CENTER

Central Park at 110th Street and Lenox Avenue
(212) 860–1370
www.centralparknyc.org

Sitting majestically on the Harlem Meer at the north end of the park, the Dana Discovery Center offers a variety of free family programs and hands-on exhibits throughout the year. From April through October stop by any Tuesday through Sunday from 10:00 A.M. to 4:00 P.M. and the center will provide you with poles, unbarbed hooks, bait, and instruction booklets for you to while away the hours with some catch-and-release fishing. The Dana Center also offers a variety of educational programs, nature exhibits, jazz concerts (see page 40) and swing dancing on the plaza (see page 71).

CITY PARKS YOUTH TENNIS, TRACK & FIELD, AND GOLF

Locations throughout the five boroughs
(718) 699–4200
www.cityparksfoundation.org

Each year thousands of kids who hope to be the next Tiger Woods, Andre Agassi, or Marion Williams take to the city parks to participate in one of the most extensive youth training programs anywhere in the world. Children ages five through sixteen can take part in three separate programs supported by the City Parks Foundation and receive free lessons in tennis, track and field, and golf. Each program varies slightly, but lessons, equipment, and tournaments are free. Sometimes the kids even have a chance to meet and learn from stars of the games.

LASKER RINK
Central Park (110th Street and Lenox Avenue)
(212) 348–4867
www.centralparknyc.org

 $5.00 registration fee required for each six-week session.

Two six-week sessions of (almost) free ice-skating lessons are available for children age eight to seventeen between January and March on Tuesdays from 4:00 to 6:00 P.M. To take part you must preregister at the North Meadow recreation center (midpark at 97th Street) and lay down your $5.00 registration fee for each six-week session. Skate rentals are provided free of charge. And, those registered for the classes have free entry into the rink any other time throughout the week, though you will have to pay for your skate rental ($4.75).

LEARN TO PLAY . . . SOCCER, BASEBALL, FIELD HOCKEY, LACROSSE, BASKETBALL, BASEBALL
City recreation centers and parks throughout the five boroughs
(212) 360–3300
www.nycparks.org

These separate programs run by the City Parks Department offer girls and boys age thirteen and younger (and sometimes fourteen-year-olds) the chance not only to learn the basics of any of these sports but also to play and compete with other children throughout the city. Free and open to all, these leagues go on at different times of year and provide children with all the skills and equipment they need to enjoy the games. Call for schedules and locations.

LEARN TO SWIM PROGRAM
City pools and recreation centers throughout the five boroughs
(718) 699–4219
www.cityparksfoundation.org or www.nycparks.org

Everybody in the pool! Free swimming instruction for children ages three through fourteen is available during the summer at all thirty-three city-run outdoor pools, and lessons continue throughout the year at city-run indoor pools and recreation centers. Recreation center memberships for children younger than age thirteen are free, for fourteen- to seventeen-year-olds it costs $5.00 to $10.00. (For more information on other city recreation center offerings, see the chapter titled "Fitness, Fun, and Games: Cheap Thrills." For complete listings of recreation center locations, see Appendix D.)

HEALTH INSURANCE

CHILD HEALTH PLUS
Mayor's Office for Health Insurance Access
Human Resources Administration
330 West 34th Street (between Ninth and Tenth Avenues)
(800) 698–4543
www.nyc.gov/healthstat

This is free or low-cost health insurance available to New York City residents up to age eighteen. The cost of enrolling depends on your income and the size of your family. It's free for anyone whose income is below a certain level; if your income is higher, you may have to pay $9.00 or $15.00 per month per child. If your income is too high to qualify for these subsidized rates (around $50,000 a year for a family of four), you can still take part in the program, but you will have to pay full price for the plan (steep, but not thoroughly purse popping at about $150 a month). This is comprehensive coverage (including medical, vision, and dental) and a pretty amazing deal even if you aren't qualified to receive it for free.

MUSEUMS

BELVEDERE CASTLE/HENRY LUCE NATURE OBSERVATORY
Central Park (enter at West 81st or East 79th Streets)
(212) 772–0210
www.centralparknyc.org
Hours: Tuesday through Sunday, 10:00 A.M.–5:00 P.M.

Besides being a castle built high on a hill (a pretty desirable destination for any kid or adult), this is also the home of a nature observatory complete with your fair share of frogs, turtles, and birds and lots of hands-on exhibits. The urban park rangers who run the observatory also run guided tours (free!) on weekends. And if you prefer to explore the wilds of the park on your own, you can borrow a free Birding Kit from them. The kit is filled with useful stuff like a pair of binoculars, a field guide, a sketch pad, and colored pencils. Check out the Web site for tour schedule and details.

BROOKLYN CHILDREN'S MUSEUM

145 Brooklyn Avenue (between St. Marks and Prospect Streets)
(718) 735–4400
www.brooklynkids.org
Free hours: Every Saturday and Sunday, 11:00 A.M.–noon; the first
Thursday of every month is free all day. Also, during the summer, Friday,
5:00–7:00 P.M.

For more than a hundred years, the world's first children's museum has been
entertaining and enlightening kids with a mixture of hands-on exhibits and
performances and an extensive collection of cultural objects and natural-
history specimens. They fling the doors wide open for free entry every weekend for the early birds (11:00 A.M. to noon) and all day on the first Thursday
of each month. During the summer their Free Fridays (5:00 to 7:00 P.M.) are
not to be missed: In addition to full access to the museum, they always offer
great musical performances for young and old alike on their rooftop.

LEFFERT'S HOMESTEAD

Prospect Park (near Flatbush Avenue and Empire Boulevard)
(718) 789–2822
www.prospectpark.org
Hours: Thursday through Sunday, noon–6:00 P.M.; extended hours during
the summer months.

This is one of the few surviving Dutch Colonial farmhouses in Brooklyn, and
possibly the only children's historic house museum in the country. The
house gives children a chance to explore American history and experience
everyday life as it was in the little farming village of Flatbush through
hands-on exhibits, storytelling, and seasonal celebrations and craft workshops. Activities are free and open to all.

SONY WONDER TECHNOLOGY LAB

550 Madison Avenue (at 56th Street)
(212) 833–8100
www.sonywondertechlab.com
Hours: Tuesday through Saturday, 10:00 A.M. to 5:00 P.M., and Sunday,
noon to 5:00 P.M.

Start your visit off by meeting B. B. Wonderbot, the talking, all-knowing robot,
and wind your way through four floors of interactive fun. Then walk out with
your very own "Certificate of Achievement in the Advanced Program in
Communication Technology." This is a very popular site; you're advised to make
reservations by calling the above number at least a week in advance. They
accept reservations only Tuesday through Friday from 8:00 A.M. to 2:00 P.M. You

can get in without a reservation, but it could be a long wait in line. Also, don't miss a chance to attend their children's film screenings once a month in their amazing high-definition theater. Films for grown-ups are shown on Saturday afternoons twice a month. For schedule and reservations call (212) 833-7858.

STORES FOR THE FUN OF IT

There are a few stores around the city that are too amazingly fun to miss. Of course, the danger here is that you'll be tempted, pressured, or whined into spending some actual money. If you can think of these as incredible interactive museums (without gift shops!), then you'll have a great time playing with their "exhibits."

F.A.O. SCHWARZ
767 Fifth Avenue (at 58th Street)
(212) 644-9400
www.fao.com
They have crowned themselves "The Ultimate Toy Store"—and they live up to the billing. Three huge floors of the newest, biggest, best, most state-of-the-art (and most expensive!) toys and games to be found anywhere in the world, and almost all of them are available for you to play with. Plenty of costumed characters, roving magicians, and ridiculously friendly staff make any visit a fun and memorable one.

HALLOWEEN ADVENTURE
104 Fourth Avenue (at 11th Street)
(212) 673-4546
www.halloweenadventure.com
Make a day of walking around this store, playing with all the unusual novelty items and gags, trying on the wild costumes, masks, and hats. And for an extra little treat of tricks, head downstairs to the magic department where they are always demonstrating some amazing magic tricks, or maybe even see a whole magic show at their brand new theater, where they plan to offer free magic shows throughout the year (except during October).

NBA STORE
666 Fifth Avenue (at 52nd Street)
(212) 515-6221
www.nba.com/nycstore
If you're a basketball fan, this place is a slam dunk. Of course, you'll find every piece of NBA and WNBA paraphernalia you could imagine, but you don't

need to buy a thing to have a great time. Lots of free video games, basket-ball carnival games, and even a full-size cushioned basketball court make the spot worth a visit. They also host a full schedule of special events, including in-store appearances and workshops by basketball greats and concerts. Check the Web site for a schedule of special events.

NEW YORK DOLL HOSPITAL
787 Lexington Avenue (between 61st and 62nd Streets)
(212) 838–7527
This trauma center for teddy bears and other cuddlies in critical condition is unlike any shop you've been in before. If you're prepared for piles of decap-itated dolls, unstuffed animals, and just some of the oddest and rarest (and most unique-looking) dolls anywhere, then stop by to see who has checked in recently. The doctor on call is sure to be the third-generation owner Irving Chase, a seemingly curmudgeonly fellow who turns kindhearted when kids come by to visit his patients.

STORYTELLING

BANK STREET BOOKSTORE
610 West 112th Street (at Broadway)
(212) 678–1654
www.bankstreet.edu/bookstore/
Considered one of the best bookstores for and about children in the city. Every week you'll find many author readings, musical performances, and cos-tumed characters for children, as well as discussions and presentations for parents. Events are scheduled at various times throughout the week. Call or check their Web site for details. Almost all events are free, though some require reservations.

BARNES & NOBLE BOOKSELLERS
www.barnesandnoble.com
At every Barnes & Noble superstore, you'll find lots of free readings every week for kids and adults. At these locations you'll find story times where B&N staff, authors, costumed characters, and other guest readers gather children around to hear a book or a story. Of course, the kind folks at Barnes & Noble wouldn't mind if you decided to buy the book, but that's up to you. Call stores to confirm dates and times.

Playtime!

From the countries that brought you Lego and Brio comes a chance to bring your children (age five and younger) for an informal playtime every Saturday, noon to 5:00 P.M., in the Heimbolt Family Children's Learning Center at the Scandinavia House. Lots of toys to play with (coincidentally, Lego and Brio), Scandinavian costumes, storybooks in the Scandinavian languages (and English), and even a stage. Children, parents, and caregivers from all backgrounds are welcome. The Scandinavia House is located at 58 Park Avenue (between 37th and 38th Streets). For more information, call (212) 879-9779 or check the Web site www.scandinaviahouse.org.

EAST SIDE

CITICORP BUILDING, 160 East 54th Street (at Third Avenue); (212) 750-8033; Saturday at 2:00 P.M.

240 EAST 86TH STREET (between Second and Third Avenues); (212) 794-1962; Saturday at 11:00 A.M.

UNION SQUARE, 33 East 17th Street (between Park Avenue and Broadway); (212) 253-0810; Saturday at 2:30 P.M.

WEST SIDE

2289 BROADWAY (at 82nd Street); (212) 362-8835; Sunday at 10:00 A.M. (once a month).

GREENWICH VILLAGE, 396 Avenue of the Americas (at 8th Street); (212) 674-8780; Wednesday at 11:00 A.M.

LINCOLN CENTER, 1972 Broadway (at 66th Street); (212) 595-6859; Sunday at noon.

BROOKLYN

BROOKLYN HEIGHTS, 106 Court Street (at State Street); (718) 246-4996; Tuesday at 11:00 A.M.

PARK SLOPE, 267 Seventh Avenue (at 6th Street); (718) 832–9066; Tuesday at 11:00 A.M.

QUEENS

BAYSIDE, 23-80 Bell Boulevard (at Northern Boulevard); (718) 224–1083; Sunday and Monday at 11:00 A.M.

FOREST HILLS, 70-00 Austin Street (between 69th Road and Continental Avenue); (718) 793–1395; Tuesday at 10:30 A.M., and Friday at 1:30 P.M.

THE BRONX

BAY PLAZA, 290 Baychester Avenue; (718) 862–3945; Thursday at 6:00 P.M.

STATEN ISLAND

2245 RICHMOND AVENUE (between Nome and Travis Streets); (718) 982–6983; Tuesday and Saturday at 10:30 A.M.

BOOKS OF WONDER
16 West 18th Street (between Fifth and Sixth Avenues)
(212) 989–3270
www.booksofwonder.com
Every Sunday at noon.
This is a literary wonderland for kids and one of the few remaining independent bookstores in the city devoted solely to children's books. They host an overflowing schedule of readings and events (almost all free) that varies from week to week. You can join them every Sunday for story time: Staff members read their favorite classic and contemporary children's stories.

CITYPARKS KIDS
Various parks throughout the five boroughs
(212) 360–8290
www.cityparksfoundation.org or www.nycparks.org
May through August.
Forget about the hassle of getting on a train or in a car to entertain the kids—CityParks Kids brings the fun to you. Throughout the summer, this program schedules a series of performances (storytellers, children's theater, puppet shows) in large and small public parks throughout the five boroughs. Call or check their Web site for locations and schedules.

HANS CHRISTIAN ANDERSEN STATUE
Central Park
Enter at 72nd Street and Fifth Avenue
Saturday, 11:00 A.M.–noon, June through September (rain or shine).
This is storytelling at its purest: No reading, just master storytellers recount-
ing tales from around the world (and, of course, featuring many by Mr. H. C.
Andersen himself). Once the weather turns cooler, the storytelling moves to
the comfortable confines of the Scandinavia House (58 Park Avenue between
37th and 38th Streets) on the second Saturday of each month at 11:00 A.M.
(from October through May). For more information on the Scandinavia House
schedule, call (212) 879–9779 or check the Web site www.scandinavia
house.org. The stories are appropriate for children age five and older.

LOGOS BOOKSTORE
1575 York Avenue (between 83rd & 84th Streets)
(212) 517–7292
www.logosbookstorenyc.com
Monday at 3:00 P.M.
Join the wonderfully energetic staff storyteller Devorah Hankin every Monday
afternoon at 3:00 P.M. for story time. Devorah picks out a few of her favorite
new and classic children's stories and shares them with the little ones for a
delightful afternoon.

NEW YORK PUBLIC LIBRARY
www.nypl.org/branch/events/
Almost every branch of the NYPL has a children's section with regularly scheduled readings for kids at least once a week. Many—such as the Donnell Library
(20 West 53rd Street, between Fifth and Sixth Avenues; 212-621-0618)—
have lots of special classes and workshops in everything from poetry to cat's
cradles. For more details, pick up a copy of the monthly *Events for Children and
Young Adults* catalogs at any branch or check out the library's Web site. (For
branch locations, see Appendix C.)

NYU PROGRAM IN EDUCATIONAL THEATRE
Provincetown Playhouse
133 MacDougal Street (between West 3rd Street and Washington
Square South)
(212) 998–5868
www.nyu.edu/education/music/edtheatre
Sunday at 3:00 P.M.
A popular series of professional storytellers from around the country and
around the world. The program also presents a couple of free theater produc-

tions for children and young adults each year in the Black Box Theater. Call for schedule and details.

THE SCHOLASTIC STORE

557 Broadway (between Prince and Spring Streets)
(212) 343–6166
www.scholastic.com/sohostore

Drop by this colorful, energetic store almost anytime and you'll find something going on for you to enjoy. Every month the people who brought you Clifford the Big Red Dog and Harry Potter put together a full schedule of special events and hands-on activities, including author signings, celebrity appearances, craft workshops, and, of course, regular story times (Tuesday at 2:00 P.M.). Check the Web site or drop by the store for the schedule of events.

"We haven't the money,
so we've got to think."

—Lord Rutherford

ROM IVY LEAGUE colleges to technical schools, from GED to Ph.D., from continuing education to just-for-fun classes, if you can think of it (and even if you can't), you can learn it in New York. Many classes are offered completely free of charge and with no catch, while others can be had for nothing (or next to nothing) if you're willing to volunteer your time instead of paying. When volunteering, you're put to work in administrative offices, studios, or classrooms and your work hours are exchanged for classroom hours. You will find the math for these exchanges spelled out in each listing, but always check with the school to confirm these details. The economics of these work-study programs can change over time.

ARTS

CHAMBERS POTTERY

153 Chambers Street, second floor (between Church Street and West
Broadway)
(212) 619–7302
www.chamberspottery.com

Work-study in exchange for free classes. The math: 3
hours of work = 1 hour of free class time.

This small Tribeca pottery studio offers classes for children and adults. A
limited amount of space is available for work-study students.

DIEU DONNE PAPERMILL

433 Broome Street (between Broadway and Crosby Street)
(212) 226–0573
(877) DD–PAPER (toll-free outside New York only)
www.dieudonne.org

Internship/work-study program. The math: 8 hours of
work = 1 hour of studio time, plus after 6 to 8 weeks of
work you can take a class for free.

This is the place to go in New York to learn everything about the art of hand
paper making. This studio, gallery, and mill in Soho is a very small operation,
so interns often get the chance to work in the studio assisting masters of the
art, as well as performing all the usual glamorous intern duties (cleaning, filing, running errands, etc.). You will need to commit to working one full day
a week (11:00 A.M. to 6:00 P.M.), and they would like you to stay for at least
six months.

DOWNTOWN COMMUNITY TV CENTER (DCTV)

87 Lafayette Street (between White and Walker Streets)
(212) 966–4510
www.dctvny.org

Interns work sixteen hours a week in exchange for free
classes and equipment and facilities rental.

Learn the creative and technical skills you need to produce your own television programs. DCTV offers interns the use of top-of-the-line equipment and studios and classes in every aspect of television production, in exchange for time spent working in their offices or on their cable TV productions.

DOWNTOWN THIRD THURSDAY
Various historic locations around downtown
(212) 835–2789
www.downtownny.com

 Free admission, but reservations are required.

You are cordially invited into some of the most exclusive and eye-popping locations throughout downtown to hear some of the most informed authors and historians tell you what they know. This delightful lecture series runs the third Thursday of every month from January to May. The public gains access to some hidden architectural gems, both classic and modern, and gets to hear talks by some of New York's smartest folks on the issues, history, and architecture of the downtown area. Reservations are required, but all events are free.

FILM/VIDEO ARTS
462 Broadway, Suite 520 (at Grand Street)
(212) 941–8787
www.fva.com

Interns work sixteen hours a week in exchange for free classes and equipment and facilities rental.

Michael Moore, the producer and director of the documentaries *Roger and Me, Bowling for Columbine, Fahrenheit 9/11,* and *The Awful Truth* on Bravo—and an F/VA alumnus—says this about F/VA: "Film/Video Arts puts this art form in the hands of people who really aren't supposed to be doing it because it is really such an expensive process. What Film/Video Arts has done is to say, 'Money should not be in the way of getting these resources in the hands of people whose stories we should hear.'" F/VA provides state-of-the-art facilities, equipment, and a full schedule of classes for film and video production to all for low rates, but for interns it's all free.

GREENWICH HOUSE POTTERY
16 Jones Street (between Bleecker and West 4th Streets)
(212) 242–4106
www.greenwichhousepottery.com

 Work-study assistants work in the office, gallery, library, studio, or classes in exchange for free or reduced-rate pottery classes.

A full schedule of pottery classes for children, teens, and adults. Greenwich House also has a very fluid and somewhat negotiable work-study program. Students can work in a variety of positions for one to eight hours a week to be a part of the program. Depending on what skills you have and the job you take on, you can get anywhere from $100 off tuition to full tuition plus free firing time and twenty-four-hour access to the studio.

INSTITUTE FOR FINE ARTS AT NYU
The James B. Duke House
1 East 78th Street (at Fifth Avenue)
www.nyu.edu/gsas/dept/fineart/
Though they don't like to advertise it, every Friday at 4:00 P.M. during the school year the institute invites the public to the elegant and monumental halls of the Duke mansion to attend the Silberberg Lectures in the Fine Arts. This is a series of lectures by leading scholars from institutions around the country. The lectures are aimed at the institute's grad students, so this is pretty serious stuff. For more information and a schedule of lecturers, check out their Web site.

MANHATTAN NEIGHBORHOOD NETWORK (MNN)
537 West 59th Street (between Tenth and Eleventh Avenues)
(212) 757–2670
www.mnn.org

 You must be a resident of Manhattan and agree to produce a program for public access TV.

These organizations administer public access for cable TV services in Manhattan and Queens. The federally mandated obligation of cable TV is that they must provide a channel for all residents to exercise their First

Amendment right of freedom of expression. They provide training on production equipment (video production, studio production, editing, audio, basic
lighting, digital video and editing, and so on) as well as equipment for programs aired on public access TV. Classes and equipment are also provided in
each of the other four boroughs, but there's a small fee charged for classes
and materials that runs between $50 and $100 per class. (Contact Queens
Public Television (QPTV), 718–886–8160, www.qptv.org; Brooklyn Community
Access Television (BCAT), 718–935–1122, www.brooklynx.org/bcat; Staten
Island Community Television, 718–727–1414, www.sictv.org; or BronxNet,
718–960–1180, www.bronxnet.org.)

URBAN GLASS
647 Fulton Street (entrance on Rockwell, between DeKalb and Fulton
Streets)
Brooklyn
(718) 625–3685
www.urbanglass.org

> **THE CATCH** Studio and office volunteers are "paid" at a rate of $7.50
> an hour. This amount is applied to the cost of any class.

This is New York's only glass-art studio open to the general public. They
offer classes in glassblowing, neon, lamp working, casting, and anything
else that has to do with glass. The classes can be very expensive ($600 for
beginning glassblowing), so it can take a while to gain enough hours to
work off the class. The good news is that many of your volunteer hours can
be spent in the studio. So you can get a lot of useful hands-on experience
while you work (and you may even pick up a few great bits of discarded
glass art while tooling around). The bad news is that it gets awfully hot in
the studio; dress appropriately.

FOOD AND WINE

THE NATURAL GOURMET INSTITUTE FOR FOOD AND HEALTH
48 West 21st Street, second floor (between Fifth and Sixth Avenues)
(212) 645–5170
www.naturalgourmetschool.com

Work as a kitchen assistant or in their office to audit classes.

Slice and dice, scrub the pots, and *Bam!* you can become the next Emeril (but healthier—the school offers classes in "Health Supportive Cooking"). They have a full schedule of classes to satisfy everyone from the novice cook to the most experienced chef. All classes are vegetarian and have a holistic healing bent. The classes range from basic cooking how-tos like "Knife Skills," "Snack Attack: Healthier 'Junk' Food," and "Choosing Safe Foods" to healthful vegetarian and ethnic specialties like "Dazzling Vegan Desserts," "The Miracle of Miso," and "Authentic Indian Buffet." Kitchen assistants begin working an hour before the class, preparing ingredients and the kitchen; participate in and nibble their way through the classes; and clean up the kitchen after the class is over.

NEW SCHOOL CULINARY ARTS PROGRAM
131 West 23rd Street (between Sixth and Seventh Avenues)
(212) 255–4141
www.nsu.newschool.edu/culinary

 Work as a kitchen assistant to audit classes or as a work-study office assistant in exchange for classes. Office assistant math: 3 hours of work = 1 hour of class.

The kitchen assistant program is similar to the one at the Natural Gourmet Institute, except the classes are not limited to vegetarian subjects and can be much more indulgent. The schedule includes classes in basic techniques ("How to Boil Water," "Introduction to French Cooking," and "Creative Hors d'Oeuvres"), light and vegetarian cooking ("Low-Fat Sauces," "Light Italian Cooking," and "Cooking for the Way We Eat Today"), holiday cooking and baking ("The Hanukkah Feast," "For Pumpkin Lovers Only," and "Czech Christmas Cookies"), desserts ("Introduction to Cake Decorating," "Strudel Workshop," and "New Chocolate Desserts"). Kitchen assistants do not participate in the classes they work; they only observe. Work-study students are able to take part in classes. Everyone gets to feast on the results of the class work.

THE WINE WORKSHOP
160 West 72nd Street (between Columbus Avenue and Broadway)
(212) 875–0222
www.ackerwines.com/workshop

As part of Acker Merral Wine Store, "America's oldest and finest wine shop" (if they don't say so themselves), The Workshop offers a full schedule of classes on wines. Prices range from $85 to $1,000 a class, but you can get in on these for nothing as a pourer. Pourers may not always get the chance to actually taste the pricey wines they are pouring for the paying students; this depends on the number of people in the class. If there is room, pourers are welcome to drink up. Of course, volunteer pourers must be prepared to show up early to help set up, pitch in during the class, and stay after to help clean up. Call the workshop to add your name to the list, and they will call you when they have an opening in a class. You can also stop by the store any Saturday afternoon (2:00 to 5:00 P.M.) to sample some of their fine wines (they will do all the pouring then).

MIND

BROOKLYN PUBLIC LIBRARY'S BUSINESS LIBRARY
280 Cadman Plaza West (between Tillary and Pierrepont Streets)
(718) 623–7000
www.biz.brooklynpubliclibrary.org

 "You should only be successful and make us proud."

 An abundance of classes and workshops are offered throughout the year targeted toward entrepreneurs, small-business owners, students, small investors, and anyone interested in Brooklyn business. Some highlights include an entrepreneur series, a business fair in May and June, and the "Made in Brooklyn" breakfast series (Yes! Including a free continental breakfast) highlighting specific industries in Brooklyn, from music and film to Key lime pies and Caribbean beef patties. They also play host to the SCORE program, in which small-business start-ups get personalized mentoring from established and retired business owners. Free Internet access is available as well.

THE COOPER UNION FOR THE ADVANCEMENT OF SCIENCE AND ART
Cooper Square (8th Street between Bowery and Third Avenues)
(212) 353–4120
www.cooper.edu

Brains, brains, talent, and brains, plus a $50 application fee.

Every one of the 900 students at this top college of art, architecture, and engineering attends completely tuition-free. They do have to cover their own room, board, books, and a $600 student fee per year, but the $25,000 tuition bill is on the house. It shouldn't surprise you that the competition to get into this premier school is pretty stiff. Each year about 2,400 men and women from around the world apply for Cooper Union, and only about 300 are accepted. Gentlemen, start your slide rulers.

EGLISE FRANÇAIS DU ST-ESPRIT
109 East 60th Street (between Park and Lexington Avenues)
(212) 838–5680
www.stespritnyc.net
Free beginning and intermediate French classes are taught every Sunday from 10:00 to 11:00 A.M. These are very small and intimate classes (they have room for no more than ten students per class). They run from September through December and January through June.

ENGLISH CLASSES FOR SPEAKERS OF OTHER LANGUAGES
New York Public Library
Various branches in Manhattan, the Bronx, and Staten Island
(212) 340–0918
www.nypl.org
Beginner and intermediate English classes are offered three times a year (fall, winter, and spring). Space is limited, and registration is required. Check the Web site for branch locations and class schedules.

HENRY GEORGE SCHOOL OF SOCIAL SCIENCE
121 East 30th Street (between Park and Lexington Avenues)
(212) 889–8020
www.henrygeorgeschool.org
Free adult education classes that deal with the hidden factors at work in the economy. Classes include "Progress and Poverty" and "Applied Economics and Economic Science." The classes meet once a week for ten weeks; preregistration is required. They also offer free film forums and upper-level courses such as "Current Events," "The Genesis of Modern Economics," and "Money and Banking." All courses and forums are offered in Spanish as well.

Libraries with Class!

At branches of the New York Public Library (www.nypl.org), Brooklyn Public Library (www.brooklynpubliclibrary.org), and Queens Public Library (www.queenslibrary.org), you will find literally thousands of free classes, lectures, and workshops in everything imaginable offered throughout the year. Here is just a sampling of classes. For details and schedules, stop into any branch or check the Web sites.

401(k) Rollover
How to Do a Term Paper
Fashion Design for Teens
Arts and Crafts
Ballroom Dancing
Basic and Intermediate Internet
Basic Mouse Skills
Bead Making Workshop
Jewelry Making
Become a Stamp Collector
Breaking the Rules Again: Teens Writing Poetry
Career Exploration Inventory
Citizenship Preparation Workshop in Mandarin
College and You
Computers for Seniors
Conserving Home Energy
Create a Quilt
Create Your Own Photo Album
Create Your Own Shadow Puppet
Crocheting Class
Dance with a Mexican Touch
Doing Business in Taiwan
Drum Clinic
E-mail Basics
ESOL Class
Estate Planning
GED Class

Get Connected to Consumer Health Information
Book Discussions
Health Information on the Internet
How to Read the NYC Subway Map
Illustrated Bookmaking
Internet Search Strategies
Introduction to Computers
Introduction to Excel
Introduction to PowerPoint
Introduction to Word
Investing: How to Research Companies and Industries
Job and Résumé Resources Online
Knitting Classes for Beginners
Knitting Club
Learning about the Rights of Immigrants
Makeup Tips and Techniques
Making Your Assets Last
Open Mike Night
Origami
Picture Book Hour
Poetry Writing Workshop
Polish Your Résumé!
So You Want to Be a Songwriter
Sorting through the Life Insurance Maze

Stay C.O.O.L. Under Fire: Dealing with Difficult People
Staywell Exercise for Older Adults
Success in Math
Great Ideas Forum
Checking and Credit 101 Workshop
Cantonese Program for Parents
Bridge Club
Tai Chi for Seniors
Telescope Moon Watching
The Art of Breathing and Relaxation
The Art of Public Speaking
The Big Apple on the Big Screen
The History of Greenwich Village
The Write Stuff: A Writing Workshop for Adults
Toddler Time
Understanding the 2001 Tax Relief Act
Using MS Word for Your Newsletter
Using Music in Literacy and ESOL
Voice-Over Workshop: How to Break into the Lucrative World of Voice-Overs
Watercolor Class
Work for the U.S. Postal Service

HOUSING EDUCATION PROGRAM
NYC Department of Housing Preservation and Development
100 Gold Street, Room 6C
(212) 863-8830
www.nyc.gov/hpd

 You must be a New York City resident or property owner.

Get a Job, Get a Degree

New York is home to many top-ranked universities and countless other colleges and technical schools throughout the five boroughs. Like any business, these schools need a large support staff to keep the doors open and the students happy—and that's where you come in. From office assistants and administrative staff to maintenance and mailroom clerks, almost all of these jobs include the fringe benefit of free or seriously reduced tuition for classes at these and affiliated schools. So instead of paying $30,000 a year for that graduate degree, why not have them pay you for your time? Forget about paying $10,000 to become a computer systems analyst; you can take advantage of the system to get it for nothing. Salaries at the schools vary, but you probably won't be making the kind of money you can retire on. Still, this extra benefit can make it a very profitable position. Here are some places to start your search:

COLUMBIA UNIVERSITY, *475 Riverside Drive, Room 1901 (between 119th and 120th Streets); (212) 870-2425; www.columbia.edu/cu/jobs.*

NEW YORK UNIVERSITY, *7 East 12th Street, first floor (at Fifth Avenue); (212) 998-1250; www.nyu.edu/hr.*

WWW.UNIVERSITYWORK.COM

This city-run program offers a comprehensive set of courses to help home-owners learn how to keep their properties in good fiscal and physical health. Classes include "Basic and Advanced Building Management," "Building Finances," "Tenant Relations," "Building Maintenance," and others. Courses are generally offered three to five times a year, but many fill up quickly; early registration is recommended.

SMALL BUSINESS DEVELOPMENT CENTER (SBDC)

Pace University, 163 William Street, sixteenth floor (Ann and Beeckman Streets); (212) 618–6655

Baruch College, 1 Bernard Baruch Way (between 24th and 25th Streets on Lexington Avenue); (212) 721–5465
www.nyssbdc.org

Ready to start your own business but haven't got a clue what to do? Well, you are going to want to get to know the folks at these SBDCs. Basically, this is your uncle in the business who is going to help you do it right. These centers (two of eighteen throughout the state) are sponsored by the federal government, New York State, and the local universities. They are there to help you through every step of the start-up process and will continue to offer assistance for as long as you're in business, with one-on-one coaching and workshops in everything from business plan development and financial planning to marketing strategies and management. There is never a charge for any of their counseling services, and most classes and workshops are free as well.

BODY

BIKRAM YOGA NYC

797 Eighth Avenue, fourth floor (between West 48th and West 49th Streets)
(212) 245–2525
www.bikramyoganyc.com
Friday at 11:30 A.M., pay-what-you-wish class.

Work the front desk for five hours a week for unlimited free classes.

Bikram has become the hottest craze in yoga, in more ways than one. This popular yoga studio literally turns the heat up to more than one hundred degrees for its ninety-minute classes, guaranteeing you will be dripping and exhausted from this vigorous workout. This can be an addictive and expensive habit, with each class running $20. Of course, there is a way to stretch your dollars here. Every Friday at 11:30 A.M., they offer a pay-what-you-wish class where anyone can show up and pay as little as they want for the class. All proceeds from that weekly class go to benefit the AIDS organization Equity Fights AIDS. And if one class a week doesn't satisfy your need for sweat, you can sign up to work one five-hour shift a week at the desk for unlimited free classes. Students are required to take classes for a few months before they can take part in the work-study program. They have three other studios around the city where you can do your work-study, but you have to fill out an application and interview at this location.

DIAS Y FLORES

520–522 East 13th Street (between Avenues A and B)
(212) 260–9344
www.greenthumbnyc.org/events.html

This community garden offers free yoga, tai chi, and drawing classes during the summer months. All supplies for the drawing classes are provided free, but bring your own yoga mats and towel for the others. Class offerings vary from summer to summer; call for schedules and details. The Green Thumb Web site (listed above) is also a great resource for free happenings in community gardens all around the city.

GUARDIAN ANGELS TRAINING ACADEMY

763 Eighth Avenue (between 46th and 47th Streets)
(212) 397–7822
www.guardianangels.org

THE CATCH They would like you to volunteer for at least one four-hour patrol in exchange for free classes, but it is not required.

They offer free self-defense training, Capoeira, and Thai boxing classes to volunteers. The Guardian Angels are those (in)famous red-bereted folks who patrol the subways, streets, and public events to "offer assistance and protection to any member of the public and will not hesitate to physically protect victims of crime." Since they were founded by Curtis Sliwa in 1979, they have been called vigilantes by some and by others . . . guardian angels.

HIGH VIBE HEALTH & HEALING

138 East Third Street (between First Avenue and Avenue A)
(212) 777–6645
www.highvibe.com

This "living food" and health supplements store offers free classes on such subjects as fasting, family nutrition, essential oil treatments, and gallbladder and liver detox. They also hold raw food preparation workshops, but they charge for those.

HIMALAYAN INSTITUTE

East West Books
78 Fifth Avenue (between 13th and 14th Streets)
(212) 243–5995
www.himalayaninstitute.org/hinyc/

 Work-study students exchange classes for office work. The math: 1 hour of work = 1 hour of class.

Offers a full schedule of classes, seminars, and workshops on yoga, meditation, and vegetarian cooking.

THE OHASHI INSTITUTE

147 West 25th Street, sixth floor (between Sixth and Seventh Avenues)
(646) 486–1187 or (800) 810–4190
www.ohashiatsu.org

 Work-study students may work in the office, on the cleaning crew, or on special projects in exchange for credit toward classes. The math: 1 hour of work = $10 credit toward class for the first year, $12 thereafter.

Ohashi offers a six-level curriculum on its own style of shiatsu massage (Ohashiatsu) that can be taken by both professionals and laypeople. Ohashiatsu is a stretching, relaxing, and energizing acupressure type of massage that works with the Eastern healing philosophies of chi (energy) and the meridians (energy channels) of the body.

SPIRIT

THE ASIAN CLASSICS INSTITUTE/
THREE JEWELS COMMUNITY CENTER

61 Fourth Avenue (between 9th and 10th Streets)
(212) 475–7752 or (212) 475–6650
www.world-view.org

The institute offers general-interest and teacher-training courses in Tibetan Buddhism, meditation, and Tibetan language, all free of charge. The general-interest courses are drop-in classes open to all, and the formal study teacher-training courses are open to those "willing to make a serious commitment to their studies." These courses have attendance requirements, homework assignments, and tests. The Three Jewels Community Center offers free meditation classes, free coffee and tea, free Internet access, and a free lending library. They are also associated with Godstow Retreat Center, where you can get away from the city for a free retreat in exchange for household chores (see page 226 for more information on Godstow).

FALUN DAFA

Central Park (Fourth Avenue and 73rd Street) and many other sites throughout the city
(212) 978–9511 or (877) FALUN–99
www.falun-ny.net

 THE CATCH   None (as long as you aren't in China)

From the folks who brought you tai chi comes a new, very old traditional Chinese exercise, Falun Dafa (or Falun Gong). It's a practice that aims to improve mental and physical well-being through a series of easy-to-learn exercises, meditation, and development of "one's Heart/Mind Nature." And from the folks who brought you Tiananmen Square comes a whole new wave of oppression. This is the group that has gained a lot of attention recently by being banned in China and has seen brutal suppression of its practitioners by the Chinese government. So there must be something to it. They offer free introductory classes as well as weekly group practices.

MANHATTAN JEWISH EXPERIENCE (MJE)

131 West 86th Street (between Columbus and Amsterdam Avenues)
5 East 62nd Street (between Fifth and Madison Avenues)

(212) 787–9533
www.jewishexperience.org

If you're like me and all you remember about Hebrew school as a kid was falling asleep, then here's your chance to try it again. The big difference is that this time you'll stay awake and maybe even enjoy it. MJE offers a full schedule of basic courses for free, including the Monday Night Lounge, which includes a sushi dinner and interesting discussions of how current issues (sexuality, free will, business and medical ethics) relate to the ancient religion, followed by music and dessert. They also offer free basic Learn to Read Hebrew classes (and intermediate and advanced courses for $5.00 a class). Classes are fun, unintimidating, interactive, and geared for all Jews, particularly those with little or no background in Judaism. These classes are not meant to recruit Jews into a particular sect, but to help you gain a deeper understanding of the age-old traditions and how they fit into modern life. Plus, it's not a bad place to meet a nice Jewish girl or guy and make your mother happy. They also have a full program of inter-mediate and advanced courses and lectures for which they do charge a small fee ($5.00 per class). Hey, they even set out some free soft drinks and noshes.

THE OPEN CENTER

83 Spring Street (between Broadway and Lafayette Street)
(212) 219–2527, ext. 117
www.opencenter.org

Volunteer four hours a week for unlimited free classes (depending on availability).

They offer a huge array of classes and workshops in holistic learning and living. There are classes in everything from feng shui, reflexology, belly dancing, and salsa aerobics to Taoism, Kabbalah, tantric sex, and herbal-ism. You can also find ongoing yoga and meditation classes here, as well as a number of certification programs. They treat their volunteers with great respect and support. If you're interested in alternative learning, this is the place for you.

SHAMBHALA CENTER OF NEW YORK

118 West 22nd Street, sixth floor (between Sixth and Seventh Avenues)
(212) 675–6544
www.ny.shambhala.org

Three free classes each week (donations requested, but not required). Work-study is also available for other classes. The math: 1 hour work = $10 class credit.

The Shambhala Center offers a full schedule of classes and lectures on all forms of meditation, yoga, and Buddhist and eastern practices. Each week they hold two "Learn to Meditate" classes (Wednesday at 6:00 P.M. and Sunday at noon) and an "Open Dharma Gathering" (Tuesday at 7:00 P.M.), which includes a guided meditation and lectures by noted teachers. Both of these classes are on a donation basis. You can also take part in their work-study program to take any of their classes for free. Each hour of work nets you $10 credit toward classes.

> "Always laugh when you
> can. It is cheap medicine."
>
> —Lord Byron

HEALTH AND MEDICAL:
LIVE FREE OR DIE

NEW YORK SURELY ranks among the most expensive places to stay healthy. From ordinary checkups to health insurance, getting sick here will cost you. The good news is, New York is also one of the major centers for medical schools and clinical studies, which provide many opportunities for free and low-cost care, often with cutting-edge treatments (excuse the pun). New York is also a center for bleeding-heart liberals, so in this town big government still plays some role in providing services to those in need of low-cost health care through the extensive Health & Hospitals Corporation system and at some community clinics.

TO YOUR HEALTH: FREE CLINICS

In a day and age when medical costs are sky-high and the cost of health insurance is just as stratospheric, it would seem to be just a fantasy that such a thing as a free clinic still exists, right? Well, stop dreaming and start dialing to get yourself an appointment, because it really does, and not just one but two are right here in New York City. These two clinics, one in Manhattan and one in the Bronx, provide free medical care, health education, and social work services to anyone who is uninsured and older than age nineteen. Both clinics are open only on Saturday mornings and are staffed by the medical students and physicians from NYU Medical School in Manhattan and the Albert Einstein College of Medicine in the Bronx.

ECHO FREE CLINIC
Walton Family Health Center
1894 Walton Avenue (at East 177th Street)
Bronx
(718) 583–3060
www.echo-clinic.org
To make an appointment call between 9:00 A.M. and 4:45 P.M. Monday through Friday. Appointments are usually about two months from the day you call. The clinic does take a limited number of walk-ins every Saturday, but you should be prepared to wait a while.

NYC FREE CLINIC
The Institute for Urban Family Health
16 East 16th Street, third floor (between Fifth and Madison Avenues)
(917) 544–0735
http://endeavor.med.nyu.edu/freeclinic/
Appointments made by calling on Monday between 4:00 and 5:00 P.M. No walk-ins are accepted.

WHATEVER AILS YOU: CLINICAL STUDIES

Medical centers throughout New York run clinical trials for almost any condition imaginable, from cancer to acne, from athlete's foot to weight loss. People

Guinea Pigs: Student Clinics

Calling all brave souls with sore feet, aching muscles, off-balance polarity, and clogged chi. Students at Alternative Health schools throughout the city are waiting to rub, prick, and stretch you back to health. All over New York there are schools for everything from acupuncture and herbal medicine to polarity therapy and shiatsu. Many of these schools have clinics attached to them where they offer low-cost (and sometimes free) appointments to the public, on whom the students try out their new skills. It may seem a bit scary to let a newbee acupuncturist loose on you with his needles, but rest assured that these are all advanced students, and they're always watched over by professionals. Here is a list of schools and the services they offer:

AYURVEDA'S BEAUTY CARE SPA & BIOTICARE HOLISTIC CENTER, *99 University Place, Fifth Floor (between 11th and 12th Streets); (212) 529–3300; www.ayurvedasbeautycare.com; free Ayurveda nutritional counseling is offered at various times throughout the year. They also plan to start offering free or low-cost facials and other skin-care services from students soon. Check their Web site or call for schedule and details.*

PACIFIC COLLEGE OF ORIENTAL MEDICINE & ACUPUNCTURE, *915 Broadway (between 20th and 21st Streets); (212) 982–4600; www.pacificcollege.edu; low-cost acupuncture and herbal medicine.*

THE OPEN CENTER, *83 Spring Street (between Broadway and Lafayette Street); (212) 219–2527, ext 116; www.theopencenter .org; free reiki, reflexology, and polarity-therapy sessions. Call to put your name on the list of available clients, and a student will call you when they need a warm body to attend a class or to practice on.*

THE SWEDISH INSTITUTE, *226 West 26th Street (between Seventh and Eighth Avenues); (212) 924–5900; www.swedishinstitute.edu; massage, $150 for six one-hour sessions or $250 for twelve one-hour sessions; acupuncture, $300 for a consultation plus twelve sessions.*

TRI-STATE COLLEGE OF ACUPUNCTURE, *80 Eighth Avenue (at 14th Street); (212) 242–2254 for acupuncture, (212) 242–4307 for herbal medicine; www.tsca.edu; $35 for one-hour acupuncture appointments; $20 for herbal medicine appointments (plus the cost of herbs, about $15).*

are always needed to participate in these studies, and all medication and care are provided free of charge—in fact, you can even get paid for participating in many of these studies.

COLUMBIA-PRESBYTERIAN MEDICAL CENTER
Department of Dermatology
161 Fort Washington Avenue, Room 750 (between 165th and 168th Streets)
(212) 305–6953
cpmcnet.columbia.edu

Constantly organizing new trials for medication and treatment of various skin conditions including acne, toe fungus, wounds, and more. Treatment and medication are free, and compensation is provided.

Pick a Study, Any Study

To find a study for a particular condition, check out these Web sites:

NATIONAL DATABASES

CENTER WATCH, *a friendly consolidated listing by category; www.centerwatch.com.*

NATIONAL CANCER INSTITUTE, *a searchable database for clinical trials throughout the country for all forms of cancer; www.cancer.gov/clinicaltrials.*

AIDS CLINICAL TRIAL INFORMATION SERVICE, *(800) 874–2572; www.aidsinfo.nih.gov.*

VERITAS MEDICINE, *a database of clinical studies by condition; www.veritasmedicine.com.*

NATIONAL INSTITUTES OF HEALTH, *a national database of conditions and studies for clinical trials in everything from Acidosis to Zellweger Syndrome; www.clinicaltrials.gov.*

NEW YORK MEDICAL CENTERS

BETH ISRAEL MEDICAL CENTER, *www.wehealny.org/studies.*

NYU MEDICAL CENTER, *www.med.nyu.edu/clinicaltrials.*

NYU AIDS CLINICAL TRIALS UNIT, *(212) 263–6565; www.hivinfosource.org.*

COLUMBIA-PRESBYTERIAN, *www.columbiaclinicaltrials.org.*

NEW YORK HEADACHE CENTER
30 East 76th Street, second floor (at Madison Avenue)
(212) 794–3550
www.nyheadache.com
Conducts clinical trials on different medication and treatments for migraines and other types of headaches. All research-related examinations and treatments are free, and financial compensation is often provided.

RESEARCH TESTING LABORATORIES
255 Great Neck Road
Great Neck, Long Island
(516) 773–7788
www.rtlab.com
Runs studies in everything from weight loss to hair loss. Compensation is provided.

HHC TO THE RESCUE

New York City Health & Hospitals Corporation (HHC) was created to provide comprehensive medical care to all people "regardless of their ability" to pay. The corporation consists of eleven acute-care hospitals, six diagnostic and treatment centers, four long-term care facilities, and more than eighty community health clinics. HHC also operates MetroPlus Health Plan, a health maintenance organization (HMO) for Medicaid recipients. You can expect waits to be a bit longer for all appointments and at emergency rooms at these facilities than at private hospitals, but sit tight and they'll get to you. For more information, check the Web site www.nyc.gov/hhc or call (212) 788–3321.

MANHATTAN

BELLEVUE HOSPITAL CENTER, 462 First Avenue (at 27th Street); (212) 562–4141.

COLER-GOLDWATER MEMORIAL HOSPITAL,
1 Main Street (Coler); (212) 848–6000.
900 Main Street (Goldwater); (212) 318–8000.
Roosevelt Island

GOUVERNEUR NURSING FACILITY AND DIAGNOSTIC & TREATMENT CENTER, 227 Madison Street (between Jefferson and Clinton Streets); (212) 238–7000.

HARLEM HOSPITAL CENTER, 506 Lenox Avenue (at 135th Street); (212) 939–1000.

METROPOLITAN HOSPITAL CENTER, 1901 First Avenue (97th Street, between First and Second Avenues); (212) 423–6262.

RENAISSANCE DIAGNOSTIC & TREATMENT CENTER, 215 West 125th Street (between Seventh and Eighth Avenues); (212) 932–6500.

THE BRONX

JACOBI MEDICAL CENTER, 1400 Pelham Parkway South (at Eastchester Road); (718) 918–5000.

LINCOLN MEDICAL AND MENTAL HEALTH CENTER, 234 East 149th Street (between Park and Morris Avenues, near the Grand Concourse); (718) 579–5000.

MORRISANIA DIAGNOSTIC & TREATMENT CENTER, 1225 Gerard Avenue (between East 167th and East 168th Streets); (718) 960–2777.

NORTH CENTRAL BRONX HOSPITAL, 3424 Kossuth Avenue (210th Street, between Gunhill and Jerome Avenues); (718) 519–5000.

SEGUNDO RUIZ BELVIS DIAGNOSTIC & TREATMENT CENTER, 545 East 142nd Street (between Brock and St. Anns Avenues); (718) 579–4000.

BROOKLYN

CONEY ISLAND HOSPITAL, 2601 Ocean Parkway (between Avenue Z and Shore Parkway); (718) 616–3000.

CUMBERLAND DIAGNOSTIC & TREATMENT CENTER, 100 North Portland Avenue (between Park and Myrtle Avenues); (718) 260–7500.

DR. SUSAN SMITH MCKINNEY NURSING AND REHABILITATION CENTER, 594 Albany Avenue (at Rutland Road); (718) 245–7000.

EAST NEW YORK DIAGNOSTIC & TREATMENT CENTER, 2094 Pitkin Avenue (between Pennsylvania and New Jersey Avenues); (718) 240–0400.

KINGS COUNTY HOSPITAL CENTER, 451 Clarkson Avenue (between Albany and New York Avenues); (718) 245–3131.

WOODHULL MEDICAL AND MENTAL HEALTH CENTER, 760 Broadway (at Flushing Avenue); (718) 963–8000.

QUEENS

ELMHURST HOSPITAL CENTER, 79–01 Broadway (at 79th Street); (718) 334–4000.

QUEENS HOSPITAL CENTER, 82–70 164th Street (at the Grand Central Parkway); (718) 883–3000.

STATEN ISLAND

SEA VIEW HOSPITAL REHABILITATION CENTER AND HOME, 460 Brielle Avenue (Bradley and Rockland Avenues); (718) 317–3000.

DEPRESSION/MENTAL HEALTH STUDIES AND CLINICAL TRIALS

A number of hospitals and research centers throughout New York conduct ongoing clinical studies of depression and medications for mental illnesses such as Prozac, Zoloft, Wellbutrin, and others. If you qualify for a study, they can provide you with up to one year of free medication and medical care. All studies are supervised and monitored by doctors and psychiatrists adhering to strict clinical testing protocols, some of which could involve the use of a placebo.

MOUNT SINAI MEDICAL CENTER, Compulsive, Impulsive and Anxiety Disorders Clinic, 99th Street and Madison Avenue; (212) 241–4657; www.mssm.edu/psychiatry/ciadp.

NEUROPSYCH RESEARCH ASSOCIATES, 1236 Park Avenue (at 96th Street); (212) 722–6604.

NEW YORK PRESBYTERIAN/CORNELL MEDICAL CENTER, Depression Treatment Study Program, 525 East 68th Street (at York Avenue); (212) 746–5705.

NEW YORK PSYCHIATRIC INSTITUTE, Depression Evaluation Service, 1051 Riverside Drive, Suite 3300; (212) 543–5734; www.depression-nyc.org.

ST. LUKE'S/ROOSEVELT HOSPITAL, Mood Disorders Research Program, 910 Ninth Avenue (at 58th Street); (212) 523–7666.

STD CLINICS

There are eleven city-run STD (sexually transmitted disease) clinics located throughout the five boroughs that provide free testing and treatment for all common STDs. They also provide anonymous and confidential HIV testing and counseling. Of course, you can also get free condoms at all locations. These clinics all operate on a take-a-number-and-wait-on-line basis, so you can never predict how long the wait will be. Most clinics are open Monday through Friday from 8:30 A.M. to 4:00 P.M. and some offer Saturday hours, but always call to check hours and services before heading down to one of these clinics. For more information, call the hotline at (212) 427–5120 or check the Web site www.nyc.gov/health.

MANHATTAN

CENTRAL HARLEM STD CLINIC, 2238 Fifth Avenue (at 137th Street); (212) 690–1760.

EAST HARLEM STD CLINIC, 158 East 115th Street (off Lexington Avenue); (212) 360–5962.

CHELSEA STD CLINIC, 303 Ninth Avenue (at 28th Street); (212) 239–1718 or (212) 239–0843.

RIVERSIDE STD CLINIC, 160 West 100th Street (between Columbus and Amsterdam Avenues); (212) 865–7757.

THE BRONX

MORRISANIA STD CLINIC, 1309 Fulton Avenue (at East 169th Street, off Third Avenue); (718) 579–7714.

BROOKLYN

BUSHWICK CLINIC, 335 Central Avenue (between Linden and Grove Streets); (718) 573–4820 or (718) 573–4823.

Safety First: Free Condoms

A Cheap Bastard can be a sexy bastard, but there's no reason you can't also be a safe bastard. Here is a list of places to pick up your free condoms.

GAY MEN'S HEALTH CRISIS (GMHC), *119 West 24th Street (between Sixth and Seventh Avenues). Provides a huge amount of free services for people with AIDS and everything you need for AIDS prevention, including condoms-a-plenty. Check out the front desks on the fourth and seventh floors. For more information on other services they provide, call (212) 807–6655 or (800) AIDS–NYC, or check the Web site www.gmhc.org.*

THE LESBIAN, GAY, BISEXUAL & TRANSGENDER COMMUNITY CENTER, *208 West 13th Street (between Seventh and Eighth Avenues). The newly renovated center is home to a full schedule of weekly meetings, support groups, workshops, and social activities, many of which are free. You'll also find the free Pat Parker/Vito Russo Library, and there are always free condoms available at the front desk. For more information on schedule and activities, call (212) 620–7310, or check the Web site www.gaycenter.org.*

FORT GREENE STD CLINIC, 295 Flatbush Avenue Extension, fifth floor (at Willoughby Street); (718) 643–4133.

QUEENS

CORONA STD CLINIC, 34–33 Junction Boulevard (between Roosevelt and Northern Avenues); (718) 476–7815.

JAMAICA STD CLINIC, 90–37 Parsons Boulevard, first floor (off Jamaica Avenue); (718) 262–5572.

ROCKAWAY STD CLINIC, 67–19 Rockaway Boulevard (at Beach 67th Street); (718) 945–7150.

STATEN ISLAND

RICHMOND STD CLINIC, 51 Stuyvesant Place (at Wall Street); (718) 420–4994 or (718) 420–4995.

> "I cannot afford to
> waste my time making
> money."
>
> —Jean Louis Agassiz

FITNESS, FUN, AND GAMES: CHEAP THRILLS

FREE TIME IS a precious commodity in New York, whether you're visiting or you live here. And no place offers more extravagant ways to drop a load of cash when you're able to break away from the hustle and bustle of life in the big city. But wait! There are also tons of things to do and places to go to wind down without breaking the bank. Here are some suggestions for great destinations, recreational activities, and other ways to take it easy for free in New York City. From kayaking along the Hudson to in-line skating lessons in Central Park and a refreshing dip in any of the many public pools throughout the city, New York City really gives you a chance to enjoy your free time. The schedules change from time to time, so be sure to call and confirm all information before showing up.

PARK IT HERE! PARKS OFFERING A VARIETY OF ACTIVITIES

BATTERY PARK CITY PARKS
Hudson River (from Chambers to Vesey Streets)
(212) 267–9700
www.bpcparks.org

This delightful park offers a real windfall of free fun-and-games activities that include volleyball, chess, backgammon, concerts, and in-line skating lessons. You can also borrow a wide variety of recreational supplies like Frisbees, basketballs, jump ropes, board games, and more from the Park House at Rockefeller Park (at Chambers Street; bring a photo ID). They even have a couple of free pool tables available near the Park House. Other programs they run throughout the season include a drumming circle, fishing, bird-watching, family dances, lots of children's programs, walking tours, concerts, and on and on. Check out the Web site for more information, or get a copy of their most recent calendar; they add new activities every season.

BRYANT PARK
Sixth Avenue (between 40th and 42nd Streets)
(212) 768–4242
www.bryantpark.org

This oasis at the dead center of the frenetic midtown bustle is awash with free activities and entertainment throughout the year. During the warmer months its beautiful lawn is the perfect destination for a quick lunchtime snooze or after-work picnic, as long as it is not crammed with throngs attending one of their many high-profile and star-studded free events. Such events include the early morning Good Morning America Concerts, the HBO Monday-night film series, Broadway and dance performances, and many others. They also offer free Pétanque lessons (pronounced *pay-TONK*), which is basically the French version of boccie with smaller balls (fill in your own joke here). Stop by the free reading room to borrow a book, newspaper, or magazine while lounging around. And in the wintertime they roll up the lawn and bring out The Pond—a state-of-the-art ice-skating rink where the skating is all free (though you will have to pay a steep $7.50 if you need to rent skates).

CENTRAL PARK
59th Street to 110th Street (between Fifth Avenue and
Central Park West)
(212) 310–6600

www.centralparknyc.org

Whole books have been written about this oasis of natural splendor amid the concrete jungle, and there are many entries in this one about specific destinations for free goings-on. Here's a quick rundown of some of the park's free delights: walking tours; in-line skating lessons; tango, salsa, and swing dance; nature exhibits; the Conservatory Gardens; fishing and birding; borrowed sports equipment from the North Meadow Recreation Center; art galleries; theater; concerts; and much more. To get information about anything going on in the park, check the Web site or stop by one of the park's three visitor centers: Belvedere Castle (midpark at 79th Street; 212–772–0210), the Dairy (midpark at 65th Street; 212–794–6564), and the Charles A. Dana Discovery Center (inside the park at 110th Street and Lenox Avenue; 212–860–1370).

HUDSON RIVER PARK

Harris Street to 59th Street (at the Hudson River)
(212) 627–2020 or (212) 414–9384
www.hudsonriverpark.org

Making the link between Battery Park City Park up to Riverside Park, the Hudson River Park is the greatest addition to New York's recreation landscape since 700 swampy acres in the center of Manhattan were made into a humble little park. Once an industrial wasteland, the West Side waterfront is now a major destination for bicyclists and skaters, who can now traverse the entire length of Manhattan. During the summer months it is one of the major epicenters of free fun in New York City. Some of the many free offerings you will find throughout the summer months include free movies, swing dancing, arts and crafts activities for the kids, Ping-Pong, catch-and-release fishing, open-air professional boxing matches, and concerts. Free kayaking is available at Pier 26 (at Canal Street, at Pier 96 at 56th Street, and at 72nd Street, and you can roll around the ramps of the state-of-the-art skate park (at Franklin Street), visit a waterpark playground on Pier 51 (at Jane Street), and enjoy lots of lush lawns for relaxing and tossing a Frisbee around. The park is still in the building stage and every year brings new activities, facilities, and free fun to the West Side.

RECREATION CENTERS

New York City Department of Parks and Recreation runs forty-two recreation centers throughout the five boroughs, and for the price of $75 a year (yes, a year!) you have access to every single one of them. Now, to be totally honest, some of these are not exactly state-of-the-art facilities, but they do have much of the same equipment you'd find at the high-price gyms around town (Nautilus machines, Lifecycles, free weights, dumbbells, et cetera). Some also offer a full schedule of classes (aerobics, yoga, tai chi, boxing, and more), and some even have indoor and outdoor pools (you won't find that at many of the more expensive clubs around town!). Many of the centers also have extensive programs for children and seniors, and all have free after-school programs for kids ages eight through thirteen. The computer resource facilities at many of the centers offer classes and instruction on the Internet and computer programs.

Some of the adult classes charge a small fee in addition to the membership.

For information, check the Web site www.nycgovparks.org and click on "Things to Do," or call the chief of recreation's office in each borough (see Appendix D for recreation center locations).

CHIEF OF RECREATION'S OFFICE

(212) 408–0243 (Manhattan)

(718) 965–8935 (Brooklyn)

(718) 430–1858 (the Bronx)

(718) 520–5936 (Queens)

(718) 390–8020 (Staten Island)

GROUP SKATES

Organized group skates have become quite popular in the city. Each one has a slightly different attitude, ethos, and skill level, but all demand that you be prepared to skate through the streets and that you hone your flirting-while-blading skills. There are groups skating almost every night of the week, spring through fall. All require you to wear helmets and wrist guards.

EMPIRE SKATE CLUB OF NEW YORK
(212) 774–1774
www.empireskate.org

This is a membership organization that welcomes all skaters to join in a number of group skates every week. The Tuesday Night Skate (meets at Blades West, 120 West 72nd Street, between Columbus and Amsterdam Avenues, at 8:00 P.M.) is for high-intermediate and advanced skaters. The Thursday Evening Roll (convenes at the Columbus Circle entrance to Central Park at 59th Street at 6:30 P.M.) is for all levels. The Sunday Morning Skate (also meets at the Columbus Circle entrance to Central Park at 59th Street, at 11:00 A.M.) is open to all levels. All skates are canceled in the case of rain or wet streets; call to confirm.

TIME'S UP

(212) 802-8222

www.times-up.org

An environmental activist organization puts together bike and skate rides throughout the year with a point: Get rid of the cars! Critical Mass is an "organized coincidence" that aims to exercise the rights of skaters and cyclists as road users. Meet at Union Square (14th Street and University Place) at 7:00 P.M. on the last Friday of every month, year-round. The Moonlight Ride/Roll through Central Park happens on the first Friday of every month at 10:00 P.M. The group meets at the Columbus Circle entrance to Central Park at 59th Street. The Prospect Park Moonlight Ride/Roll is the second Saturday of every month at 9:00 P.M. and starts at Grand Army Plaza (Flatbush Avenue and Eastern Parkway). Both are relaxing and easygoing tours through these parks. They also run many other rides throughout the five boroughs; check their Web site for details.

Meet the Mets!

Besides being the best, most exciting baseball team in New York City (that's my opinion and I'm sticking to it), the New York Mets were made for Cheap Bastard baseball fans. There are two great ways to see a Mets game free, and legally, too.

1. *Any Wednesday night they're playing at Shea, just be one of the first 1,000 people to bring a Pepsi can or bottle to the picnic area in center field and get in free. Get there early!*

2. *During any home game, join the hardiest of the Mets faithful watching the game from the walkway of the subway station for the 7 train looking out over right field.*

For schedule and information, call (718) 507-8499 or check the Web site www.mets.com.

Get In-Line:
Central Park Skate Patrol

Not too steady on those skates? Don't let that stop you from getting out there and hitting the road, but make your first stop (or crash!) at the Free Braking and Safety Clinic in Central Park, taught by certified volunteers. Stationed at the East and West Side 72nd Street entrances to the park every Saturday and Sunday from 12:30 to 5:30 P.M. (mid-April to mid-October), these kind and patient volunteers will hold your hand while you master the art of staying in an upright position with blades on your feet. Be sure to pick up a copy of their free Central Park Pocket Guide for Skaters, *which offers a great map and lots of useful information for the beginning skater. They also offer advanced group classes and lessons (but they charge for those). For more information, call (212) 439–1234 or check out the Web site www.skatepatrol.org.*

WEDNESDAY EVENING SKATE CLUB

North end of Union Square (17th Street, between Broadway and Park Avenue)
www.weskateny.org

This very popular skate tours different sections of the city each week and meets between 7:30 and 8:00 P.M. The group rides for about two hours. Open to all levels.

BOATING

THE DOWNTOWN BOATHOUSE

Pier 26 (Hudson River, between Canal and Chambers Streets); Saturday and Sunday, 9:00 A.M.–6:00 P.M.; some weekdays, 5:00–7:00 P.M. (call the status line).

Pier 96 (56th Street and the Hudson River); Saturday and Sunday, 10:00 A.M.–5:00 P.M.

Riverside Park (at 72nd Street); Saturday and Sunday, 10:00 A.M.–5:00 P.M.

(646) 613–0375 (recorded information), (646) 613–0740 (daily status line)
www.downtownboathouse.org
May through October.
These three locations offer free kayaking on a first-come, first-served basis. They provide the boats, safety equipment, and brief instructions, and you provide the muscle. You can take a leisurely ride in the local embayment, and once you have some experience, you can join them on their free three-hour rides to the Statue of Liberty or the Intrepid Museum. The long rides leave from Pier 26 at 8:00 A.M. every Saturday and Sunday; get there earlier to put your name in the lottery for a slot. They also hold introductory kayaking classes every Wednesday evening from 6:00 to 8:00 P.M. at Pier 96. The boathouse is entirely volunteer-run. Volunteer and get yourself some advanced lessons and extra access to the boats.

FLOATING THE APPLE

Pier 40 (Hudson River at Houston Street); Tuesday and Thursday, 6:00 P.M. to dusk.

Pier 84 (Hudson River at 44th Street); call for schedule.
(917) 929–3670 or (212) 564–5412
www.floatingtheapple.org
Join the crew and hit the high seas . . . well, the choppy Hudson . . . for an exhilarating afternoon of rowing. This volunteer organization builds their own vintage-style Whitehall gigs and puts land-loving New Yorkers on the water. No experience necessary. These friendly folks will deftly guide you through the whole experience, and you will soon feel like you were born with an oar in your hand. If you are lucky, you might even get dinner out of the deal. Once a month or so, they fire up the grill and cook up some free hot dogs and burgers. Now *that's* cruising in style.

THE GOWANUS DREDGERS CANOE CLUB

Red Hook, Brooklyn
(718) 243–0849
www.waterfrontmuseum.org/dredgers
Weekday evenings and weekends by appointment, spring through fall.
Question: What do Venice and Brooklyn have in common? Answer: Great Italian food, pigeons, and canals. Yes, canals—but you can take a ride through Brooklyn's canals for free! (though the "O Solo Mio" may not be quite as good). E-mail a member of the club through the Web site and they will be happy to take you on a canoe trip down this undiscovered trail. They also offer introductory canoe classes many Wednesday evenings and Sunday

afternoons and the occasional walking or bicycle tour. Check their Web site for schedule and details.

EVERYBODY IN! PUBLIC POOLS

In addition to the pools at the recreation centers (see Appendix D), there are a number of city-run outdoor pools to cool yourself off in during those steamy summer months. These pools are all free and are open from Memorial Day through Labor Day. Daily hours are generally 11:00 A.M. to 7:00 P.M. You can get more information by clicking on "Things to Do" at the Web site www.nyc-govparks.org or by calling the pools directly.

MANHATTAN

DRY DOCK (EAST VILLAGE), East 10th Street between Avenues C and D; (212) 677–4481.

JOHN JAY (UPPER EAST SIDE), East 77th Street east of York Avenue; (212) 794–6566.

LASKER (CENTRAL PARK), 110th Street and Lenox Avenue; (212) 534–7639 (Olympic-size pool).

MARCUS GARVEY (CENTRAL HARLEM), 124th Street and Fifth Avenue; (212) 410–2818.

SHELTERING ARMS, West 129th Street and Amsterdam Avenue; (212) 662–6191.

THOMAS JEFFERSON, East 112th Street and Amsterdam Avenue; (212) 860–1372 (Olympic-size pool).

WAGNER (EAST HARLEM), East 124th Street between First and Second Avenues; (212) 534–4238.

THE BRONX

CLAREMONT, 170th Street and Clay Avenue; (718) 901–4792.

HAFFEN, Ely and Burke Avenues; (718) 379–2908.

MAPES, East 180th Street (between Mapes and Prospect Avenues); (718) 364–8876.

Everything and Anything

Be sure to get yourself one of the invaluable New York City Department of Parks and Recreation special-events calendars for the year. It lists the vast numbers of activities going on in parks throughout the five boroughs from April through October. Many of these are one-day events that you don't want to miss—the Urban Park Rangers' Falcon Olympics, Haunted Halloween Walks, ethnic celebrations from every corner of the world in every corner of the city, opera, symphony, and philharmonic performances, sports tournaments, and much more. Call (212) 360–1480 to get a copy, call the hotline at (212) 360–3456 for an up-to-date schedule, or check the Web site www.nycparks.org. And fear not: The schedule is free, and all the activities are gratis as well.

VAN CORTLANDT, West 242nd Street and Broadway; (718) 548–2415.

BROOKLYN

BUSHWICK HOUSES, Flushing Avenue and Humboldt Street; (718) 452–2116.

COMMODORE BARRY, Flushing and Park Avenues (between Navy and North Elliot Streets); (718) 243–2593.

DOUGLAS AND DEGRAW, Third Avenue and Nevins Street; (718) 625–3268.

HOWARD, Glenmore and Mother Gaston Boulevard (at East New York Avenue); (718) 385–1023.

KOSCIUSKO (between Marcy and Dekalb Avenues); (718) 622–5271 (Olympic-size pool).

SUNSET PARK, Seventh Avenue (between 41st and 44th Streets); (718) 965–6578 (Olympic-size pool).

QUEENS

ASTORIA, 19th Street and 23rd Drive; (718) 626–8620 (Olympic-size pool).

FISHER, 99th Street and Thirty-second Avenue; (718) 779-8356.

LIBERTY, 173rd Street and 106th Avenue; (718) 657-4995.

STATEN ISLAND

FABER, Faber Street and Richmond Terrace; (718) 816-5259.

LYONS, Pier 6 and Victory Boulevard; (718) 816-9571.

TOTTENVILLE, Hylan Boulevard and Joline Avenue; (718) 356-8242.

WEST BRIGHTON, Henderson Avenue (between Broadway and Chappel Street); (718) 816-5019.

BEACHES

While no one would confuse New York City with Maui, it does have its fair share of sandy beaches within city limits. The city parks department maintains 14 miles of public beaches, all of which are open from Memorial Day through Labor Day. And you know New York has a much better subway system than Maui. In fact, all city beaches are accessible by public transportation, though some more easily than others. For more information, go to www.nycparks.com and click on "Things to Do," then click "Activities/Facilities."

BRIGHTON BEACH AND CONEY ISLAND
Brighton 1st Street to West 37th Street
Brooklyn
(718) 946-1350
www.nycgovparks.org
These two beaches are really one long stretch of shoreline that's a very popular destination because of its legendary reputation and easy accessibility. It's located at the end of the F, B, W, and Q subway lines. The throngs also show up because the area offers so much more than just sand and sun. A trip to Coney Island isn't complete without a walk through Astroland (what remains of the famous amusement park) and a ride on the oh-so-rickety and oh-so-thrilling roller coaster, the Cyclone (a kick worth paying $5.00 a ride; 718-372-0275; www.astroland.com). Astroland also has a fireworks display every Friday night with free cabaret performances

beginning at 8:00 P.M. during the summer. Don't miss the stalls of antiques/junk/whatever being hawked along Surf Avenue. Farther down the boardwalk is Brighton Beach. Known as "Odessa by the Sea," Brighton has become the home of New York's thriving Russian immigrant community, and a walk along Brighton Avenue certainly makes you feel like you've been transported to the heart of Mother Russia. There are also some amazing deals to be found on fresh fruits, vegetables, and rugelach along the avenue.

JACOB RIIS PARK
Fort Tilden, Gateway National Park
Rockaway, Queens
(718) 318–4300
www.nps.gov/gate

Run by the National Park Service, this small strip of sand located just a short hop from Brooklyn is a very popular destination, particularly on the weekends. When the public beach is overrun, venture onto the private beaches of Rockaway, just a short walk along the dunes. From Brooklyn, take the Q35 bus, and from Queens take the Q35 or the Q22 bus.

MANHATTAN BEACH
Oriental Boulevard (from Ocean Avenue to Mackenzie Street)
Brooklyn
(718) 318–4000
www.nycgovparks.org

Located just a bit farther down the shore from Brighton Beach, this more secluded beach isn't quite as populated as the big guys next door and also

Open the Gate:
Gateway National Recreation Area

Administered by the National Park Service, Gateway is made up of 26,000 acres of parkland that runs through Brooklyn, Queens, Staten Island, and into northern New Jersey. There's a huge array of activities for kids and adults, from nature walks, concerts, and campfire sing-alongs to sailing lessons, gardening classes, and yoga on the beach. All activities run by the NPS are free and open to all. For a guide to their programs, locations, and activities, call (718) 338–3799 or check their Web site, www.nps.gov/gate.

offers areas for you to fire up the barbecue and picnic. The buses B1 and B49 will take you to the beach.

ORCHARD BEACH
Pelham Bay Park
The Bronx
(718) 885–2275
www.nycgovparks.org
Looking out on Long Island Sound, this is the beach of choice for Bronx residents. The waters are generally calm and the promenade is quite lively, especially on weekends. They offer free Latin music concerts on the beach every Sunday in the summer. Take the number 12 bus from the Pelham Bay subway station (6 train).

ROCKAWAY BEACH
Beach 9th Street in Far Rockaway to Beach 149th Street
Neponsit, Queens
(718) 318–4000
www.nycgovparks.org
Popular with Brooklyn and Queens residents, this long stretch of beach (7 miles) runs almost the entire length of Rockaway. Take the A train toward Far Rockaway; there are many beach stops along the way.

SOUTH AND MIDLAND BEACHES
Fort Wadsworth to Miller Field
Staten Island
(718) 987–0709
www.nycgovparks.org
Staten Island's own secret beach that's hardly ever crowded.

"No entertainment is so cheap as reading, nor any pleasure so lasting."
—Lady Mary Wortley Montague

LIBRARIES ARE THE ultimate resource for anyone who wants it all but doesn't want to spend anything to get it. After all, the libraries were established by Mr. "A Penny Saved Is a Penny Earned" himself, Benjamin Franklin. New York has three public library systems: the New York Public Library (in Manhattan, the Bronx, and Staten Island), the Brooklyn Public Library, and the Queens Borough Public Library. The three systems have a network of research libraries and local branches with more than 200 locations throughout the five boroughs (see Appendix C for a complete list of branch locations). At each of these branches, you'll find not only bookshelves full of reading material but also a wide selection of videos and CDs of every kind of music conceivable. Some locations, like the Mid-Manhattan and Donnell Libraries, can rival Blockbuster and Tower Records in their video and CD selections.

You also have access to computers and the Internet as well as computer classes. In fact, you can find free classes in everything from origami and quilting to job placement and starting a small business. Many branches also have a regular schedule of music, films, theater, and readings. There are many private libraries in New York, too; some charge a membership fee to borrow materials, but all can be a great source for in-house research.

RESEARCH CENTERS

THE NEW YORK PUBLIC LIBRARY HUMANITIES AND SOCIAL SCIENCES LIBRARY

Fifth Avenue and 42nd Street
(212) 930–0830
www.nypl.org/research/chss

This landmark Beaux Arts building is home to more than one million books, 135 miles of hidden bookshelves, and two friendly lions named Patience and Fortitude. You cannot take any books out of this library, but you are welcome to spend endless hours in their stunning reading rooms—and you will want to. The building recently underwent a multimillion-dollar renovation and the grandeur of these rooms, particularly the Rose Reading Room, guarantees you'll be thinking exceptionally intelligent thoughts. Don't miss the one-hour tours of the historic facility every Tuesday through Saturday at 11:00 A.M. and 2:00 P.M. Tours of changing exhibitions in Gottesman Hall begin at 12:30 and 2:30 P.M. They also offer an array of classes at the South Court Training Center.

THE NEW YORK PUBLIC LIBRARY FOR THE PERFORMING ARTS

40 Lincoln Center Plaza (65th Street and Amsterdam Avenue)
(212) 870–1630
www.nypl.org/research/lpa/lpa.html

Returned to its home at Lincoln Center after a three-year renovation, this is home to one of the world's most extensive collections of materials in the performing arts. Not limited to books, the library is particularly well-known for its huge collections of historic recordings, videotapes, CDs, records, autograph manuscripts, correspondence, sheet music, stage designs, press clippings, programs, posters, and photographs. You can borrow a great deal of the materials in the library, though the archival collections are only available for reference. Being the performing arts library, you would expect they might have a performance or two every now and then—and they certainly don't disappoint.

You'll find a full schedule of presentations by prominent actors, composers, musicians, writers, choreographers, and dancers throughout the week.

SCHOMBURG CENTER FOR RESEARCH IN BLACK CULTURE
515 Malcolm X Boulevard (at 135th Street)
(212) 491–2200
www.nypl.org/research/sc

This is a national research library devoted to collecting, preserving, and providing access to resources documenting the experiences of peoples of African descent throughout the world. Their collection is entirely noncirculation, but they make many of the historic materials available to the public through an extensive schedule of exhibitions, publications, and educational, scholarly, and cultural programs. They do charge for some performances, but many are free. Be sure to grab a free MP3 audio tour when viewing any of their exhibitions.

SCIENCE, INDUSTRY, AND BUSINESS LIBRARY
188 Madison Avenue (at 34th Street)
(212) 592–7000
www.nypl.org/research/sibl

The nation's largest public information center devoted solely to science and business, the research center houses both a circulating library and an extensive noncirculating collection (1.4 million volumes). The library's Electronic

Reference Desk

You will find mentions throughout this book of various goings-on at public libraries around the city. Here's a rundown of which chapters contain detailed information on these happenings:

For the complete list of **PUBLIC LIBRARY BRANCH LOCATIONS** *in the five boroughs, see Appendix C.*

For listing of branch libraries that offer **REGULARLY SCHEDULED FILMS,** *see pages 54–55.*

For **FILMS FOR KIDS** *at libraries, see pages 133–36.*

For **STORYTELLING AND READING,** *see pages 142–46.*

For **CLASSES** *at libraries, see page 155.*

For **CONCERTS** *at libraries, see page 35.*

"Get Ya Free Money Heeere!"

Okay, it's not as simple as that, but there is plenty of it out there in the form of grants and scholarships from private and public organizations, and the Foundation Center can help you find it (free of charge, of course). The library will help you sift through the more than 47,000 private and corporate giving programs to find the ones that are the best targets for your project. They have free training sessions on funding research, proposal writing, proposal budgeting, and even the occasional networking breakfast (with free pastries and coffee!). The Foundation Center (79 Fifth Avenue, second floor, at 16th Street) is open Monday, Tuesday, Thursday, and Friday, 10:00 A.M. to 5:00 P.M.; and Wednesday until 8:00 P.M. For more information, call (212) 620–4230 or check the Web site www.fdncenter.org.

Information Center connects users to the hundreds of internal and external electronic information resources, including Internet databases, CD-ROMs, electronic journals, and online services. The Electronic Training Center offers ongoing classes in computer programs, the Internet, research, and business and industry issues. Combined, the two centers have more than a hundred computer workstations ready for public use. Take the free one-hour tour Tuesday or Thursday at 2:00 P.M. to learn more about the facilities. For tour information, call (212) 592–7000.

PRIVATE LIBRARIES

FRENCH INSTITUTE/ALLIANCE FRANÇAISE
22 East 60th Street (between Park and Madison Avenues)
(212) 355–6100
www.fiaf.org
Hours: Monday through Thursday, 1:30–8:00 P.M.; Saturday, 9:30 A.M.–1:30 P.M.

THE CATCH Nonmembers do not have borrowing privileges. Membership is $75 a year.

This is the largest collection of all-French materials in the United States. You're welcome to spend all day in the spacious library reading any of the

30,000 French books, perusing the hundreds of French magazines, watching any of the 1,000 French videos, or listening to the many French CDs, French books on tape, or French cassettes. In other words, if it's French, it's here.

GOETHE INSTITUTE
1014 Fifth Avenue (between 82nd and 83rd Streets)
(212) 439–8700
www.goethe.de/uk/ney
Hours: Tuesday and Thursday, noon–7:00 P.M.; Wednesday, Friday, and Saturday, noon to 5:00 P.M.

Nonmembers do not have borrowing privileges. Membership is $10 a year.

This is the German version of the French Institute. The big difference here is that they have half as many books, videos, CDs, newspapers, and magazines. (And, of course, they're in German, not French.)

Got a Question? Get an Answer!

Q: *Need to know the capital of Lithuania or the correct spelling for Engelbert Humperdinck? Then give a call to free library reference lines. They are there to answer any question you have, from the most obscure facts to the most commonly asked question on all subjects. The New York Public Library's telephone reference line is (212) 340–0849 (Monday through Saturday, 9:00 A.M. to 6:00 P.M.). The Brooklyn Public Library's reference phone is (718) 230–2100, ext. 5 (Monday and Friday, 9:00 A.M. to 6:00 P.M.; Tuesday through Thursday, 9:00 A.M. to 9:00 P.M.; Saturday, 10:00 A.M. to 6:00 P.M.; and Sunday, 1:00 to 6:00 P.M.), and the folks at the Queens Borough Public Library can help you at (718) 990–0714 or (718) 990–0728 (Monday through Friday, 10:00 A.M. to 8:45 P.M. and Saturday, 10:00 A.M. to 5:15 P.M.).*

A: *The capital of Lithuania is Vilnius. Answer courtesy of the Brooklyn Public Library Telephone Reference Line.*

A: *The correct spelling for both the 1960s nightclub singer and the nineteenth-century German composer of Hansel and Gretel is Engelbert Humperdinck. Answer courtesy of the New York Public Library Telephone Reference line.*

INSTITUTO CERVANTES LIBRARY

211-215 East 49th Street (between Second and Third Avenues)
(212) 308-7720, ext. 104
www.cervantes.org
Tuesday and Wednesday, 11:30 A.M.–7:30 P.M; Thursday and Friday,
noon–7:00 P.M.; Saturday, 10:00 A.M.–1:30 P.M.

Nonmembers do not have borrowing privileges. Membership is $50 a year.

Okay, this time take the French Institute, double the size of the collection, translate everything into Spanish, and you have the Instituto Cervantes Library.

THE NEW YORK ACADEMY OF MEDICINE LIBRARY

1216 Fifth Avenue (at 103rd Street)
(212) 822-7300
www.nyam.org
Hours: Monday, Tuesday, Thursday, and Friday, 9:00 A.M.–5:00 P.M.;
Wednesday, 9:00 A.M.–7:00 P.M.

This noncirculating research library houses the second-largest medical collection in the United States, following the National Library of Medicine in Bethesda, Maryland. Its extensive facilities include more than one million volumes, more than 1,400 current journal subscriptions, and a variety of electronic resources. They also offer a full curriculum of free classes in various research methods and techniques to make your use of their library (and all libraries!) much more effective.

PAT PARKER/VITO RUSSO CENTER LIBRARY

The Lesbian, Gay, Bisexual & Transgender Community Center
208 West 13th Street (between Seventh and Eighth Avenues)
(212) 620-7310
www.gaycenter.org
Hours: Monday through Thursday, 6:00–9:00 P.M.; Saturday,
1:00–4:00 P.M.

The collection at this library is geared toward everything to do with gay, lesbian, bisexual, transgender, and AIDS studies. This circulating library is open to all (a membership fee is requested but not required). The library has a collection of about 12,000 books and more than 500 videos (documentaries and features). When you borrow videos, they ask you to leave a refundable deposit for the one-week loan.

"Opinions are the cheapest commodities on Earth."

—Frank Bacic

NEWSPAPERS: THE FREE PRESS

IMES, SHMIMES. You don't need to throw away $1.00 a day ($3.50 on Sunday!) to get your fill of information in New York City. Whatever your interest or point of view, there's a free newspaper out there for you. Granted, the news you get from some of the free presses in the city might have a bit of a skewed worldview. But if you're looking for community news, local entertainment listings, and happenings around town, there are plenty of papers to pick up that you don't need to drop a quarter, a dime, a nickel, or even a penny to get. You'll find most of these papers in those ubiquitous newspaper boxes on almost any major street corner in Manhattan. Some can be found throughout the boroughs but are easiest to come by in Manhattan.

AM NEW YORK

(212) 239–5555

www.am-newyork.com

Headline: Pint-sized Publication Packs a Punch. One of the newest and most welcome additions to the freescape of New York City, this easily digestible daily newspaper gives you all the news that fits in twenty pages. The perfect companion for your subway ride to work, the tabloid touches on local, national, and international topics and has sections (okay, pages) devoted to travel, food, sports, classifieds, and local events. My favorite feature is their *4 for Free* section, which lists four free events going on around New York every day. Pick up your free copy any weekday at street-corner boxes throughout the five boroughs.

BIG APPLE PARENT, BROOKLYN PARENT, AND QUEENS PARENT

(212) 889–6400 (*Big Apple Parent*)

(718) 638–8600 (*Brooklyn Parent*)

(718) 347–5700 (*Queens Parent*)

www.parentsknow.com

This monthly magazine is dedicated entirely to parenting in New York City. Each month's issue has intelligent and informative articles, an extensive calendar of events, and lots and lots of advertising. Be aware that the magazine is targeted toward parents with no shortage of cash, so there's no focus on doing things on the cheap. There is, however, some very useful information

Extra! Extra!

I have to confess that there are times when even I read one of the big daily newspapers, either to get better informed or, in the case of the Post, *just for laughs. Still, that's no excuse to spend money. If you have access to the Web, you have free access to the newspapers. Every one of the major dailies publishes practically its entire contents, along with even more information, on the Web every day. For the* New York Times, *check out www.nytimes.com. The* New York Daily News *is at www.nydailynews.com,* Newsday *is at www.nynewsday.com, and the* New York Post's *Web site is www.nypost.com. If you feel the need to get some ink on your hands, you can always find a copy at any local library.*

for all to be found within their pages. You can find copies in street-corner boxes and stores throughout Manhattan, in Brooklyn Heights, Carroll Gardens, and Park Slope in Brooklyn, and throughout Queens. Check the Web site or call for specific locations.

DOWNTOWN EXPRESS
(212) 242-6162
www.downtownexpress.com

Downtown Express is a biweekly newspaper covering all the goings-on in Tribeca, Battery Park City, the South Street Seaport, and the Wall Street area in lower Manhattan. This slim publication manages to cover the huge amount of local news, arts, sports, and other happenings below Canal Street. The listings section includes local theater, music, and particularly good coverage of art galleries in the area. The paper is widely distributed in street-corner boxes and stores below Canal Street.

GO NYC
(888) 466-9244
www.gonycmagazine.com

This glossy monthly mini-magazine is the place to GO for all things lesbian in NYC. You can find copies in bars and stores all around downtown and selected locations in Brooklyn and Queens. Check their Web site to find a copy near you.

HX
(212) 352-3535
www.hx.com

As you can tell from the full name of this weekly, *Homo eXtra* is a gay magazine. *HX* occasionally touches on such subjects as politics and current events but is best relied on for its bar and club listings, reviews, gossip, and nothing-left-to-the-imagination advertising. You can find copies at every gay bar and store in the city as well as some street-corner boxes in Chelsea.

JEWISH SENTINEL
(212) 244-4949

As you might imagine, this is the source for all things Jewish around New York—from articles on Israel and the Jewish perspective on New York to a selected listing of cultural events, gatherings, galleries, and performances that might be of interest to the Jewish community. You can pick up a copy at street-corner boxes placed randomly around Manhattan; call for specific locations.

METRO SPORTS

(212) 563–7329

metrosportsny.com

The source for everything on the go in New York. Articles and listings on running, cycling, skiing, skating, marathons, triathlons, sports medicine, and new equipment. Most of all, the magazine is a vehicle for a lot of advertising, though the calendar of events is particularly thorough and useful. *Metro Sports* is published once a month and can be found in any sporting goods store around the city.

NEW YORK BLADE NEWS

(212) 268–2701

www.nyblade.com

New York's weekly gay community newspaper covers local and national issues, personalities, and events affecting gay men and lesbians in the city. It's also a good source for arts listings and community events. The paper is distributed widely on street corners and stores throughout Manhattan and at selected locations throughout the boroughs; call or check the Web site for specific locations.

NEW YORK PRESS

(212) 244–2282

www.nypress.com

New York's *alternative* alternative newspaper, the *Press* is chock-full of opinionated and often very funny articles on the politics, characters, events, and arts of the city. Its film, music, and events listings are among the best in the city. You'll find copies on almost any street corner in Manhattan and parts of Brooklyn (downtown, Park Slope, and Cobble Hill). Like the *Voice,* grab a copy early in the week; you may have a hard time finding one once the weekend rolls around.

NEW YORK RESIDENT

(212) 993–9410

www.newyorkresident.com

A weekly magazine with a focus on the culture and politics of the city. You'll find regular articles on health, fashion, travel, and restaurants, as well as weekly theater, film, and music picks. The *Resident* is distributed widely in street-corner boxes in Manhattan.

NEXT MAGAZINE

(212) 627–0165

www.nextmagazine.net

Almost an exact clone of *HX.*

THE ONION

(212) 627–1972

www.theonion.com

This on-target satirical news weekly takes on national issues, news figures, and "local" events all over the country. While their view on the news can be hysterically funny, their arts section, "The A.V. Club," is surprisingly serious and extensive. The section doesn't include timetables or movie locations, but they do include in-depth reviews and features on almost every film in the theaters at any given time, from Hollywood blockbusters to independents and documentaries. You'll also find good articles on videos and local music picks. You can grab a copy from their boxes located all over Manhattan (most plentifully below 23rd Street and in the Columbia University area) and in Park Slope and Williamsburg in Brooklyn.

VILLAGE VOICE

(212) 475–3300

www.villagevoice.com

The original and still the largest alternative news weekly. Since 1955 the *Voice* has been the place to go to get the other view on anything: politics, art, theater, film, literature, sex, and even a unique take on horoscopes. The paper is sure to annoy you with some of its articles and engage you with others, but you will almost always find them provocative. Even if you never agree with what they have to say, the *Voice* is always worth picking up for the extensive music, film, theater, dance, and art listings, and the sprawling classifieds, which include their no-holds-barred personals. Grab a copy out of one of the red boxes on most street corners around the five boroughs or free at newsstands and stores around the city. Get your copy early in the week; by the time the weekend rolls around, the boxes are usually empty. You can always find a pile of papers outside their downtown office on Bowery between 5th and 6th Streets. Check the Web site to find a place to pick up a copy near you.

WEST SIDE SPIRIT AND OUR TOWN

(212) 268–8600

www.ourtownnyc.com

Both put out by the same publisher and editorial staff, these two weekly papers are basically mirror images of each other, with *Our Town* covering the East Side and the *West Side Spirit* covering (you guessed it) the West Side. Both cover the local politics, crime, and events of their areas and share a good citywide listing of arts and community events, with a strong focus on free activities. Both can be found in corner boxes and stores on their respective sides of town between 59th and 110th Streets.

"There are many things that we would throw away, if we were not afraid that others might pick them up."

—Oscar Wilde

FURNITURE AND HOUSEHOLD GOODS: ONE MAN'S TRASH . . .

ALL AROUND THE city you'll spot them every other day of the week. Some people call them piles of trash, but the trained eye clearly recognizes them as mountains of treasures. Furnishing New York apartments by "recycling" is not only good for the environment, it's great for the bank account. It's a long-held tradition and a way of life for students, artists, collectors, and anyone with an open mind and a creative eye. You will be shocked at the high caliber of items some people consider garbage, but it makes sense. Consider the fact that New Yorkers on average earn a great deal of money but are forced to live in some of the smallest apartments this side of a shoe box. The result is, folks end up throwing away some mighty fine used stuff to make room for some newer, finer stuff.

Freecycle:
A Little Give & Take

Here is the scenario: Someone across town has just upgraded to a brand-new couch and wants to get rid of that oh-so-cozy but slightly shoddy pullout that has seen him through the leaner times. You are new to town and just finished shelling out every dime you have to secure that pricey New York studio, but now you have to furnish it. It is a match made in heaven, but how do we make the connection. Freecycle! This Web-based recycling group is in existence to empty out your spare closet and fill your neighbor's, or vice versa. All you have to do is go to their Web site, www.freecycle.com, and connect to the New York branch (this is an international movement verging on two million members worldwide). Once you become a member, for free of course, your inbox will literally be flooded with e-mail offers for stuff (useful and not so useful) every day. A typical day's offerings can run the gamut from the worthwhile (including furniture, books, appliances, clothes) to the kooky (advice, leftovers, broken glass bottles) to the incredibly specific (2 yards of yellow felt, size 9.5 women's sensible brown shoes, 75 small packets of soy sauce). You are even able to post "Wanted" messages for practically anything you might need. The New York list has a membership of more than 20,000 members (and growing) so, anything you want you can get, anything you want to get rid of someone else wants, and many things you did not know you needed are up for grabs.

FAVORITE FINDS

Almost anything you need or want can be found on the street. I can't tell you how many times I have said "I need" this or that, only to come across that exact "this or that" a few days later on the street. You are limited only by your willingness to forage and schlep. Obviously, the smaller the item you're in the market for, the more effort you'll have to put into your search. If you're interested in larger furnishings, however, the sky's the limit. Here are some of my favorite items I've picked up from the street over the years:

Antique trunks	Ironing board
Antique wooden milk crate	Leather easy chair
Artwork	Luggage
Bookcases	Microwave oven
Chest of drawers	Mirrors
Coffee table	Oriental rugs
Couch	Ottoman
Decorative window flower box	Plates, bowls, silverware
Desk	Power Mac computer, monitor,
Desk chairs	and printer
Director's chairs	Spice rack
Doctor's office scale	Storage boxes
End tables	Telephone
Exercise mat	Toaster oven
File cabinets	Vacuum cleaner
Footstool	Wicker basket
Halogen torch lamp	Window screens

Who knows what *you* might find!

CURBSIDE SHOPPING TIPS

Here are some helpful rules to live by when you are on the prowl:

1. **SHOP IN THE BEST NEIGHBORHOODS:** The better off the neighbors, the better the garbage.

2. **KNOW WHEN THE SHOPS ARE OPEN FOR BUSINESS:** Consult the accompanying map to see what days the Department of Sanitation will be around to take away the merchandise. It's best to do your hunting the night before scheduled pickups. You'll generally start to notice piles appearing in the late afternoon and early evening.

3. **WHEN IN DOUBT, DON'T LEAVE IT OUT:** If you're considering an item, take it. Undoubtedly it will not be there if you decide to come back for it. But if you take it and it doesn't work or fit your need, you can always redonate it. Nothing ventured, nothing gained.

The Big Salvation (Army)!

Not that I'm endorsing the idea of spending cash, but there are times when you can't wait to stumble across that perfect headboard, desk, or butcher-block countertop, and money must be spent. The best option is always to shop at any of New York's many thrift stores. While whole books have been written on this subject alone, there are some standout shops to head for when you're in the market for furniture, appliances, or knickknacks of any kind. Most local thrift stores offer a smattering of sofas, chairs, and china, but their space is limited, so the selection is as well. Still, in each borough you'll find a main Salvation Army Thrift Store (usually connected to a warehouse) with huge assortments of goods. While these stores may not be around the corner, the prices and selection make them worth the trip. For some other shopping ideas, see the shopping chapter, and for a good list of thrift stores throughout the city, check out the Web site www.salvationarmy.usaeast.org. Here are the super Salvation Army stores in each borough:

MANHATTAN: 536 West 46th Street (between Tenth and Eleventh Avenues); (212) 757–2311.

BROOKLYN: 436 Atlantic Avenue (between Bond and Nevins Streets); (718) 834–1562.

22 Quincy Street (between Classon and Downing Streets); (718) 622–5686.

THE BRONX: 4109 Park Avenue (at 175th Street); (718) 583–3500.

QUEENS: 34–02 Steinway Street (between Thirty-fourth and Thirty-fifth Avenues); (718) 472–2414.

STATEN ISLAND: 2052 Clove Road (at Mosel Avenue); (718) 442–3080.

4. **DON'T BE A HOG:** If you find something that turns out not to fit your need, set it back out on the street right away. The temptation is to hold on to this great find and hope you can find a use for it someday. The problem is, you'll end up cluttering up your small studio apartment with stuff you can't use, and the longer you hold on to it, the harder it will be to part with it. Just like ripping off that Band-Aid, do it quick and it will be less painful. And no doubt, someone else will pick it up and be very grateful to you.

School's Out!

For a few short weeks from late May to early June, the pickings are prime down in the Village around NYU and up in Morningside Heights around Columbia University. As the students of these hoity-toity schools close up their apartments for the year, one of the lesser-known traditions of graduation season begins: the Dumping of the Dorms. These students, many of them well heeled, set out an abundance of useful items (desks, chairs, futons, couches, filing cabinets, microwaves, lava lamps . . . anything you might find in the IKEA catalog that can fit in a dorm room makes its way to the street) as the young intelligentsia make their way out of town for the summer, or into the real world forever. Keep your eyes open.

5. **A LITTLE WORK GOES A LONG WAY:** Repaint it, refinish it, change the knobs, or reupholster the cushion and presto! It's good as new!

6. **CLEAN IT.** (Hey, you never know.)

7. **ENJOY IT.**

HAPPY HUNTING!

"I always say shopping is cheaper than a psychiatrist."
—Tammy Faye Bakker

SHOPPING:
A TALE OF TWO STREETS

1F YOU *MUST* SPEND MONEY—and as a rule I do not endorse the practice—there are a couple of streets you should know about to keep this awful habit in check. Of course, there are thousands of stores throughout the city where you can find "a deal." There are also tons of books that tell you where to find these stores, but I'm just going to include a few of the best. On 17th and 32nd Streets, you'll find clusters of some of my favorite shops in New York City—the places where I shop almost to the exclusion of any other stores in town. What makes them so great? You guessed it: great stuff, really cheap.

On West 32nd Street you will find a couple of stores that can supply you with all the essentials of life (food, dishes, books, clothes, furnishings, office supplies, cosmetics, electronics, toys . . .) and many of the absurdities of life ("As seen on TV" items, last year's fad items, "has-been" pop star paraphernalia, and more) at ridiculously low prices. West 17th Street is the place to head to check out three of the best thrift stores around. These secondhand shops are not necessarily the cheapest in the five boroughs, but you can snag some amazingly high-quality finds at very respectable prices at these shops.

32ND STREET: BARGAIN PARADISE

JACK'S 99¢ STORES
110 West 32nd Street (between Sixth and Seventh Avenues)
(212) 268–9962

You may have come across other 99-cent stores in your travels, but Jack's is hands-down the best there is. This huge store is overflowing with bargains, from the frozen foods section to every household item or office supply you could ever need. While some of the goods are made by companies you may not recognize, a surprisingly large amount of the merchandise is brand name. The wares change on a daily basis, so you could walk the aisles every day and be almost guaranteed of finding something you can't live without (for 99 cents, that is). Located upstairs is Jack's World where they have another great selection of bargains on higher-ticket items (appliances, furniture, clothes, housewares, toys and games), but here they don't keep to the 99-cent limit. There is a second Jack's 99¢ location at 16 East 40th Street (between Fifth and Madison Avenues) and another Jack's World at 45 West 46th Street (between Fifth and Sixth Avenues).

WEBERS CLOSEOUTS
116 West 32nd Street (between Sixth and Seventh Avenues)
(212) 564–3606

Just a couple of doors down from Jack's, Webers is another great source for steals, though they no longer rise to the challenge of keeping everything priced less than a buck. Still, there are plenty of good deals to be had if you're willing to do a little work sifting through the schlock. There are many other Webers located throughout the city, but none quite as expansive as this one.

17TH STREET: FIRST IN SECONDHAND

HOUSING WORKS THRIFT SHOPS
143 West 17th Street (between Sixth and Seventh Avenues)
(212) 366–0820
www.housingworksthrift.com

Fruit of the Streets

Over the last few years, fruit stands have begun to sprout up on almost every street corner in the city. But one seems to stand above all others as the place to get more bananas for your buck. A guy named Smiley, or "The Fruit Nazi" (depending on whom you talk to), runs a few Midtown stands where you're likely to find the kind of produce you don't usually see other street vendors selling: plump strawberries, mangos, mesclun, kiwis, as well as the usual apples, tomatoes, peppers, and more. The catch is that he sells them for pennies, but only in large quantities—10 large tomatoes for $1.00, four pounds of grapes for $2.00, five pounds of gourmet salad mix for $3.00. Also, he doesn't take too kindly to you picking out the fruit (hence "The Fruit Nazi"). Let him pick your pears and you'll stay on his good side. The main stand is on 48th Street, just east of Sixth Avenue. He runs another stand with much of the same selection at 42nd Street and Third Avenue. These stands are open for business Monday through Friday, after 3:00 P.M. He also has a Web site that doesn't give you much information, but does lay out his strict fruit-handling philosophy: www.expage.com/smileysproduce.

Think of Housing Works Thrift Shops as the Bergdorf Goodman of secondhand. The designer clothing, furniture, housewares, art, antiques, books, CDs, and records are certainly a cut above what you would find in your neighborhood Salvation Army or Goodwill. The prices are also a bit higher, but not much. They often run daily specials making the place a steal. There are four other locations around the city (202 East 77th Street, between Second and Third Avenues; 306 Columbus Avenue, between 74th and 75th Streets; 157 East 23rd Street, between Third and Lexington Avenues; 245 West 10th Street, between Hudson and Bleecker Streets). Housing Works is New York's largest provider of housing and supportive services to homeless, formerly homeless, and at-risk men, women, and children living with HIV and AIDS.

ANGEL STREET
118 West 17th Street (between Sixth and Seventh Avenues)
(212) 229–0546
www.angelthriftshop.org

Continue along 17th Street a bit farther and you'll come across Angel Street. Much like Housing Works, it gets great high-quality donations but with more of an emphasis on furnishings and accessories than clothes (though the clothes they do sell, they sell very cheaply). You'll also find enticing daily specials at this boutiquelike shop. All proceeds from Angel Street benefit individuals and families affected by substance abuse, HIV, AIDS, and mental illness.

17 @ 17 THRIFT STORE
17 West 17th Street (between Fifth and Sixth Avenues)
(212) 727–7516
www.thriftshopscharity.org
Walk farther down the street. Okay, you do actually have to cross an avenue, but since you're in the neighborhood, it's worth stopping in. This store is almost always so overflowing with furniture, clothes, and tchotchkes that you can count on them having a 50 to 75 percent off sale going on. All proceeds benefit the Women's Campaign of the UJA-Federation of New York, helping Jewish people in need around the world.

"And the turtles, of course . . .
all the turtles are free.

As turtles and, maybe,
all creatures should be."

—Dr. Seuss

PETS: CANINE, FELINE, BOTTOM LINE

HETHER YOUR PREFERENCE is cats or dogs (or hamsters, rabbits, or even the occasional turtle), there are plenty of little companions to be had for the asking. By opting for an adopted pet, you will not only be saving a cage full of cash and giving a home to a needy (and loving) buddy, but you will also be doing your part to put an end to the animal mills that churn out unhealthy dogs and cats for pet stores. Most of the shelters around the city do require some "donation" to offset their expenses, but here are some ways to increase the size of your household without decreasing the size of your bank account. Also here are some suggestions on where to go to keep your Pekinese in the pink without spending much green.

Surfing for Pets

Here are a couple of good Web sites to check out for free pet adoptions. There is also no charge to list pets on these sites for adoption.

WWW.ANIMALALLIANCENYC.ORG, *New York City's official animal information site, provides information and links to practically everywhere you can possibly adopt a pet in the five boroughs as well as information on licensing, low-cost spay, neuter, and pet-care options, events, and discounts for services.*

WWW.NEWYORK.CRAIGSLIST.ORG, *the classified section of the Internet, has a listing for every pet need from pet portraits to adopting or buying every kind of pet you can think of. New listings are added every day and throughout the day. Craigslist includes my favorite section, "Free," where you will find listings for furniture, tickets, appliances, books, antiques, classes, and so much more.*

WWW.PETFINDER.ORG, WWW.PET-ARK.COM, *national and local clearinghouses for shelters and rescue organizations that list thousands of animals by breed and location. Many of these shelters do suggest donations ranging from $30 to $100.*

LOW-COST PET CARE AND ADOPTIONS

ASPCA
Bergh Memorial Animal Hospital & Clinic
424 East 92nd Street (between York and First Avenues)
(212) 876–7700
www.aspca.org

 Charges $70 for an appointment with a doctor and $100 for an emergency visit.

The granddaddy of all humane organizations, the ASPCA's clinic and hospital provide low-cost health care for your little loved ones. They provide the full range of medical care for pets, including spaying and neutering ($40 to $65), vaccines, and an on-site pharmacy. They also offer adoptions of all sorts of pets for a $75 donation. The adoption package includes microchip

ID, spaying or neutering, follow-up exams, medical support, vaccines, literature, private behavior counseling, and starter equipment.

BIDE-A-WEE

410 East 38th Street, second floor (between First Avenue and FDR Drive)
(212) 532–5884 (clinic)
(212) 532–4455 (adoptions)
www.bideawee.org

 Charges $32.50 for exams, $42.50 for emergency visits, and $70 to $80 for adoptions.

This full-service veterinary clinic provides everything to keep your feline feeling fine. Appointments are available about a week in advance. They also have a large shelter and offer adoptions for a $70 to $80 fee, which includes spay or neutering, all vaccinations, and two weeks of free clinic services.

NORTH SHORE ANIMAL LEAGUE

25 Davis Avenue
Port Washington, Long Island
(516) 883–7575
www.nsalamerica.org

 They do charge a small fee for spay and neutering and vaccinations that runs between $25 and $135 depending on the kind of pet and its size and age.

This huge shelter is overflowing with hundreds of dogs and cats at any given time, both purebreds and mixed breeds. It's a short forty-five-minute ride from Manhattan on the Long Island Railroad—and it's worth the trip. Not only is this the only shelter that will let you adopt pets over three years old for free (or for whatever donation you feel like making), but all pets are spayed or neutered, vaccinated, and have ID tags. You also get free medical care for your pet for thirty days, free training advice for the life of the pet, very low-cost training classes, and a free starter kit when you take your new pal home (worth $100!). They will check you out before they let you adopt a pet, so bring two picture IDs and phone numbers of references. If you can't make it to Long Island, they'll come to your neighborhood. Their mobile adoption center travels throughout the city and the tristate area. Check the Web site or call for schedule and details. The shelter is open for adoptions seven days a week from 10:00 A.M. to 9:00 P.M.

PET POSTINGS

Another way to find a free companion is to check out the bulletin boards and windows of local pet stores and veterinarians for notices from your neighbors who need to give up their pets. Whether it's because they're moving and can't take the Tonkinese to Tupelo, or their Labrador just had a litter, or the new hubby is allergic to the husky, often owners and their pets must be parted. Here are some places where you're sure to find postings:

EAST SIDE

ANIMAL ATTRACTIONS, 343 East 66th Street (at First Avenue); (212) 734–8400.

CALLING ALL PETS, 1590 York Avenue (at 84th Street); (212) 249–7387.

CALLING ALL PETS, 301 East 76th Street (at Second Avenue); (212) 734–7051.

THE COUNTRY VET, 430 East 75th Street (between First and York Avenues); (212) 535–3250.

THE NATURAL PET, 238 Third Avenue (between 19th and 20th Streets); (212) 228–4848.

PETCO, 560 Second Avenue (at 31st Street); (212) 779–4550.

PETCO, 860 Broadway (at East 17th Street); (212) 358–0692.

WEST SIDE

ANIMAL GENERAL, 558 Columbus Avenue (at 87th Street); (212) 501–9600.

BARKING ZOO, 172 Ninth Avenue (between 20th and 21st Streets); (212) 255–0658.

CLINTON VETERINARY CENTER, 357 West 52nd Street (between Eighth and Ninth Avenues); (212) 333–5548.

THE PET HEALTH STORE, 440 Amsterdam Avenue (at 81st Street); (212) 595–4200.

PET STOP, 564 Columbus Avenue (between 87th and 88th Streets); (212) 580–2400.

SPOILED BRATS, 340 West 49th Street (between Eighth and Ninth Avenues); (212) 459–1615.

WESTSIDE ANIMAL HOSPITAL, 733 Ninth Avenue (between 49th and 50th Streets); (212) 247–8600.

DOWNTOWN WEST

PARROTS AND PUPS, 45 Christopher Street (east at Seventh Avenue); (212) 352–8777.

PET BAR, 132 Thompson Street (between Prince and Houston Streets); (212) 253–9250.

DOWNTOWN EAST

ANIMAL CRACKER, 26 First Avenue (at 2nd Street); (212) 614–6786.

WHISKERS, 235 East 9th Street (between Second and Third Avenues); (212) 979–2532.

EXPLORING NEW YORK

"Afoot and lighthearted I take to the open road,

Healthy, free, the world before me,

The long brown path before me, leading wherever I choose."

—Walt Whitman

WHETHER YOU'RE A visitor to New York or a native, there is always so much to discover about every corner of the city. The best way to get to know New York is to walk the streets with someone who knows it well. There are free guided tours of every fashion: leisurely strolls; historical, architectural, and nature tours; one-on-one explorations and groups. Most of the tours happen at regularly scheduled times every week, and some can be scheduled at your convenience.

AUSTRIAN CULTURAL FORUM
11 East 52nd Street (between Fifth and Madison Avenues)
(212) 319–5300
www.acfny.org
Monday to Friday at noon and 3:00 P.M.

A unique addition to the New York skyline, this building is a pure example of making the most out of a little. Stop in any day for a free tour of this nar-

WALKING TOURS BY THE WEEK

TIME	MONDAY	TUESDAY	WEDNESDAY	THURSDAY	FRIDAY	SATURDAY	SUNDAY
8:30 A.M.						New York Youth Hostel's 16-hour Grand Tour	
9:00 A.M.							
9:15 A.M.	Steinway Factory Tour (spring & fall only)	Steinway Factory Tour (spring & fall only)					
9:30 A.M.	Federal Reserve Bank (9:30 A.M.–2:30 P.M.)	Federal Reserve Bank (9:30 A.M.–2:30 P.M.)	Federal Reserve Bank (9:30 A.M.–2:30 P.M.)	Federal Reserve Bank (9:30 A.M.–2:30 P.M.)	Federal Reserve Bank (9:30 A.M.–2:30 P.M.)		
10:00 A.M.							
10:30 A.M.							
11:00 A.M.	Columbia University	Columbia University NYPL WNET	Columbia University NYPL	Columbia University NYPL	Columbia University NYPL	NYPL Lincoln Square June–September	Orchard Street March–December
11:30 A.M.						8th Street June–September (selected dates)	
12:00 NOON	Austrian Cultural Forum	Austrian Cultural Forum	Austrian Cultural Forum	Wall Street Austrian Cultural Forum	Times Square Austrian Cultural Forum	Brooklyn Brewery (12:00 –5:00 P.M.) Prospect Park Audubon Center Wall Street	
12:30 P.M.	Pennsylvania Station 4th Monday of month		Grand Central Terminal	34th Street	The Grand Tour		
1:00 P.M.		WNET	WNET	WNET			
1:30 P.M.							
2:00 P.M.	Columbia University Trinity Church	Columbia University NYPL Trinity Church	Columbia University NYPL Trinity Church	Columbia University NYPL Trinity Church	Columbia University NYPL Trinity Church	Union Square NYPL Trinity Church	Trinity Church
2:30 P.M.							
3:00 P.M.	Austrian Cultural Forum	Austrian Cultural Forum	Austrian Cultural Forum	Austrian Cultural Forum	Austrian Cultural Forum	Prospect Park Audubon Center April–November	Prospect Park Audubon Center April–November
3:30 P.M.							

row twenty-four-story glass-and-concrete skyscraper that looks like a huge totem pole designed for a science fiction movie. They also host a full schedule of other free events including readings, concerts, art exhibitions, film screenings, and panel discussions.

BATTERY PARK CITY WALKING TOURS

Battery Park City Parks Conservancy
2 South End Avenue (at West Thames Street)
(212) 267–9700
www.bpcparks.org
Various dates May through October.
They offer a variety of walking tours, including nature walks, garden tours, river walks, art tours, and historic tours. Some tours are offered weekly, others on occasion. Check the Web site or call for schedules.

BIG APPLE GREETERS

1 Centre Street, Room 2035 (at Chambers Street)
(212) 669–8159
www.bigapplegreeter.org
Any day, any place, year-round.
This is your dream-come-true tour of New York. You choose the time and day, you choose the place, and you don't pay anything—in fact, they'll even give you a one-day unlimited-use MetroCard for the subway. You think I'm kidding, don't you? Well, I'm not. Friendly and knowledgeable New Yorkers volunteer their time for this amazing organization to show you around any neighborhood in the city. They usually live in the area they show, so they can give you firsthand accounts of the area's history, off-the-beaten-trail spots, and great tips for finding some tasty (and cheap!) food and drink. Walks can run from two hours to all day. They don't accept tips, but if you offer to buy them lunch, they probably won't argue with you. Call at least two weeks in advance.

BROOKLYN BREWERY

79 North 11th Street (between Wythe Avenue and Berry Street)
Williamsburg, Brooklyn
(718) 486–7422
www.brooklynbrewery.com
Saturday, noon–5:00 P.M. (last tour at 4:30).
Brooklyn's mom-and-pop brewery walks you through the process of mixing up a batch of beer in intricate detail, right down to the molecular physics. And

somehow it seems so very interesting once you've been plied full of generous samples of their fine (and fresh!) brew. Also, on Friday night they have free music and cheap beer.

CENTRAL PARK
Central Park Conservancy
(212) 360–2727 (tour hotline)
www.centralparknyc.org
Various days and times throughout the week, year-round.
Explore the wilds of New York City with the many tours led by volunteers for the Central Park Conservancy. With a wealth of knowledge about the flora, fauna, history, trivia, secret passageways, and hidden trails of Central Park, these tours are always worthwhile for natives and visitors alike. Call the hotline for schedule information.

COLUMBIA UNIVERSITY
213 Low Library (116th Street and Broadway)
(212) 854–4900
www.columbia.edu
Monday through Friday, 11:00 A.M. and 2:00 P.M., year-round.
This one-hour tour of New York's very own Ivy League school uncovers the history, architecture, and personalities behind these prestigious walls.

DOWNTOWN WALKING TOUR
NYC Heritage Tourism Center (between Vesey and Barclay Streets)
(212) 606–4064
Tuesday at noon.
Explore the historic past and classic architecture of the neighborhood surrounding City Hall. This ninety-minute tour touches on City Hall, Tweed Courthouse, the Woolworth Building, St. Paul's Chapel, the African Burial Ground, the Brooklyn Bridge, and many other landmarks that shaped New York from its earliest settlements to today.

8TH STREET WALKING TOUR
The Village Alliance
(212) 777–2173
www.villagealliance.org
Every other Saturday at 11:30 A.M., late May through September.
The ninety-minute tour called "Discover Places, Tidbits & Gossip That Even New York's Cognoscenti Don't Know" delivers just what it promises as it

traipses through the East and West Villages. The tour meets at the northwest corner of Second Avenue and St. Marks Place (8th Street). Call or check the Web site for the schedule.

THE FEDERAL RESERVE BANK
33 Liberty Street (between Nassau and William Streets)
(212) 720–6130
www.newyorkfed.org
Monday through Friday at 9:30 A.M., 10:30 A.M., 11:30 A.M., 1:30 P.M., 2:30 P.M.; make a reservation one month ahead.
You've heard the sayings "Follow the money" and "Show me the money," right? Well, here's your chance to do both. This sixty-minute tour of the richest bank in the world takes you through their gold vaults, tells you all about the Fed's cash-processing procedures, and even gives you some free money at the end of the tour! Okay, so it happens to be shredded. You can't have everything.

GRAND CENTRAL TERMINAL
42nd Street and Vanderbilt Avenue
(212) 439–1049
www.mas.org
Wednesday at 12:30 P.M., year-round.

 While there's no charge for the tour, they do ask for a donation of any amount, though you aren't obligated to give one.

For more than twenty-five years, the Municipal Art Society has been showing folks around this Beaux Arts landmark. The tour includes the history of the terminal as well as a look at the major restorations completed in 1998. The tour runs a little more than an hour and meets at the main information booth on the main level of Grand Central.

THE GRAND TOUR: GRAND CENTRAL STATION AREA
42nd Street and Vanderbilt Avenue
(212) 883–2420
www.grandcentralpartnership.org
Every Friday at 12:30 P.M., year-round.
This free ninety-minute walking tour organized by the Grand Central Partnership leaves from the Philip Morris Building across the street from

Grand Central. This walk points out some of the architectural splendors of East 42nd Street, including Grand Central Station, the Chrysler Building, the Chanin Building, and many others, as well as passing along some of the area's rich history and curious events.

JOHN J. HARVEY FIREBOAT
Pier 63 (Hudson River and 23rd Street)
www.fireboat.org
Various days and times, year-round.

Since she was put into service in 1931, the *John J. Harvey* fireboat has greeted every passenger cruise ship that has made its way into New York Harbor with a spectacular water display. But this boat wasn't made just for show. To this day, although she was officially retired from service by the New York City Fire Department in 1994, she remains one of the most powerful and fastest fireboats ever to take to the water. The ship is now under private ownership and does not rest on her impressive laurels. She's now pressed into action for tours up and down the Hudson and around New York Harbor. The schedule of events is erratic, but they go on throughout the year (more from spring through fall and less in the winter). Some tours have themes and knowledgeable guides, like their "History of Garbage" tour and a tour of historic fires the Harvey worked on. Other tours are just pleasant days on the water. All are free, because the boat doesn't meet the strict standards set by the U.S. Coast Guard for the carriage of passengers for hire. If you come onboard, it's as private guests of the boat, and you may be asked to sign a release to this effect. Trips are limited to the first fifty passengers. And yes, they do "fire up" the powerful hoses at some point on every trip and, yes, you will get wet. For schedule information, check out the Web site or sign up for their mailing list though the Web site.

LINCOLN SQUARE
Columbus Circle fountain (59th Street and Broadway)
(212) 581-3774
www.lincolnbid.org
Saturday at 11:00 A.M., June through November.

This ninety-minute tour (that can actually run as long as three hours) explores the historic Lincoln Square district, which has become a world center for arts and entertainment—and is also full of historic treasures, architectural jewels, peaceful green areas, and surprising enclaves of public art. The tour meets at the Columbus Circle fountain.

NEW YORK CITY HALL
Murray Street and Broadway
(212) 788–2170
www.nyclink.org
Monday through Thursday, year-round.
Stroll through this early-nineteenth-century Federal-style building that's home to the mayor's office and city council chambers and is chock-full of historic American portraits and artifacts. Tours are offered Monday through Thursday with the Tuesday tour including a peek inside the newly restored Tweed Court House right behind City Hall. Reservations are required.

NEW YORK INTERNATIONAL YOUTH HOSTEL
891 Amsterdam Avenue (between 103rd and 104th Streets)
(212) 932–2300
www.hinewyork.org
Saturday at 8:30 A.M.
Clear your calendar and join the Hostel's Grand Tour, which takes place every Saturday. This is truly an all-day affair. Led by their indomitable volunteer guide Jerry Balch, it can run as long as sixteen hours and cover up to an exhausting 22 miles. The schlep hits everywhere from downtown Brooklyn to 59th Street, including a walk over the Brooklyn Bridge, a ride on the Staten Island Ferry, South Street Seaport, Little Italy, Chinatown, and on and on. The haul attracts throngs of people, not just those staying at the hostel. And, don't worry, you can drop out of the marathon when your feet have had enough. The hostel also offers a host of other tours that vary from week to week, including trips to such destinations as 42nd Street, Greenwich Village, and others. Stop by or check out their Web site for a schedule. And if you are looking for a bed in New York, the hostel is the way to go. It is clean, friendly, fun, and most importantly, cheap. With beds running only $30 to $38 a night, this is just about the best deal you're going to find in the city.

NEW YORK PUBLIC LIBRARY (NYPL)
Humanities and Social Science Library, 476 Fifth Avenue
(entrance at 42nd Street)
(212) 930–0501
www.nypl.org
Tuesday through Saturday at 11:00 A.M. and 2:00 P.M., year-round.
The lions welcome you to a one-hour walk through the stunningly renovated

main branch of the public library. They also offer guided tours through their major art exhibits daily at 12:30 and 2:30 P.M.

ORCHARD STREET WALKING TOUR
Katz's Deli
205 East Houston Street (at Ludlow Street)
(212) 226–9010
www.lowereastsideny.com
Sunday at 11:00 A.M., March through December.
From pushcarts to pulsing beats, this tour explores a neighborhood that started out as a hub for immigrants from Russia and Eastern Europe and is now turning into the newest chic area on the isle of Manhattan. Tours run about ninety minutes.

PENNSYLVANIA STATION TOURS
34th Street Partnership tourist information kiosk
32nd Street and Seventh Avenue
(212) 719–3434
www.34thstreet.org
The fourth Monday of every month at 12:30 P.M., year-round.
Tour the grandeur that once was New York's Penn Station. The tour resurrects this behemoth by using vintage photographs and surviving remnants to tell the story of New York's lost railroad station. This ninety-minute walk tells the tale from Penn Station's turn-of-the-twentieth-century beginnings to the forces that brought about its destruction in the 1960s.

PROSPECT PARK AUDUBON CENTER
Lincoln Road and Ocean Avenue
Brooklyn
(718) 287–3400
www.prospectparkaudubon.org
Saturday at noon: Bird-Watching Tour.
Saturday and Sunday at 3:00 P.M.: Discovery Tour.
The newly restored boathouse is home to this state-of-the-art wildlife preserve and education center. Their busy schedule abounds with free events, activities, and tours through the wilds of Brooklyn's only forest with a gorge and water-fall (okay, even without the gorge and waterfall, it would still be Brooklyn's only forest). Take the Discovery Tour offered every Saturday and Sunday at 3:00 P.M., the Bird-Watching Tour every Saturday at noon, or stop in for any other of the tons of ongoing activities for kids and adults throughout the week.

STEINWAY & SONS
1 Steinway Place (Nineteenth Avenue and 38th Street)
Long Island City, Queens
(718) 721–2600
www.steinway.com
Monday and Tuesday at 9:15 A.M., spring and fall only.
Take a walk back in time through the Steinway factory, where they still craft each of their world-famous pianos by hand using the same techniques created and patented by Henry Engelhard Steinway (and his sons) starting in 1853. From bending and shaping one long piece of wood into the entire outer rim of the piano to hand-sanding, sawing, rubbing, regulating, voicing, and stringing the instruments, the tour is an in-depth two-and-a-half-hour master class in the art of piano making from those who do it best. Tours are held on Monday and Tuesday mornings during the spring and fall only, and reservations are required.

TAKE A WALK, NEW YORK!
(212) 228–3126
www.walkny.org
Various locations throughout the five boroughs, year-round.
Your government thinks you're getting too fat. So they want you to hit the streets and start exercising. This federally funded local group organizes guided walks all around the city that aim to stimulate you intellectually and visually so they can sucker you into walking, walking, walking. This is a great chance to explore sections of the city you've never visited before (or may not have even known existed). The walks are always easily accessible by public transportation, led by knowledgeable guides, and free.

THIRTEEN/WNET
450 West 33rd Street (between Ninth and Tenth Avenues)
(212) 560–2711
www.thirteen.org
Tuesday at 11:00 A.M.; reservations required.
A fascinating one-hour peek inside the country's largest public television station.

34TH STREET HISTORY TOUR
Empire State Building
350 Fifth Avenue (between 33rd and 34th Streets)
(212) 719–3434
www.34thstreet.org
Thursday at 12:30 P.M., year-round.

This ninety-minute architectural history tour of 34th Street tells the stories behind such buildings as the Empire State Building and Macy's, and introduces you to characters and events like "Andy Warhol versus Con Edison," architect Stanford White, and "Mary Murray's Tea Party." The tour meets at the Fifth Avenue entrance to the Empire State Building, and is led by noted architectural historians.

TIMES SQUARE WALKING TOUR
Times Square Visitors Center
1560 Broadway (between 46th and 47th Streets)
(212) 869–1890
www.timessquarebid.org
Friday at noon.

What was once a center for horse trading has now become the center of the commercial theater world. This two- to three-hour tour fills you in on all the history, intrigue, and ever-changing architecture of Broadway and its surrounding areas. The visitor center also offers free Internet access, loads of information, and clean bathrooms!

TRINITY CHURCH
Broadway and Wall Street
(212) 602–0800
www.trinitywallstreet.org
Daily at 2:00 P.M., year-round.

A short fifteen- to twenty-minute tour that covers the long history of one of New York's oldest churches (established 1697). Concerts are also offered every Thursday at 1:00 P.M.

UNION SQUARE WALKING TOUR
16th Street between Union Square East and West (Park Avenue and Broadway)
(212) 460–1200
www.unionsquarenyc.org
Saturdays at 2:00 P.M., year-round.

Take a ninety-minute, opinionated, totally interactive tour of Union Square's past, present, and future. Meet at the Lincoln statue midpark at 16th Street.

URBAN PARK RANGERS
Parks throughout the five boroughs
(866) NYC–HAWK (692–4295)
www.nyc.gov/parks

Various times, days, and locations, year-round.

Yogi Bear has nothing on New York. Yes, we have our own pack of park rangers, and they're a useful bunch of folks to know. They run an extensive and ever-changing array of walks, hikes, nature explorations, canoe trips, and even camping trips. Call to get a schedule or check out the Web site.

WALL STREET WALKING TOUR

Museum of the American Indian
1 Bowling Green (at the end of Broadway, across from Battery Park)
(212) 606–4064
www.downtownny.com
Thursday and Saturday at noon, year-round.

Explore this area that takes in everything from founding fathers of the United States to the financial capital of the world. This free ninety-minute tour weaves together the history, events, architecture, and people of downtown with stops at the U.S. Custom House, Trinity Church, New York Stock Exchange, and many other sites along the way. No two walks are ever the same, so join in often.

"We're gonna see America. We take no map. We'll follow the sun. Stay in cheap motels and steal what we need along the way."

—Al Bundy

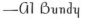

TRAVEL: FREE-WHEELIN'

JUST BECAUSE YOU'RE low on cash is no reason to sit at home. Whether it's getting around the city or getting out of town, there are some great options. Of course, the best way to get to see New York is the cheapest—by foot (biking and in-line skating are great choices as well). More than any other place in America, New York is a walking city—logically laid out, compact, lots to see, and plenty of people to bump into along the way (figuratively and literally). While New York is undoubtedly a big city, as you walk the streets, you realize that it's also very much a small town. There may be eight million people, but you'll be amazed at how many friends and acquaintances you'll run into on the streets and how many familiar faces in the crowds you'll see over and over again. When walking is out of the question, though, the subway is the answer. The unlimited-use MetroCard ($7.00 for one day, $24.00

for one week, $76.00 for one month) makes getting from here to there a bargain. The MetroCard is good for all subways and buses (see below). Here are some other suggestions for getting around and out of New York.

GETTING AROUND NEW YORK

MTA NEW YORK CITY TRANSIT
(718) 330–1234
www.mta.nyc.ny.us/nyct
Okay, I know I'm not offering you any special deals here. Yes, you do have to pay to get on the trains. This isn't Germany; there ain't no such thing as an honor system on these trains. You pay your fare and you ride your train. You will be ticketed if you hop the turnstiles. Don't try it. But the unlimited-use MetroCards make it easy and cheap to get to anywhere in the five boroughs by subway and/or bus.

STATEN ISLAND FERRY
Whitehall Terminal (at Whitehall and South Streets)
311 or (718) 727–2505
www.nyc.gov/dot
This not-to-be-missed trip runs about every twenty minutes most times, but once an hour late at night. It's absolutely free, and with the spectacular views of lower Manhattan and the Statue of Liberty, how can you pass it up? Particularly dramatic views at sunset, but any time of day it's an awe-inspiring voyage.

GETTING OUT OF NEW YORK

AUTO DRIVEAWAY COMPANY (ADC)
225 West 34th Street, #1201 (between Seventh and Eighth Avenues)
(212) 967–2344
www.autodriveaway.com
www.nycdriveway.com

 There's a $15 registration fee and a $350 refundable deposit. The registration fee is good for one year and at all locations.

Forget about flying, Greyhound, or Amtrak; here's your chance to see America the way it was meant to be seen, behind the wheel of your very

Hacking It in New York

You won't be surprised by this recommendation: Don't ever take a cab. Besides the fact that it's expensive (just hopping in a cab seems to always cost you at least $5.00), the wild ride will invariably take you longer than grabbing the nearest subway. Fahgeddaboutit!

own gas-guzzling, pedal-to-the-metal, "where the hell is the next rest stop" automobile. With sixty-four locations throughout the United States and Canada, these folks can provide you with the free use of a late-model car to practically any major city you want to visit. If your plans are somewhat flexible, this is a great way to drive yourself around the states. The deal is: ADC acts as a kind of matchmaker between people or companies that need vehicles moved from place to place and drivers who want to get from here to there. Call them up to see what's available, pay your registration and deposit, and hit the road. Cars go on a first-come, first-served basis to drivers twenty-three years or older with two photo IDs. They give you time to do plenty of sightseeing along the way by allotting you extra time to get to where you're going (four days to Florida, for instance, and ten days to the West Coast). When you deliver your car, you get back your deposit and call the nearest ADC office to see when you can get a car back or off to your next destination. The looser your travel plans, the better this system will work for you. The cars come with a free first tank of gas; otherwise, all gas and lodging costs along the way are your responsibility.

CLUB GETAWAY
Kent, Connecticut
(800) 643–8292
clubgetaway.com

 You must have the ability to teach something fun or provide some useful service to campers in exchange for free weekends.

This summer camp for adults is a "Club Med in Connecticut" and is always on the lookout for volunteers to commit to spending some weekends with their swinging singles. If you can offer some useful service to the paying campers—teaching yoga, arts and crafts, or in-line skating, say, or even cooking up a killer pie—they will give you room, board, and free run of the extensive grounds and facilities in exchange for the time you spend working with the campers. Even if you don't necessarily think you have some great expertise, they're pretty open to any idea; it's definitely worth a shot. The camp has been rated "one of the top ten hottest destinations for singles" by the Travel Channel and has everything you need to do almost any sport under the sun.

GODSTOW RETREAT CENTER

Redding, Connecticut
(203) 938–2330 or (212) 475–7752
godstow@world-view.org
www.godstow.org

 Help with the upkeep of the grounds through such duties as trimming trees and foliage, planting, pruning, raking, cleaning, making repairs, or painting.

Escape the hustle and bustle of the city for a couple of days of contemplative meditation and housecleaning. This restored mansion is run as a retreat for the Asian Classics Institute of New York and is situated on ninety-eight beautiful acres of woods and meadows, rolling hills, streams, and ponds. Volunteers spend part of their time helping to keep the center looking beautiful and are free to enjoy the grounds for the rest of their stay. Volunteers are welcome weekends or weekdays.

KRIPALU CENTER FOR YOGA & HEALTH

Lenox, Massachusetts
(413) 448–3123
www.kripalu.org

 Volunteers work thirty-five hours per week in exchange for a stay at this yoga retreat.

This world-renowned center for karma yoga offers free one- to four-week stays at the breathtaking mountain retreat to volunteers through the Seva Program. In exchange for a vigorous thirty-five-hour workweek that could include chopping vegetables, cleaning bathrooms, washing dishes, or performing basic maintenance tasks, you can take part in all the classes and activities that are part of their Retreat and Renewal schedule, including classes in hatha yoga, meditation, Kripalu DansKinetics, and more. They will also provide you with a dormitory room and three vegetarian meals a day. The weeks are scheduled from Sunday to Sunday. And if you want more once

The Virtual Thumb

There are a number of Web sites where you can find yourself a free ride out of town or a companion to ride with you wherever you're going. These Ride Share listings are a great way to travel to or from New York, save a load of cash, and maybe even make a good friend along the way. You are usually expected to split the cost of gas, but not always. Check out these sites for details:

www.erideshare.com

www.newyork.craigslist.org

www.hitchhikers.org

your stay is over, they also offer other longer-term volunteer programs that could run from three to twenty-one months.

ROWE CAMP & CONFERENCE CENTER

Rowe, Massachusetts
(413) 339–4954
www.rowecenter.org

Chop wood and carry water in exchange for a peaceful week in the mountains.

For one week every spring and fall, the Rowe Center holds "Work Weeks" where folks from far and wide, both young and old, come to help spiff up the grounds and have a great time. This community-oriented camp offers lots of fun activities and free room and board for all those helping out these weeks. Throughout the year they also offer various conferences on a wide variety of artistic and spiritual subjects, and you can work off the cost of these programs through other work-study programs. Check the Web site for more details and schedule.

VIPASSANA MEDITATION CENTER

386 Colrain-Shelburn Road
Shelburn Falls, Massachusetts
(413) 625–2160
www.dhamma.org

Donations of any amount are accepted, but not required, at the end of the ten-day retreat.

Vipassana offers its ten-day meditation "Boot Camp" free of charge (including all accommodations, meals, and instructions)—the only hitch is you can't say a word about the service. In fact, you can't say a word about anything; this is a completely silent retreat. No meditation experience is required to take part, and their focus in not religion-based at all. They are all about the technique and practice of meditation as a "universal remedy for universal ills." Fill out an application at their Web site and make a reservation one to two months in advance.

THE TRAIN TO THE PLANE

Getting to New York's three major airports can be an expensive affair. It can cost you $60 by cab, $18 by shuttle van, or $13 by bus service, but it can be done for next to nothing if you have some time and patience.

KENNEDY AIRPORT
This is the easiest and most user-friendly airport to get to by public transportation, with four cheap options for getting there (two dirt cheap and two not-quite-as cheap). The pricier and slightly more convenient plan is to pick up the AirTrain at either the Howard Beach Station (A train) or at the Sutphin Boulevard Station (E, J, or Z trains). The AirTrain is officially part of the MTA system, but your MetroCard will not get you on board. To take the ten-minute monorail ride to the terminals, you will have to cough up an additional $5.00. But if you are a purist like me, you will hop on one of the two city buses that will get you to the terminals for just the swipe of your unlimited MetroCard or a $2.00 subway fare (free transfer from the subway!). Grab the Q10 bus from the Kew Gardens/Union Turnpike subway station (E or F trains) or Q3 at Jamaica Center/Parsons/Archer subway station (E, J, or Z trains). The travel time from Manhattan for any of these routes is about sixty to ninety minutes. The big difference is the AirTrain is a bit plusher and luggage friendly, while the buses are, well, buses.

LA GUARDIA AIRPORT
Getting here can be an adventure, but it can be done for the cost of a subway token as well. From 106th Street and Broadway or 125th Street and

Next Year in Jerusalem

How about an all-expenses-paid ten-day trip to Israel? Well, if you're between eighteen and twenty-six years old, Jewish, and have never been to the Holy Land before, Birthright Israel wants to take you for free.

Sound inviting? To date they have sent more than 90,000 people from all around the country (including many groups from New York City), and they're looking for more every year. The aim is to build a strong link between young American Jews and Israel. While they try to keep the proselytizing to a minimum, there are many discussions of all things Jewish while you visit historic sites like Masada, the Wailing Wall, and the Dead Sea. Of course, they wouldn't mind you spending your own cash to come back to Israel in the future, or even deciding to settle in Israel, but there's no pressure to do either.

Birthright Israel puts together more than thirty groups to make the trip each winter and spring. These trips take into account the full spectrum of ideological, religious, educational, and cultural backgrounds of the Jewish community. There are groups for those who are nonobservant, Reform, Conservative, and Orthodox. Some trips have a traditional hotel and sightseeing agenda, while others are for those with special interests like biking, sports, or history. In recent years they have also begun to coordinate their activities with the Israeli government to ensure the safety and security of those on the trips. For more information, stop by the Birthright Israel offices at 521 Fifth Avenue, twenty-seventh floor (at 43rd Street); call (888) 99–ISRAEL (994–7723); or check the Web site www.birthrightisrael.com.

Lenox Avenue, hop on the M60 bus. The bus winds its way around Upper Manhattan and Queens and takes you directly to the airport. Travel time is forty-five to ninety minutes (depending on traffic). Another option is to take the E or the F train to the 74th Street and Roosevelt Avenue stop, then catch the Q33 bus. Neither of these are specifically meant to be airport shuttles. That means they make many stops along the way before getting to the terminals, and they do not have any special luggage racks. You won't be making friends with your fellow passengers if you block the aisle with your steamer trunk. For information on all MTA buses and subways, call (718) 330–1234 or check the Web site www.mta.nyc.ny.us/nyct.

NEWARK LIBERTY AIRPORT

Making it to Newark Liberty Airport from Manhattan can be pretty cheap and easy, as long as you know the schedules ahead of time. If you head off without a plan, it could take you a while or wind up costing you a few more bucks than you planned on. The easiest option is to hop on the New Jersey Transit bus #107 ($4.00) at Port Authority in midtown (41st Street and Eighth Avenue) and take it straight to the airport. The good news is this bus will get you to the airport in about thirty minutes and for only $4.00; the bad news is it has a very limited schedule. If that doesn't work for you, take the Path Train to Newark Penn Station ($1.50) and get the New Jersey Transit bus #62 ($1.25) to the airport. The bus runs about every ten to twenty minutes and is about a twenty-minute ride. The more convenient but much pricier option is to take the AirTrain from Penn Station in Manhattan directly to the airport ($14), or you can save a few bucks by taking the Path Train to Newark Penn Station and grabbing the AirTrain there ($7.50). For detailed schedules and more information, call (800) 772–2222 or check the Web site www.panynj.gov.

GARDENS AND GARDENING: DIRT CHEAP

GARDENS MAY NOT be the first thing you think of when you think of New York, but there's a surprising amount of greenery to be found within this urban jungle—and I'm not just talking about fire-escape gardens. From quaint community gardens to grand botanical gardens, you can delight in some of the most stunning horticulture anywhere in the world within the city limits. Not only can you partake in the sights and smells of the gardens, but you can also produce some lovely flowers and vegetables yourself. Cultivate your own free plot of land in one of New York's many community gardens, get free bulbs and cuttings, or develop your own green thumb through free gardening classes around town.

PUBLIC GARDENS

THE BROOKLYN BOTANIC GARDEN (BBG)
1000 Washington Avenue (at Flatbush Avenue)
(718) 623–7200 (info) or (718) 623–7333 (events hotline)
www.bbg.org

 Free Hours: All day Tuesday and Saturday from 10:00 a.m. to noon; seniors are also free all day Friday.

Hailed by the *New York Times* as "the premier horticultural attraction in the region," the BBG's endless gardens and greenhouses will bring your senses to life. They also provide free gardening and composting classes and workshops throughout the year (see below for details).

THE CENTRAL PARK CONSERVATORY GARDENS
105th Street and Fifth Avenue
(212) 360–2766 or (212) 310–6600
www.centralparknyc.org

Always free, this is the only formal garden in Manhattan open to the public. It covers a relatively small area (when compared to the other botanical gardens in New York) but provides a welcome escape from the clamor of city life. They offer free tours of the gardens from spring through fall on Saturday at 11:00 A.M. Also be on the lookout for their annual plant giveaways—tulips in May and mums in November.

THE NEW YORK BOTANICAL GARDEN
200th Street and Kazimirov Boulevard
The Bronx
(718) 817–8700
www.nybg.org

 Free Hours: All day Wednesday and Saturday from 10:00 A.M. to noon. Additional fees apply to certain exhibits within the garden.

Who could want anything more than 250 acres of flora from every corner of the world, including forty-eight gardens and plant collections and fifty acres of forestland? This is one of the oldest and largest gardens in the world and should not be missed. They offer free admission to the grounds on Wednesday and Saturday mornings, but you will still have to pay additional fees to gain entry into some venues within the gardens. They also run an extensive adult education curriculum, which you can get free or at reduced tuition by taking part in their work-study program.

THE QUEENS BOTANICAL GARDEN (QBG)
Flushing Meadows Park, 43–50 Main Street (at Dahlia Avenue)
(718) 886–3800
www.queensbotanical.org

Always free admission to this twenty-acre garden (closed Monday). QBG also presents a free concert series during the summer and many free classes throughout the year.

THE STATEN ISLAND BOTANICAL GARDEN
1000 Richmond Terrace
(718) 273–8200
www.sibg.org

Free admission to the garden grounds, but they do charge admission to the Chinese and Secret Gardens.

This is a small garden when compared to the big guys in the Bronx and Brooklyn, but it makes a lovely place to take a respite. Admission to the garden grounds is free every day, but you will need to pay your way into the enticing and well-regarded Chinese Scholar's Garden.

WAVE HILL PUBLIC GARDEN AND CULTURAL CENTER
675 West 252nd Street (enter at 249th Street and
Independence Avenue)
The Bronx
(718) 549–3200
www.wavehill.org

Free Hours: All day Tuesday and Saturday from 9:00 A.M. to noon; no admission charges during December, January, and February.

This former private estate, now a city-owned garden, offers some outstanding views of the Hudson River and New Jersey (yes, it is possible), and some gorgeously maintained gardens.

GARDENING EDUCATION

BROOKLYN GREENBRIDGE & URBAN COMPOSTING PROJECT
Brooklyn Botanic Gardens
1000 Washington Avenue (at Flatbush Avenue)
(718) 623-7250 or (718) 623-7209
Compost Help Line (718) 623-7290
www.bbg.org

Classes and workshops are free, but you must register at least one week in advance.

Classes and workshops offered throughout the year on such topics as "Composting in the City," "Perennial Flowers Basics," "Introduction to Horticulture Therapy," "Gardening with Native Plants," and "Battle the Asian

Get The Dirt

Visitors occasionally comment on how dirty New York is. Well, this just might be the reason why. Through a program of the Department of Sanitation and the various botanical gardens of New York, every New Yorker is entitled to an unlimited amount of compost free of charge. Compost is considered to be the "black gold" of gardening and is an essential ingredient for any lush fire-escape garden, window box, or houseplant. The compost give-back days are scheduled each spring and fall. Call or check the Web site for the dates and locations you can show up to shovel yourself a load of this messy but useful, nutrient-rich, organic plant food. They also sell discounted compost bins for $20 ($70 retail price); visit www.nyccompost.org or call (718) 817-8543 (the Bronx and Manhattan); (718) 623-7290 (Brooklyn); (718) 539-5296 (Queens); or (718) 362-1007 (Staten Island).

And if you can't wait for those official give-back days, you can grab some free compost to go anytime at any local Starbucks Coffee. Yes, the ubiquitous coffee pusher gives away its used grounds to anyone who wants them. The nitrogen-rich grinds and any soil make the perfect blend to wake up any houseplant. To find a location near you, walk down any street or check the Web site www.starbucks.com.

Long Horn Beetle!" The classes are targeted toward community gardeners, but all are welcome.

NEW YORK BOTANICAL GARDEN SCHOOL OF CONTINUING EDUCATION

200th Street and Kazimirov Boulevard
The Bronx
(718) 817–8610
www.nybg.org/edu/conted

 Work-study is available: Perform administrative duties in exchange for free or discounted classes. The math: 1 hour of work = 33 percent reduction in price per classroom hour; 2 hours of work = 66 percent reduction in price per classroom hour; 3 hours of work = 1 free classroom hour.

Choose from more than 700 courses in botanical art and illustration, botany, crafts, floral design, gardening, commercial horticulture, landscape design, and horticultural therapy. Take a short how-to class, explore a topic in depth, or pursue a new career in one of their seven certificate programs.

COMMUNITY GARDENS

Community gardens are generally free to join. They provide you with a plot of land to plant in and all the supplies and materials you need, from seeds and soil to how-tos and hothouses. Some long-established, centrally located gardens have long waiting lists, while newer, off-the-beaten-trail gardens have many spots available. These gardens are not only a good place to grow rutabagas but also great gathering spots for the communities they are in. Many of the gardens have full schedules of free classes, performances, and activities for all.

GREEN GUERILLAS

151 West 30th Street, tenth floor (between Sixth and Seventh Avenues)
(212) 402–1121
www.greenguerillas.org
A good starting point to find a community garden in your neighborhood to participate in.

GREENTHUMB

49 Chambers Street, Room 1020 (between Broadway and
Center Street)
(212) 788–8070
www.greenthumbnyc.org

This organization has more than 600 member community gardens in practically every neighborhood in the five boroughs. The Web site also has a great
events calendar where you will find all kinds of free goings-on in the gardens:
classes (tai chi, writing, yoga, drawing), concerts, barbecues, community
gatherings, film screenings, and more. Check the Web site or call for the
community garden near you.

"I hate flowers. I paint them because they're cheaper than models and they don't move."

—Georgia O'Keeffe

ART GALLERIES: SHOW ME THE MONET

NEW YORK IS HOME to hundreds, perhaps thousands, of art galleries, and every one of them is free for you to wander through. In this city where space is at a premium, many of these are small single-room galleries with limited exhibition space, yet there are others that rival some of the major museums around town in the caliber of artists they show and their vast spaces. In some cases, in fact, the line between commercial gallery and museum is hard to define. Ultimately, though, the prime difference between the two remains simple and clear: money. You will never pay an admission charge at a commercial gallery, because everything you see hanging on the walls, lying on the floor, and dangling from the ceiling is for sale. Does the Gap charge you to browse? New York being the center of the art world, the artists you'll find at these galleries are the same ones you'd see at any major contemporary or modern art museum around the world. The styles of works you will find in these galleries run the full spectrum from fine art to the kind of contemporary installations that keep right-wing Republicans in business.

While there are galleries scattered all over the city, you'll find a large concentration of them clustered in just a few neighborhoods: Chelsea, Soho, and Williamsburg, Brooklyn. Each of these areas caters to a different clientele and mind-set, but all have a huge variety of styles, techniques, and talents within their own worlds. The galleries I'm including in this listing are those where you're sure to find some of the most intriguing, world-class, cutting-edge, or otherwise eye-opening works in these neighborhoods and around the city. Don't take this list as the comprehensive survey of galleries in the five boroughs but as a jumping-off point. Galleries generally change shows every four to six weeks. The best way to take them in is to wander these neighborhoods with an open mind (but you can keep the purse closed).

CHELSEA

Chelsea has become the most popular area in Manhattan for galleries. Most of those located here are considered blue-chip galleries that work with lists of established, well-known, high-profile artists. In other words, the galleries can charge thousands of dollars for any given work. There are about 150 galleries crammed into a 10-block area, and most are open Tuesday through Saturday, 10:00 A.M. to 6:00 P.M. Below are some of the big-shot galleries you don't want to miss, but the best way to discover a favorite spot is to walk the streets and check out everything that looks inviting. Most of the galleries are located between 21st and 26th Streets, and between Tenth and Eleventh Avenues.

BARBARA GLADSTONE GALLERY
515 West 24th Street (between Tenth and Eleventh Avenues)
(212) 206–9300
www.gladstonegallery.com
Known for presenting high-minded shows with a focus on conceptual sculpture.

CHEIM & READ
547 West 25th Street (between Tenth and Eleventh Avenues)
(212) 242–7727
www.cheimread.com

This large gallery presents the works of such artists as Diane Arbus, Louise Bourgeois, Robert Mapplethorpe, and Andy Warhol.

FEATURE INC.
530 West 25th Street (between Tenth and Eleventh Avenues)
(212) 675–7772
www.featureinc.com

Specializes in contemporary artists that they consider to be on the cutting edge.

GAGOSIAN GALLERY
555 West 24th Street (between Tenth and Eleventh Avenues)
(212) 741–1111
www.gagosian.com

Shows are always headline grabbing, and the huge space allows them to present works on a grand scale.

GALERIE LELONG
528 West 26th Street (between Tenth and Eleventh Avenues)
(212) 315–0470
www.galerie-lelong.com

The gallery's long history includes a dedication to abstract and minimalist paintings, contemporary sculpture, and contemporary Latin American artists.

Where Else to (van) Gogh

Stop into any gallery along the way and pick up a copy of ChelseArt *and Art Now's* Gallery Guide. ChelseArt *is a concise map and up-to-date listing of all the goings-on in the Chelsea area. The* Gallery Guide *is a monthly publication of happenings at every major gallery in Manhattan and selected listings in the other boroughs and beyond. You can get both of these free at any gallery. You may notice the $3.00 price tag on the* Gallery Guide, *but don't pay any attention; everyone gives it away for free. You can also check out the Web site www.galleryguide.org for more information.*

A Feast for the Eyes
(With an Open Bar!)

You are cordially invited to rub shoulders with the trendsetters of the New York art scene, be the first to see what's happening at the happening galleries, and grab yourself a glass (or three) of fine wine or a few bottles of beer. Whenever you stop in to view a gallery, be sure to put your name on their mailing list, and you will start receiving invitations to their upcoming shows, including information about the opening reception. Every gallery holds an opening reception a couple of days before the show opens to the public, where anyone has a chance to meet the artist(s), mix and mingle, drink, and sometimes even eat. These events are almost always open to anyone in the know, and now that means you. Another way to find out about openings is to check out the Web site dks.thing.net, pick up a free copy of the Gallery Guide *at any gallery, or check the Web site www.galleryguide.org.*

LUHRING AUGUSTINE GALLERY

531 West 24th Street (between Tenth and Eleventh Avenues)
(212) 206–9100
www.luhringaugustine.com
Cutting-edge, big-budget shows.

MATTHEW MARKS GALLERY

521 West 21st Street (between 10th and 11th Streets)

522 West 22nd Street (between Tenth and Eleventh Avenues)

526 West 22nd Street (between 10th and 11th Streets)

523 West 24th Street (between Tenth and Eleventh Avenues)

(212) 243–0200
www.mmarks.com
One of the first galleries to settle in Chelsea, its four spaces are always home to an unpredictable but intriguing array of works.

METRO PICTURES
519 West 24th Street (between Tenth and Eleventh Avenues)
(212) 206-7100
www.metropicturesgallery.com

Primarily presents photography shows by such artists as Cindy Sherman and Robert Longo.

PACEWILDENSTEIN
534 West 25th Street (between Tenth and Eleventh Avenues)
(212) 929-7000
www.pacewildenstein.com

The list includes such artists as Chuck Close, Isamu Noguchi, Pablo Picasso, Robert Rauschenberg, Mark Rothko, and Julian Schnabel.

PLUS ULTRA
637 West 27th Street (between Eleventh and Twelfth Avenues)
(917) 517-0761
www.plusultragallery.com

This upstart gallery started out as one of the notable Williamsburg galleries before migrating to Chelsea. They have held on to their edgier sensibility as they have moved in among the more established galleries of Chelsea by still working with a slate of young and up-and-coming artists and, best of all, continuing to serve beer and not wine at their openings.

303 GALLERY
525 West 22nd Street (between Tenth and Eleventh Avenues)
(212) 255-1121
www.303gallery.com

Represents a battery of young artists working in a variety of forms, including photography, film, painting, sculpture, and whatever else moves them.

SOHO

Soho is the original art gallery neighborhood of New York, and while gentrification and skyrocketing real estate prices have forced many galleries to relocate, it still remains well populated by galleries presenting vital work. The galleries are often smaller than those in Chelsea, but they display works that are generally more cutting edge and riskier. The spaces are sometime storefronts and clearly marked, but they're often up a few flights and out of the way. Most galleries are open Tuesday through Saturday, 11:00 A.M. to 6:00 P.M. You will find most of the galleries located between West Broadway and Mercer, from Grand to Houston. There's a good map and extensive area listings in the *Gallery Guide,* available free at any gallery. Here are some of the highlights.

ARTISTS SPACE

38 Green Street (between Grand and Broome Streets)
(212) 226–3970
www.artistsspace.org

This nonprofit gallery is often the first stop in a professional career for artists. Since 1972 this large gallery has played host to the first works of many artists who've gone on to international recognition working in almost any style and medium.

DEITCH PROJECTS

18 Wooster Street (between Canal and Grand Streets)

76 Grand Street (between Wooster and Greene Streets)

(212) 343–7300
www.deitch.com

These two galleries play host to wildly diverse solo and group shows of contemporary artists.

DIA CENTER FOR THE ARTS

393 West Broadway (between Spring and Broome Streets)

141 Wooster Street (between Prince and Houston Streets)
www.diacenter.org

Without giving too much away about these two long-term installations, they are worth viewing if only to ponder the question, *What would Starbucks give to get this real estate?* These two works, the *Earth Room* and the *Broken Kilometer,* have been on display in these spaces since 1977 and 1979, respectively. Open Wednesday through Saturday noon to 6:00 P.M., but closed from 3:00 to 3:30 P.M.

THE DRAWING CENTER

35 and 40 Wooster Street (between Grand and Broome Streets)
(212) 219–2166
www.drawingcenter.org

A cross between a museum and a gallery, this is the only institution in the United States dedicated exclusively to the exhibition, study, and promotion of the medium of drawing. The larger space at 40 Wooster is home to major historical and contemporary shows. They do occasionally ask for "suggested donations" for large historical shows. The smaller space across the street at 35 Wooster always shows contemporary works and is always free to view.

RONALD FELDMAN FINE ARTS
31 Mercer Street (at Grand Street)
(212) 226–3232
www.feldmangallery.com

One of the oldest and best-respected galleries in Soho, they have a strong focus on performance, installation, political, and conceptual works from both emerging and long-established artists. Among the collection is the largest selection of Andy Warhol prints of any gallery.

ROSENBERG + KAUFMAN FINE ART
115 Wooster Street (between Prince and Spring Streets)
(212) 431–4838
www.artnet.com/rosenberg+kaufman.html

Up four flights you'll find this small gallery that's well worth the haul. Working with emerging and midcareer artists, the studio specializes in what it calls contemporary contemplative art. They seek out art that reveals itself slowly to the viewer, operating under the motto, "The more you look, the more you see."

WILLIAMSBURG, BROOKLYN

The Williamsburg art galleries are the newest and freshest additions to the New York art world. Since the late 1990s a set of young, brash, daring, less serious, more innovative galleries has begun to sprout up in some unusual settings in this formerly industrial/working-class, now artsy-hip neighborhood. Spread throughout the area, there are about forty spaces located in lofts, storefronts, and even a backyard toolshed. The spaces are a mix of larger studios and some closet-size galleries that are not always clearly marked, and can be off the beaten trail, but a hearty stroll around the neighborhood should give you a chance to see most of the sights. There is a good continually updated map of all the area galleries at the Web site www.wburg.com. Most galleries are open Friday through Monday or just on weekends. Here are some of the area galleries where you can always count on seeing something interesting.

HOLLAND TUNNEL

61 South 3rd Street (between Berry and Wythe Avenues)
(718) 384-5738
Hours: Saturday and Sunday, 1:00–5:00 P.M.

You might call it intimate, petite, confined, even claustrophobic, but whatever you call it, there's no getting around the fact that this gallery started out in life as a toolshed from Home Depot. This space has gained quite a reputation partly because of the space itself, but also because of its daring programming. At times, this two-by-four of a gallery has hosted as many as one hundred artists in a single show.

MOMENTA ART

72 Berry Street (between North 9th and 10th Streets)
(718) 218-8058
www.momentaart.org
Hours: Thursday through Monday, noon–6:00 P.M.

Momenta is a not-for-profit gallery dedicated to giving opportunities to emerging artists. Many exhibitions are the first solo shows by these artists.

PIEROGI 2000

177 North 9th Street (between Bedford and Driggs Avenues)
(718) 599-2144
www.pierogi2000.com
Hours: Friday through Monday, noon–6:00 P.M.

One of the oldest, best-respected, and most spacious of the area galleries, Pierogi 2000 highlights the works of Brooklyn artists in a series of mostly solo shows.

Beer Here!

If your style is more Budweiser than Beaujolais, Williamsburg art may be right up your alley. At these decidedly less pretentious Brooklyn galleries, beer is the official drink of choice for the opening receptions. So chugalug your way down to these opening nights for some free beer and intriguing art. For information on openings, check out the calendar at www.wburg.com or put your name on each gallery's mailing list to receive invitations.

ROEBLING HALL

390 Wythe Avenue (at South 4th Street)
(718) 599–5352
www.roeblinghall.com
Hours: Friday through Monday, noon–6:00 P.M.

Considered one of the powerhouses of the area, Roebling Hall displays the works of neighborhood and international artists working in all forms. The shows are always daring, insightful, filled with humor, and thought-provoking. In recent years they have also opened a larger space in Chelsea (606 West 26th Street at Eleventh Avenue, 212–929–8180), where they generally show more established artists.

OTHER GALLERIES AND SHOWS AROUND NEW YORK

BROADWAY WINDOWS

Broadway at East 10th Street
(212) 998–5751
www.nyu.edu/pages/galleries
Hours: 24/7.

Five innocent-looking shop windows that serve as a gallery. They display a wide range of styles including paintings, sculpture, and site-specific work. Be careful when walking in this neighborhood: People are forever crashing into each other, because they can't take their eyes off these often surprising windows.

BWAC PIER SHOWS

141 Beard Street
Red Hook, Brooklyn
(718) 596–2507
www.bwac.org
Hours: Saturday and Sunday, noon–6:00 P.M., May through September only.

The Brooklyn art scene is brought to the public's eye at this series of annual events showcasing more than 200 emerging and established artists. Painting, sculpture, installation art, photography, and experimental forms are on display. It's a bit of a haul to get there, but the Civil War–era warehouse location, amazing view of the Statue of Liberty, passing barge traffic, and enough art to fill the Louvre all make it worth the effort. Call or check their Web site for a schedule of shows.

80 WASHINGTON SQUARE EAST GALLERIES

New York University
80 Washington Square East
(212) 998–5747
www.nyu.edu/pages/galleries
Hours: Tuesday, 10:00 A.M.–7:00 P.M.; Wednesday and Thursday,
10:00 A.M.–6:00 P.M.; Friday and Saturday, 10:00 A.M.–5:00 P.M.
Eight galleries consisting of different solo shows or one group show. Don't miss the "Small Works" international competition every February.

KENKELEBA GALLERY

214 East 2nd Street (between Avenues B and C)
(212) 674–3939
Hours: Wednesday through Saturday, 11:00 A.M.–6:00 P.M.
This gallery specializes in works by African-American and third-world artists, emerging artists, and experimental works.

PERFORMANCE SPACE 122 GALLERY

150 First Avenue (entrance on 9th Street)
(212) 228–4249
www.ps122.org
Hours: Thursday and Friday, noon–6:00 p.m.; Saturday and Sunday,
noon–4:00 p.m.
The gallery wing of the birthplace of downtown performance art, where you'll find shows of paintings, photography, drawings, sculptures, videos, installations, multimedia, and many other things sure to upset Jesse Helms. You can also volunteer-usher to see performances here for free. (See the first chapter, "Theater: Free Speech," for details.)

THE ROTUNDA GALLERY

33 Clinton Street (at Pierrepont Street)
Brooklyn
(718) 875–4047
www.brooklynx.org/rotunda
Hours: Tuesday through Friday, noon–5:00 P.M.; Saturday,
11:00 A.M.–4:00 P.M.
Exhibits all Brooklyn-based artists working in all forms, from painting and sculpture to installations and performance art.

SOCRATES SCULPTURE PARK
Broadway at Vernon Boulevard
Long Island City, Queens
(718) 956–1819
www.socratessculpturepark.org
Hours: Daily, 10:00 A.M.–sunset.
This four-and-a-half-acre stretch of land along the Queens side of the East River has been transformed into a delightful green space that highlights the works of up-and-coming artists. They also offer free tours and occasionally free films and music as well. Call or check the Web site for details and schedule.

WEST SIDE ARTS COALITION
On the mall at Broadway and 96th Street
(212) 316–6024
www.wsacny.org
Hours: Saturday and Sunday, noon–6:00 P.M.; Wednesday, 6:00–8:00 P.M.
From cheesy kitsch to winsome watercolors, you never know what you'll find at this little gallery showcasing the works of community artists in the middle of the road, literally (it's located on the median between the traffic running up and down Broadway). Stop by and take a look; it'll just take you a minute, again, literally.

WHITE COLUMNS
320 West 13th Street (enter on Horatio Street, between Eighth
Avenue and Hudson Street)
(212) 924–4212
www.whitecolumns.org
Hours: Tuesday through Saturday, noon–6:00 P.M.
Specializing in large-scale installations by emerging and underrepresented artists, White Columns was the first to commission works by many artists who have gone on to international fame (and infamy), including William Wegman and Andres Serrano.

"I went to the museum where they had all the heads and arms from the statues that are in all the other museums."

—Stephen Wright

THE MUSEUMS OF New York City are world class, abundant—and most of these collections can be seen free of charge. Whatever your taste or interest, whatever your age, background, or curiosities, there are museums to satisfy you. Many are completely free of charge at all times, while others have specific days and hours when they allow the public in for free or "Pay What You Want" (and you know what I want to pay!). Chances are, if the institution you would like to visit does not fit into one of those two categories, the admission charge is a "suggested donation." (Can you guess what I suggest you donate?)

ALWAYS FREE

AMERICAN FOLK ART MUSEUM
Eva and Morris Feld Gallery
2 Lincoln Square (Columbus Avenue, between 65th and 66th Streets)
(212) 595–9533
www.folkartmuseum.org
Hours: Tuesday through Saturday, noon–7:30 P.M.; Sunday, noon–5:30 P.M.
While much of the Folk Art Museum has moved down to fancier digs on 53rd
Street where they charge you to get in (except Friday evening), they still
maintain these galleries at the original location of the museum, filled with
enticing selections from their extensive permanent collection as well as temporary exhibitions. It's always a joy to take a walk through these halls and
see what new treasures they have discovered. A sign at the front desk sug-
gests a $3.00 donation, but no one seems to take any notice of that, and the
staff doesn't stop you and ask for any cash. (See pages 255–56 for more
information on the 53rd Street location.)

AUDUBON TERRACE
Hispanic Society of America, (212) 926–2234;
www.hispanicsociety.org
Hours: Tuesday through Saturday, 10:30 A.M.–4:30 P.M.; Sunday,
1:00–4:00 P.M.

American Academy of Arts and Letters, (212) 368–5900;
Broadway, between 155th and 156th Streets
www.artsandletters.org
These regal buildings in Upper Manhattan are home to two small but impressive collections. The Hispanic Society is an impressive collection of paintings,
sculpture, archaeological finds, textiles, rare books, and manuscripts from
Spain, Portugal, and Latin America dating as far back as the seventh century
B.C. and is always free and open to the public. The Academy of Arts and
Letters is a private organization of 250 preeminent American writers, composers, painters, sculptors, and architects. The building is home to many of
the works of these artists and is free, but it's open to the public only for exhibitions during the spring and fall. Call for a schedule and details.

CARNEGIE HALL
The Rose Museum
154 West 57th Street, second floor (between Sixth and Seventh
Avenues)

(212) 903-9629
www.carnegiehall.org
Hours: Daily, 11:00 A.M.–4:30 P.M., and during concert intermissions.
Explore the history of the architectural splendor and acoustical wonder that
is Carnegie Hall. From Toscanini's baton to Benny Goodman's clarinet, this
museum has hundreds of artifacts, photographs, and memorabilia from its
legendary past.

CASTLE CLINTON
Battery Park
(212) 344-7220
www.nps.gov/cacl
Hours: Daily, 8:00 A.M.–5:00 P.M.
Originally built in 1811 as the vanguard in the defense of New York Harbor
off the shores of the southwest tip of Manhattan, Castle Clinton has over its
long history served as a fort, an opera house, and the New York Aquarium; it
was finally saved from destruction and returned to its original fort design to
serve as a national monument. A small museum and video display tell you
about the long and varied history of the building, as does a well-marked self-
guided tour. Be sure to check out the tours and programs led by the park
rangers throughout the day.

FASHION INSTITUTE OF TECHNOLOGY MUSEUM
Shirley Goodman Resource Center
Seventh Avenue between 27th and 28th Streets
(212) 217-5800
www.fitnyc.edu/museum
**Hours: Tuesday through Friday, noon–8:00 P.M.; Saturday, 10:00 A.M.–
5:00 P.M.**
Located in the fashion district, this school museum is home to the largest
collection of costumes, textiles, and apparel dating from the eighteenth century in the world. You won't find all their finery on display at all times,
though; exhibitions change throughout the year. Still, whatever they have on
display is sure to thrill any fashion bug.

FEDERAL HALL NATIONAL MEMORIAL
26 Wall Street (at Broad Street)
(212) 825-6888
www.nps.gov/feha
Hours: Monday through Friday, 9:00 A.M.–5:00 P.M.
The site of George Washington's first inauguration as president and the first
home of the U.S. Congress, this building now houses a museum about its role

in the early history of the city and country. Free guided tours at 11:00 A.M. and 3:00 P.M.

FORBES MAGAZINE GALLERIES
62 Fifth Avenue (at 12th Street)
(212) 206–5548
www.forbesgalleries.com
Hours: Tuesday, Wednesday, Friday, and Saturday, 10:00 a.m.–4:00 P.M.
The business magazine shows its lighter side in their galleries with a permanent collection that includes thousands of toy soldiers, hundreds of toy boats, the untold history of the game Monopoly, and hundreds of unusual trophies. Their other galleries house changing exhibits of jewelry and historical letters and documents, as well as classical and contemporary art.

THE GARIBALDI-MEUCCI MUSEUM
420 Thomkins Avenue (at Chestnut Avenue)
Staten Island
(718) 442–1608
www.garibaldimeuccimuseum.org
Hours: Tuesday through Sunday, 1:00–5:00 P.M.
Think you know who invented the telephone? Well, think again, because back in 1850, while Alexander Graham Bell was still a child in Scotland, Giuseppe Garibaldi and Antonio Meucci were burning up the wires in Staten Island. Visit the historic home where the real first telephone conversation took place, and find out more about these two men's long list of accomplishments.

GENERAL GRANT'S NATIONAL MONUMENT
Riverside Drive and 122nd Street
(212) 666–1640
www.nps.gov/gegr
Hours: Daily, 9:00 A.M.–5:00 P.M.
Here you'll finally get an answer to that age-old question: Who's buried in Grant's Tomb? You can also see some exhibits about U. S. Grant's life (childhood, the Civil War years, and the presidency) as well as some pretty stunning views of the Hudson River.

HALL OF FAME FOR GREAT AMERICANS
Hall of Fame Terrace
181st Street and University Avenue
The Bronx
(718) 289–5161
www.bcc.cuny.edu/halloffame

FREE OR PAY-WHAT-YOU-WISH DAYS AT MUSEUMS

MUSEUM	MONDAY	TUESDAY	WEDNESDAY	THURSDAY	FRIDAY	SATURDAY	SUNDAY
American Folk Art Museum					5:30–7:30 P.M.		
Asia Society					6:00–9:00 P.M.		
Bartow-Pell Mansion Museum			Noon–4:00 P.M.				
Bronx Museum of the Arts			Noon–9:00 P.M.				
Brooklyn Museum of Art						First Saturday of Every Month 5:00–11:00 P.M.	
Dahesh Museum of Art				First Thursday of Every Month 6:00–9:00 P.M.			
Guggenheim Museum					6:00–8:00 P.M.		
International Center of Photography					5:00–8:00 P.M.		
Jewish Museum				5:00–8:00 P.M.			
Museum of Arts and Design				6:00–8:00 P.M.			
Museum of Chinese in America (MoCA)					Noon–7:00 P.M.		
Museum of Jewish Heritage			4:00–8:00 P.M.				
Museum of Modern Art (MoMA)					4:00–8:00 P.M.		
Museum of the Moving Image					4:00–8:00 P.M.		
New York Hall of Science					2:00–5:00 P.M. (EXCEPT JULY AND AUGUST)		10:00–11:00 A.M. (EXCEPT JULY AND AUGUST)
The Noguchi Museum					First Friday of Every Month 10:00 A.M.– 5:00 P.M.		
The Studio Museum in Harlem						First Saturday of Every Month 10:00 A.M.–6:00 P.M.	
Whitney Museum					6:00–9:00 P.M.		

Hours: Daily, 10:00 A.M.–5:00 P.M.
If there was a hall of fame for halls of fame, this one would certainly be in it, because this is where the whole idea began. On this covered walkway you'll find bronze busts of great American political leaders, scientists, soldiers, and authors.

LOUIS ARMSTRONG ARCHIVES

Queens College
65–30 Kissena Boulevard (at the Long Island Expressway)
(718) 997–3670
www.satchmo.net
Hours: Monday through Friday, 10:00 A.M.–5:00 P.M.
Home to more than 5,000 photographs, home recordings, scrapbooks, music, and instruments from the home of one of the (if not *the!*) greatest trumpet players in the history of jazz. They also lead tours through the Armstrong house at 34–57 107th Street in Corona, Queens, but they charge for that. The archives are free and open to the public, but by appointment only.

MUSEUM OF AMERICAN ILLUSTRATORS

128 East 63rd Street (between Park and Lexington Avenues)
(212) 838–2560
www.societyillustrators.org
Hours: Tuesday, 10:00 A.M.–8:00 P.M.; Wednesday through Friday,
10:00 A.M.–5:00 P.M.; Saturday, noon–4:00 P.M.
This East Side town house is home to a private club for illustrators, but the public is always invited to explore their two gallery spaces. They put up anywhere from fifteen to twenty-two shows a year from their extensive permanent collection of historical book and magazine covers and illustrations. Some of the true prizes of the collection reside in the upstairs dining room, which is not officially open to the public. If you ask nicely, though, they'll be happy to let you up there to see the Norman Rockwell, Maxfield Parrish, and other treasures.

NATIONAL MUSEUM OF THE
AMERICAN INDIAN

1 Bowling Green Place (between State and Whitehall Streets)
(212) 514–3700
www.si.edu/nmai
Hours: Daily, 10:00 A.M.–5:00 P.M.; Thursday until 8:00 P.M.
A branch of the Smithsonian Institution, this museum is overflowing with dazzling artifacts, interactive displays, firsthand oral histories, music, and

crafts of Native Americans. The changing exhibits explore the histories, beliefs, customs, and cultures of these once vast civilizations. The museum offers free workshops in such things as traditional basket weaving and bead-work (small materials fees are required), and free guided tours at 2:00 P.M. every day. If you miss the official guided tour, drop by the information desk on the second floor anytime—there's usually someone available to show you around free of charge. They also have a schedule of free films and live per-formances. Call or check the Web site for a schedule and details.

NEW YORK UNEARTHED
17 State Street (at Pearl Street)
(212) 748–8628
www.southstseaport.org
By appointment only.
Explore 5,000 years of New York history in fifteen minutes at this free branch of the South Street Seaport Museum. The museum is free, but you must call to make an appointment.

NICHOLAS ROERICH MUSEUM
319 West 107th Street (between Broadway and Riverside Drive)
(212) 864–7752
www.roerich.org
Hours: Tuesday through Sunday, 2:00–5:00 P.M.
Houses more than 200 works by the artist Nicholas Roerich that deal mainly with Himalayan scenery and spiritual subject matter. Sundays they also almost always present a free classical concert or poetry reading. Call or check the Web site for details.

QUEENS COUNTY FARM MUSEUM
73–50 Little Neck Parkway
Floral Park, Queens
(718) 347–FARM (3276)
www.queensfarm.org
Hours: Monday through Friday, 9:00 A.M.–5:00 P.M. (outside only);
Saturday and Sunday, 10:00 A.M.–5:00 P.M.
Where the City Mouse meets the County Mouse. This forty-seven-acre working farm is the last remaining tract of undisturbed farmland in New York City and dates back to the seventeenth century. On the weekend take a free guided tour of the farmhouse and greenhouse, wander the farmyards and *hey!* they even have hayrides (for $2.00).

TIBET HOUSE NEW YORK

22 West 15th Street (between Fifth and Sixth Avenues)

(212) 807–0563

www.tibethouse.org

Hours: Monday through Friday, noon–6:00 P.M.

The galleries host exhibitions of artworks having to do with the culture, beliefs, history, and mythology of Tibetan Buddhism. They also hold open meditations every Tuesday evening with talks afterward. They ask for a $7.00 donation or "whatever you like."

URBAN CENTER

Architectural League of New York; (212) 753–1722; www.archleague .org

The Municipal Art Society; (212) 935–3960; www.mas.org

457 Madison Avenue (between 50th and 51st Streets)

Hours: Monday through Wednesday, Friday, and Saturday, 11:00 A.M.– 5:00 P.M.

The galleries on the first two floors of the Urban Center play host to exhibitions from both of these organizations. The Municipal Art Society works usually highlight the city as a work of art, while the Architectural League's shows concentrate on the art of making the city.

WHITNEY MUSEUM AT ALTRIA

120 Park Avenue (at 42nd Street)

(917) 663–2453

www.whitney.org

Hours: Monday through Wednesday and Friday, 11:00 A.M.–6:00 P.M.; Thursday until 7:30 P.M.

A branch of the Whitney Museum, this small gallery and atrium plays host to four or five shows a year with a focus on contemporary emerging artists. There isn't much gallery here, but it's a nice indoor public space for a brown-bag lunch. They also host a series of performances every spring.

SOMETIMES FREE

AMERICAN FOLK ART MUSEUM

45 West 53rd Street (between Fifth and Sixth Avenues)

(212) 265–1040

www.folkartmuseum.org

Hours: Tuesday through Sunday, 10:30 A.M.–5:30 P.M.; Friday until 7:30 P.M.
When free: Friday, 5:30 P.M.–7:30 P.M.
This glorious new building is home to a huge collection of American folk art.
The works on display from their permanent collection or from temporary exhi-
bitions are created by artisans and artists from all walks of life throughout
American history to the present time. These mostly self-taught artists have
created pieces that are often whimsical and surprising, and could be anything
from weather vanes or painted furniture to handwoven Shaker rugs or duck
decoys. The Lincoln Center gallery is open seven days a week and always free.
(See page 249 for details on the museum's other location at 2 Lincoln Square.)

ASIA SOCIETY
725 Park Avenue (between 70th and 71st Streets)
(212) 288-6400
www.asiasociety.org
Hours: Tuesday through Sunday, 11:00 A.M.–6:00 P.M.;
Friday until 9:00 P.M.; Sunday, noon–5:00 P.M.
When free: Friday, 6:00–9:00 P.M.
A terrifically modern museum with exhibits from every corner of Asia that
encompasses antiquities as old as humankind as well as the most startling
new technologies and contemporary art commissions. They offer free guided
tours and audio tours on Free Fridays as well.

BARTOW-PELL MANSION MUSEUM
895 Shore Road North
Pelham Bay Park, the Bronx
(718) 885-1461
www.bartowpellmansionmuseum.org
Hours: Wednesday, Saturday, and Sunday, noon–4:00 P.M.
When free: Wednesday.
Travel back to the early part of the nineteenth century, when living in the
Bronx was considered living in the country. The estate predates the signing
of the Declaration of Independence, and the mansion was built and furnished in the early 1800s. The museum has returned the home, carriage
house, and gardens to their original splendor. You are welcome to make
yourself at home free of charge on Wednesday from noon to 4:00 P.M.

BRONX MUSEUM OF THE ARTS
1040 Grand Concourse (at 165th Street)
The Bronx
(718) 681-6000
www.bronxmuseum.org

Hours: Wednesday, noon–9:00 P.M.; Thursday through Sunday
until 6:00 P.M.
When free: Wednesday.
Primarily shows twentieth-century contemporary art by African, African-
American, Latino, and Asian artists as well as artists who have lived in the
Bronx.

BROOKLYN MUSEUM OF ART

200 Eastern Parkway (at Washington Avenue)
(718) 638–5000
www.brooklynmuseum.org
Hours: Wednesday through Friday, 10:00 A.M.–5:00 P.M.; Saturday and
Sunday, 11:00 A.M.–6:00 P.M.
When free: The first Saturday of every month, 5:00–11:00 P.M.
Don't miss the First Saturday event every month: free theater, free music, free
movies, free dancing, free art, free guided tours. What a night! All other times
they have a "suggested" donation of $8.00 for admission, but you can give
as much (or as little!) as you would like.

DAHESH MUSEUM OF ART

580 Madison Avenue (between 56th and 57th Streets)
(212) 759–0606
www.daheshmuseum.org
Hours: Tuesday through Sunday, 11:00 A.M.–6:00 P.M.
When free: The first Thursday of the month, 6:00–9:00 P.M.
"Make the painters copy everything beautiful in Rome, and when they are
done, if possible, make them do it again" was the philosophy of the French
Academy up through the nineteenth and early twentieth centuries. This collection specializes in this academic art by artists working to emulate
Renaissance masters like da Vinci and Michelangelo with their works depict-
ing classical mythology and biblical images. First Thursday free evenings
always include special events like historical lectures and film screenings.

GUGGENHEIM MUSEUM

1071 Fifth Avenue (at 89th Street)
(212) 423–3500
www.guggenheim.org
Hours: Sunday through Wednesday, 10:00 A.M.–6:00 P.M.; Friday and
Saturday until 8:00 P.M.
When free: Friday 6:00–8:00 P.M. is "Pay What You Want."
The art museum that is a work of art itself. Designed by Frank Lloyd Wright,

the building houses modern works that are sometimes controversial, some-times commercial, but always worth seeing.

INTERNATIONAL CENTER OF PHOTOGRAPHY (ICP)

1133 Avenue of the Americas (at 43rd Street)

(212) 857–0000

www.icp.org

Hours: Tuesday through Thursday, 10:00 A.M.–6:00 P.M.; Friday until 8:00 P.M.; Saturday and Sunday until 6:00 P.M.

When free: Friday 5:00–8:00 P.M. is "Pay What You Wish."

The huge gallery spaces of the ICP mount shows that celebrate the art, craft, and images caught in the blink of an eye by the finest photographers from around the world and throughout the history of this ever-evolving art form.

JEWISH MUSEUM

1109 Fifth Avenue (at 92nd Street)

(212) 423–3200

www.jewishmuseum.org

Hours: Sunday through Wednesday, 11:00 A.M.–5:45 P.M.; Thursday until 8:00 P.M.; Friday, 11:00 A.M. to 3:00 P.M.

When free: Thursday 5:00–8:00 P.M. is "Pay What You Wish."

Ancient traditions and modern sensibilities clash, collide, and mesh in this museum that follows the development and culture of the Jewish experience from antiquity to the present day. The walls are full of rare artifacts, inter-active displays, and intriguing works of art that span the centuries.

MUSEUM OF ARTS AND DESIGN

40 West 53rd Street (between Fifth and Sixth Avenues)

(212) 956–3535

http://nyc.mad.museum

Hours: Daily, 10:00 A.M.–6:00 P.M.; Thursday until 8:00 P.M.

When free: Thursday 6:00–8:00 P.M. is "Pay What You Want"

This elegant three-story museum essentially serves as an excuse for a very popular gift shop. The museum displays functional objects handcrafted by contemporary American artists working in such areas as glass, baskets, quilts, furniture, instruments, utensils, and even boats, kites, brooms, and paper plates. And yes, many of the artists on display in the museum have pricey items available at the gift shop.

MUSEUM OF CHINESE IN AMERICA (MOCA)
70 Mulberry Street, second floor (at Bayard Street)
(212) 923–3700
www.moca-nyc.org
Hours: Tuesday through Sunday, noon–6:00 P.M.; Friday until 7:00 P.M.
When free: Friday
A small museum dedicated to preserving and chronicling the full experience of Chinese immigrants and their descendants.

MUSEUM OF JEWISH HERITAGE
36 Battery Place (in Battery Park City Park)
(646) 437–4200
www.mjhnyc.org
Hours: Sunday through Thursday, 10:00 A.M.–5:45 P.M.; Wednesday until 8:00 P.M.; Friday and the eve of Jewish holidays, 10:00 A.M.–3:00 P.M.
When free: Wednesday, 4:00–8:00 P.M.
The museum exists as a living memorial to the Holocaust and uses the two quotes *"Remember, Never Forget"* and *"There Is Hope for Your Future"* to define its mission. The lives, culture, beliefs, and traditions of those who perished in the Holocaust are celebrated while the museum also looks forward to the present-day Jewish communities around the world that is the legacy of those Holocaust victims.

MUSEUM OF MODERN ART (MOMA)
11 West 53rd Street (between Fifth and Sixth Avenues)
(212) 708–9480
www.moma.org
Hours: Monday, Wednesday, Thursday, Saturday, and Sunday, 10:30 A.M.–5:30 P.M.; Friday, 10:00 A.M.–8:00 P.M.
When free: Friday, 4:00 P.M.–8:00 P.M.
From Monet to milk cartons, everything modern can be found here. Films, gallery talks, and jazz in the sculpture garden as well as high-profile temporary exhibitions and the permanent collection are all available during the "Pay-What-You-Wish" Friday hours.

MUSEUM OF THE MOVING IMAGE
Thirty-fifth Avenue at 36th Street
Astoria, Queens
(718) 784–4520
www.ammi.org

Hours: Wednesday and Thursday, 11:00 A.M.–5:00 P.M.; Friday, 11:00 A.M.–
8:00 P.M.; Saturday and Sunday, 11:00 A.M.–6:30 P.M.

When free: Friday, 4:00–8:00 P.M.

With the nation's largest collection of film, television, and digital media artifacts, the museum explores, catalogs, entertains, and educates visitors on the
complete history of everything having to do with the moving image. Its many
exhibits go behind the scenes and delve into every area from penny arcades
to the secrets of Yoda's puppetry. There is an additional charge for screenings
during the free hours, but there are enough fascinating galleries and interactive exhibits to keep any film buff happy.

NEW YORK HALL OF SCIENCE

47–01 111th Street
Flushing Meadows–Corona Park, Queens
(718) 699–0005
www.nyhallsci.org

Hours: Tuesday through Thursday, 9:30 A.M.–2:00 P.M.; Friday, 9:30 A.M.–
5:00 P.M.; Saturday and Sunday, 10:00 A.M.–6:00 P.M.

When free: Friday, 2:00–5:00 P.M.; Sunday, 10:00–11:00 A.M.; except in
July and August.

Kids of all ages love this place. A lot of hands-on science experiments, space
stuff, and a big glowing brain—who could ask for anything more?

THE NOGUCHI MUSEUM

32–37 Vernon Boulevard (at 33rd Road)
Long Island City, Queens
(718) 204–7088
www.noguchi.org

Hours: Wednesday through Friday, 10:00 A.M.–5:00 P.M.; Saturday and
Sunday, 11:00 A.M.–5:00 P.M.

When free: The first Friday of every month.

Housed in a former photo-engraving factory, the museum is devoted entirely
to the sculpture and art of Isamu Noguchi. Noguchi sculptures and designs
are on display in public and private spaces throughout the world, and the
museum houses many of his most striking and noted works in its thirteen galleries and garden space.

THE STUDIO MUSEUM IN HARLEM

144 West 125th Street (between Lenox and Seventh Avenues)
(212) 864–4500
www.studiomuseuminharlem.org

Hours: Wednesday and Thursday, noon–6:00 P.M.; Friday, noon–8:00 P.M.; Saturday and Sunday, 10:00 A.M.–6:00 P.M.
When free: The first Saturday of each month.
The leading museum dedicated to the works of African-American artists.

WHITNEY MUSEUM OF AMERICAN ART
945 Madison Avenue (at 75th Street)
(212) 570–3600
www.whitney.org
Hours: Wednesday, Thursday, Saturday, and Sunday, 11:00 A.M.–6:00 P.M.; Friday, 1:00–9:00 P.M.
When free: Friday, 6:00–9:00 P.M. is "Pay What You Want."
One of the most impressive collections of modern art in the world, the permanent collection follows the developments of modern work from Hopper to Pollock and from Rauschenberg to today's cutting-edge artists. A couple of floors of the museum are always reserved for changing shows, from historic solo works to daring group shows. Drop by any Friday for pay-what-you-want night and also take in the free live music and guided and audio tours.

MUSEUMS WITH SUGGESTED DONATIONS

A large selection of major and smaller museums in New York operate under a "suggested donation" system. So, while they may "suggest" a $12 "donation," you are under no obligation to make that specific donation. There's no reason to feel bad about giving less than they ask or as little as you can afford. The fact of the matter is, most of these institutions are members of the Cultural Institutions Group (CIG) and receive a tremendous amount of money from the city of New York. One of the obligations that goes along with this cash from the city is that they have to let folks into their museums for whatever they are willing to pay. In essence, you've already paid your admission when you pay your taxes. You can get away with giving as little as a penny. My standard contribution is a quarter (see, I can be generous).

AMERICAN MUSEUM OF NATURAL HISTORY, Central Park West (at 79th Street); (212) 769–5100; www.amnh.org.

BROOKLYN MUSEUM OF ART, 200 Eastern Parkway (at Washington Avenue); (718) 638–5000; www.brooklynmuseum.org.

THE CLOISTERS, Fort Tryon Park, Washington Heights; (212) 923–3700; www.metmuseum.org.

EL MUSEO DEL BARRIO, 1230 Fifth Avenue (at 105th Street); (212) 831–7272; www.elmuseo.org.

METROPOLITAN MUSEUM OF ART, 1000 Fifth Avenue (at 82nd Street); (212) 535–7710; www.metmuseum.org.

MUSEUM OF THE CITY OF NEW YORK, 1220 Fifth Avenue (at 103rd Street); (212) 534–1672; www.mcny.org.

MUSEUM OF CHINESE IN AMERICA, 70 Mulberry Street, second floor (at Bayard Street); (212) 619–4785; www.moca-nyc.org.

NEW YORK CITY POLICE MUSEUM, 100 Old Slip (between Water Street and FDR Drive); (212) 480–3100; www.nycpolicemuseum.org.

NEW YORK FIRE MUSEUM, 278 Spring Street (between Varick and Hudson Streets); (212) 691–1303; www.nycfiremuseum.org.

P.S. 1 CONTEMPORARY ART CENTER, 22–25 Jackson Avenue (at 46th Avenue), Queens; (718) 784–2084; www.ps1.org.

QUEENS MUSEUM OF ART, Flushing Meadows Park; (718) 592–9700; www.queensmuseum.org.

> "All good things are wild,
> and free."
>
> —Henry David Thoreau

T USED TO BE that the best place to see the wildlife for free in New York was to walk around Times Square on any late night. But now that 42nd Street has gotten its face-lift, the closest you will come to seeing anything too wild on those streets are the fake furs and leather worn by visitors to the Disney Shop and Madame Tussaud's. So for some real roars, New York offers some fine collections of everything from African lions, Chilean flamingos, Indian elephants, and Australian lizards to grizzly bears, Goliath beetles, lowland gorillas, and Grevy's zebras. You will find zoos in each of the boroughs, but the only ones that have free hours are the Bronx and Staten Island Zoos. Free days for both zoos are on Wednesday.

THE BRONX ZOO
Fordham Road and the Bronx River Parkway
(718) 367–1010
www.bronxzoo.com

 Free general admission all day on Wednesday, but you will have to pay to get into some exhibits (which can add up!).

The rain forest of the Congo or the African savannah may not be what you expect to see in the Bronx, but at this, the largest metropolitan zoo in the country, you'll find more than 6,000 animals and exhibits set in startlingly realistic natural habitats. As part of the Wildlife Conservation Society, the Bronx Zoo has played an integral part in saving such endangered species as the snow leopard, the American bison, lowland gorillas, Chinese alligators, Mauritius pink pigeons, and more than forty other species. And bring the family by on any Wednesday to save a fistful of cash. Wednesday is Donation Day and everyone gets in for whatever they want to pay, even if that's nothing. Beware, many of the more enticing and exciting exhibits and rides do charge additional fees (even on Wednesday), so you might want to pony up some cash for their Pay-One-Price ticket upgrade ($14.00) if you plan on taking in all the wild sights.

STATEN ISLAND ZOO
614 Broadway (off Glenwood Avenue)
(718) 442–3100
www.statenislandzoo.org

 Free on Wednesday after 2:00 P.M.

Particularly well-known for its collection of snakes and other reptiles, this small zoo also boasts an aquarium, children's zoo, rain forest, and African savannah habitats and free parking.

"If you want to say it
with flowers, a single
rose says: 'I'm cheap!'"

—Delta Burke

HEY, EVEN CHEAP BASTARDS need love. And while it's true that introducing yourself as a Cheap Bastard may not be the most successful way to get a date, being a Cheap Bastard shouldn't get in the way of having a great time. In fact, you might even score extra points by coming up with some original ideas for romantic liaisons around New York. Here are some great ways to spend days and evenings with that special someone that won't cost you a thing (except maybe your heart).

THE UNTRADITIONAL TRADITIONAL DATE: Why not put a twist on the usual date by seeing a free movie? In the summer there are any number of starlit nights for you to set out a blanket and cuddle while you watch the stars of Hollywood twinkle on the screen. My personal favorite romantic setting is the Movies With A View, at the foot of the Brooklyn Bridge—not too crowded, the skyline of New York as a backdrop, and fun films on the screen. During the cooler months move indoors with the free screenings at RiFiFi or Casa Italiana at NYU. For more details and other film ideas, see the chapter titled "Film: Cheap Shots."

THE SWEEP-HER-OFF-HER-FEET DATE: Swing down to the MoonDance at Hudson River Park any Sunday during the summer for dancing under the stars to live music. Show up early for a free lesson. During the cooler months, stick a rose in her mouth and heat things up by going down to Chelsea Market to do the Dance of Love any Saturday afternoon, when they offer a traditional Argentinean tango *milonga*. For details and more dance ideas, see the chapter titled "Dance: Free Expression."

THE SURE-WAY-TO-SCORE DATE: Spend a day of fun and games in Central Park by borrowing a free Field Day Kit from the folks at the North Meadow Recreation Center. They throw in all kinds of equipment for almost any sport you can think of. Your big sack of fun includes a basketball, bats, Wiffle balls, football, Nerf ball, horseshoe set, Frisbee, jump rope, and even hula hoops. If that doesn't get the two of you working up a sweat, nothing will. For more information, see page 283.

THE THIS-ISN'T-QUITE-VENICE-BUT-HEY-YOU-AREN'T-QUITE-SOPHIA-LOREN DATE: Your gondola awaits you at the Downtown Boathouse on Pier 26 or Pier 96. The bad news is, you have to do all the rowing and serenading yourself; the good news is, it's free. Borrow a kayak for you and your love to paddle up and down the Hudson any weekend from May through October. For details, see pages 177–78.

THE TROUBADOUR DATE: If you don't have the voice to serenade your sweetheart by yourself, here's the next best thing. Catch one of the very intimate performances at the Postcrypt Coffeehouse on the campus of Columbia University any Friday or Saturday night during the school year. Any candlelit evening of acoustic music is the perfect setting for a romantic evening for two. And hey, there's even free popcorn. For details see page 30.

THE MAKE-'EM-LAUGH DATE: A surefire way to win someone's heart is to put a smile on their face, and there are many free funny nights every week around the city. During the week you'll find some top-notch comedy performances at PSNBC and at the Upright Citizens Brigade on Wednesday and

Sunday nights. For more details and other comedy destinations, see the chapter titled "Comedy: Cheap Jokes."

THE LOVE-BIRDS DATE: See if a walk among the birds and the bees inspires anything for you. Stop by Belvedere Castle in Central Park and borrow a free Birding Kit for a delightful stroll through the wilds of the park. Your kit comes equipped with your very own set of binoculars, a field guide, a sketch pad, and colored pencils. For more details, see page 139.

THE PRETENTIOUS DATE: Show your date you can bandy around words like *cubist, conceptual, minimalistic,* and *postmodernist* with the best of them at any of the many art gallery openings that go on every week. If that doesn't have any effect, maybe all the free wine or beer will. For more details, see the chapter titled "Art Galleries: Show Me the Monet."

THE FUN-IN-THE-SUN DATE: Spend a day at any one of the local beaches. An old reliable free day. Sorry, they can't all be gems. See pages 181–83 for beaches.

THE SHOW-'EM-YOU-GOT-CLASS DATE: Take in a museum on one of the many free, suggested donation, or pay-what-you-want nights. The best one is First Saturday Night at the Brooklyn Museum—free live music and dancing, free films, and, oh yeah, there's some art there, too. For more museum details, see the chapter titled "Museums: Free to See."

THE NOT-QUITE-THE-GREAT-WHITE-WAY DATE: Take my advice: If you want a second date, don't try this on a first date. If you've been dating for a while, though, and it's clear that you're both Cheap Bastards, then why not pick a Broadway or Off Broadway show for you to volunteer-usher at together? For a list of theaters to usher at, see the chapter titled "Theater: Free Speech." If you don't want to seem chintzy, get free tickets to a production or concert at Juilliard or NYU or any of the other free theaters listed on pages 20–26.

THE YOU-THINK-*WE'VE*-GOT-PROBLEMS? DATE: Hitting one of those rough patches in the relationship? Well, there's nothing like reveling in someone else's misery to make you feel good about your own life. Take your date to see a taping of *The Montel Williams Show, The People's Court,* or *Maury* and by comparison, your troubles will surely seem insignificant. For details and more TV taping ideas, see the chapter titled "Television Tapings: Public Access."

THE GETTING-TO-KNOW-YOU DATE: Why not take the time to get to know each other as you get to know a bit of New York? There are some great walking tours that will give you the time to walk and talk your way around the city. Check out Take a Walk, New York!, Urban Park Rangers tours, or the delightful jaunts through Central Park given by the Central Park Conservancy. For more details, see the chapter titled "Walking Tours: The Freedom Trail."

THE HEY-THIS-IS-GOING-PRETTY-SWELL-I-MAY-JUST-WANT-TO-KISS-YOU SPECIAL ADD-ON TO ANY DATE: It may not be as romantic as the *Titanic,* but a ride on the Staten Island Ferry will leave you feeling like you're on top of the world. Particularly if you end that date with a romantic kiss on the boat while you ride by the dramatic New York skyline with the wind in your hair. For more details, see page 224.

FINDING A CHEAP DATE . . .

Um, I mean *finding a date, cheap.* It's a big city with lots of single folks out there trying to find each other, but hanging out in bars or going to "singles" parties and events can be costly, not to mention depressing. Here are a couple of alternative ways to make the connection by volunteering and just being your own cheap self.

DATE BAIT
(212) 971–1084
www.datebait.com
DateBaitNYC@netscape.net

 Volunteers arrive forty-five minutes early to help with registration and stay a few minutes after to help with cleanup, but they fully participate in the event.

These are structured, results-oriented mixers for single people. The way it works is that when you register, you get a name tag with a number. Once the whole group has gathered—and these events do attract large crowds—everyone gets up to one minute to introduce themselves in front of the assembled. Then there's time to mingle and get to know each other; at the end of the night, you hand in a card with the numbers of those people you're interested in having a date with. If you're on their card as well, it's a match. If not . . . well, at least there was no face-to-face rejection. They have straight, gay, and lesbian events almost every week, and they're always surprisingly unintimidating, fun, and well put together. Call or e-mail at least a few weeks in advance to make a reservation to volunteer.

HURRYDATE

(646) 435–8264

www.hurrydate.com

 Door Hosts help set up the event and welcome paying guests. They are not always guaranteed a chance to participate in the "dating" but can mingle and meet potential dates . . . and get paid for it!

Got a minute? Have a date . . . or a dozen. HurryDate puts together energetic evenings where throngs of New York singles meet each other in a rapid-fire succession of mini-dates. They hold events targeted for gay and straight daters of all ages. There are two parts to any HurryDate evening. The evening starts and ends with the usual mix-and-mingle that you'd expect in any singles soiree, but what makes this different is that you're guaranteed twelve to twenty on-the-spot dates. Each date consists of a four-minute conversation where you two can get to know the basics about each other and see if there is enough chemistry there to give the real thing a try. If you both check off "Yes" on your scorecards, HurryDate will hook you up through their Web site and let nature take its course. You can take part in the evening by being a Door Host, which basically means they will pay you about $40 to help organize the event and greet the paying daters. Door Hosts are able to participate in the face-to-face dating only when there is an odd number of participants and you fit into the age or category of the evening. In any case, you are always able to participate in the schmooze-fest part of the evening.

"Every crowd has
a silver lining."
—P.T. Barnum

NEW YORKERS DON'T need much of an excuse to throw a parade, and nobody does a parade bigger or better than us. Either celebrating a national holiday, one of New York's many ethnic groups, or just to whoop it up, if it is the weekend, there is almost always a parade heading down a major avenue near you. Here is a detailed list of most New York City parades throughout the year, including approximate dates and locations. For more information on specific dates and locations, I have included contact information wherever possible. For further information call 311, the New York City information line.

JANUARY

THREE KINGS DAY PARADE, Third Avenue from 106th to 116th Street; (212) 831–7272; www.elmuseo.org/3kings.html; January 6.

MARTIN LUTHER KING, JR. DAY PARADE, Fifth Avenue from 61st to 86th Street; third Monday in January.

IDIOT-AROD, a wild and drunken shopping cart race from Fulton Ferry Pier at the foot of the Brooklyn Bridge, over the bridge and through downtown Manhattan to Tomkins Square Park; (718) 855–8910; www.precisionaccidents.com; last weekend in January.

FEBRUARY

CHINESE LUNAR NEW YEAR CELEBRATION AND FESTIVAL, Mott Street; www.explorechinatown.com.

MARCH

ST. PATRICK'S DAY PARADE, Fifth Avenue from 44th to 86th Street; March 17; www.saintpatricksdayparade.com.

BROOKLYN IRISH AMERICAN PARADE, Park Slope, Brooklyn; Seventh Avenue and Prospect Park West from 15th to Union Street; www.brooklyn irishamericanparade.com.

There are many other local St. Patrick's Day Parades throughout the city on the weekends near March 17th; visit www.saintpatricksdayparade.com for all the listings.

RINGLING BROTHERS, BARNUM & BAILEY CIRCUS' ELEPHANT WALK, 34th Street from the Queens Midtown Tunnel to Madison Square Garden; (212) 465–6741; www.ringling.com; the parade of elephants and other circus animals usually takes place on the Tuesday night before the first performance at Madison; mid-March.

GREEK INDEPENDENCE DAY PARADE, Fifth Avenue from 62nd to 79th Street; (718) 204–6500.

PERSIAN-IRANIAN PARADE, Madison Avenue from 41st to 27th Street; www.persianparade.org.

APRIL

EASTER PARADE, Fifth Avenue between 49th and 57th Street; (212) 484–1222; www.nycvisit.com.

NEW YORK TARTAN DAY PARADE, Sixth Avenue from 45th to 58th Street; (212) 980–0844; www.tartanweek.com.

PHAGWAH: HINDU NEW YEAR'S PARADE, Queens, Liberty Avenue from 133rd to 123rd Street to Smokey Oval Park.

SIKH CULTURAL SOCIETY PARADE & FESTIVAL, Madison Avenue from 41st to 23rd Street.

MAY

CUBAN DAY PARADE (LA GRAN PARADA CUBANA), Sixth Avenue from 34th to 59th Street; (212) 348–8270; first Sunday in May.

MARIJUANA MARCH, Broadway from Houston Street to Battery Park; (212) 677–7180; www.cures-not-wars.org; the first Saturday of May.

TURKISH AMERICAN DAY PARADE, Madison Avenue and 56th Street to Second Avenue and 47th Street; www.tadf.org; a Saturday in mid-May.

HAITIAN FLAG DAY PARADE, Brooklyn; Eastern Parkway from Utica Avenue to Grand Army Plaza; third Sunday in May.

NORWEGIAN-AMERICAN 17TH OF MAY PARADE, Brooklyn; Fifth Avenue and 90th Street to Seventh Avenue and 67th Street; www.norway.org/culture/heritage.

SALUTE TO ISRAEL PARADE, Fifth Avenue from 52nd to 79th Street; (212) 472–5388; www.salutetoisrael.com.

JUNE

PHILIPPINE INDEPENDENCE DAY PARADE, Madison Avenue from 40th to 23rd Street; (212) 764–1330; www.pcgny.net.

QUEENS PRIDE PARADE, Queens; Thirty-seventh Avenue from 89th to 75th Street; www.queenspride.com; first Sunday in June.

PUERTO RICAN DAY PARADE, Fifth Avenue from 44th to 86th Street; (718) 401–0404; www.nationalpuertoricandayparade.org; second Sunday in June.

HARE KRISHNA PARADE, Fifth Avenue from 59th Street to Washington Square Park; (718) 855–6714; second Saturday in June.

BROOKLYN PRIDE PARADE AND FESTIVAL, Brooklyn; Seventh Avenue from 15th Street to Lincoln Place; (718) 670–3337.

CHILDREN'S EVANGELICAL PARADE, Third Avenue from 96th Street to 122nd Street; third Sunday in June.

BRONX WEEK PARADE, the Bronx; Moshulu Parkway; www.ilovethe bronx.com; last Saturday in June.

INTERNATIONAL CULTURES PARADE, Sixth Avenue from 35th to 56th Street; www.10.org.

MERMAID PARADE, Brooklyn; Coney Island boardwalk from Stillwell Avenue to West 15th Street; (718) 372–5159; www.coneyisland.com; last Saturday in June.

HERITAGE OF PRIDE PARADE, Fifth Avenue from 52nd Street to Christopher Street; (212) 807–7433; www.hopinc.org; last Sunday of June.

JULY

MACY'S FOURTH OF JULY FIREWORKS; FDR Drive from 14th to 42nd Street; (212) 494–4495; www.macys.com; 9:00 P.M. on July 4th.

TRAVIS FOURTH OF JULY PARADE, Staten Island; Victory Boulevard and Cannon Street.

CHINATOWN INDEPENDENCE DAY PARADE AND FESTIVAL, Canal Street to Mott Street and through Chinatown; www.explorechinatown.com; Sunday closest to July 4th.

CAPTIVE NATIONS PARADE, Fifth Avenue from 59th to 72nd Street; (718) 439–8044; third Sunday in June.

GRAN PARADA DOMINICANA DEL BRONX, the Bronx; Grand Concourse from East Tremont Avenue to 161st Street; (718) 993–4463; third Sunday in July.

COLOMBIA DAY PARADE, Queens; Northern Boulevard from 70th to 90th Street; (718) 457-3897; third Sunday in July.

AUGUST

BRONX PUERTO RICAN DAY PARADE, the Bronx; Grand Concourse from East Tremont Avenue to 161st Street; (718) 401-0404; first Sunday in August.

DOMINICAN REPUBLICAN DAY PARADE, Sixth Avenue from 36th to 58th Street; (212) 795-0107; mid-August.

BROOKLYN PUERTO RICAN DAY PARADE, Brooklyn; Graham Avenue from Broadway to Grand Street; (718) 401-0404; third Sunday in August.

INDIA INDEPENDENCE DAY PARADE, Madison Avenue from 41st to 27th Street; third Sunday of August.

PAKISTAN INDEPENDENCE DAY PARADE, Madison Avenue from 41st to 27th Street; (212) 693-1660; last Sunday of August.

SEPTEMBER

LABOR DAY PARADE, Fifth Avenue from 44th to 72nd Street.

WEST INDIAN AMERICAN DAY CARNIVAL PARADE, Brooklyn; Eastern Parkway between Utica Avenue and Grand Army Plaza; (718) 467-1797; www.wiadca.org; Labor Day weekend.

MEXICAN DAY PARADE, Madison Avenue from 41st to 23rd Street; second weekend of September.

THE STEUBEN DAY PARADE, Fifth Avenue from 61st to 86th Street; (212) 732-2422; third Sunday of September.

AFRICAN-AMERICAN DAY PARADE, Adam Clayton Powell Boulevard from 111th to 142nd Street; (212) 862-8497; third Sunday in September.

MUSLIM DAY PARADE, Madison Avenue from 41st to 26th Street; late September.

OCTOBER

NIGERIAN INDEPENDENCE PARADE, Second Avenue from 54th to 43rd Street; www.oanweb.org; first Saturday in October.

PULASKI DAY PARADE, Fifth Avenue from 26th to 52nd Street; (877) 478–5275; www.pulaskiparade.org; first Sunday in October.

KOREAN PARADE, Broadway from 41st to 23rd Street; (212) 255–6969; first Sunday in October.

COLUMBUS DAY PARADE, Fifth Avenue from 44th to 79th Street; (212) 249–9923; www.columbuscitizensfd.org; second Monday in October.

HISPANIC DAY PARADE, Fifth Avenue from 44th to 86th Street; second Sunday in October.

THE VILLAGE HALLOWEEN PARADE, Sixth Avenue from Houston to 21st Street; www.halloween-nyc.com; October 31.

NOVEMBER

NEW YORK CITY MARATHON, throughout the five boroughs; www.ing nycmarathon.org; first Sunday in November.

VETERANS DAY PARADE; Fifth Avenue from 23rd to 57th Street; (212) 693–1476; www.nationsparade.org; November 11.

MACY'S THANKSGIVING DAY PARADE, Central Park West and Broadway from 79th to 34th Street; (212) 494–4495; www.macys.com; Thanksgiving Day.

DECEMBER

TIMES SQUARE NEW YEAR'S EVE, Broadway and Seventh Avenue from 42nd to 57th Street; (212) 768–1560; www.timessquarenyc.org; December 31.

MANHATTAN

MID-MANHATTAN LIBRARY, 455 Fifth Avenue (at 40th Street); (212) 340-0833; Telephone Reference, (212) 340-0849, ext. 3; www.nypl.org

EAST SIDE

58TH STREET, 127 East 58th Street; (212) 759-7358

67TH STREET, 328 East 67th Street; (212) 734-1717

96TH STREET, 112 East 96th Street; (212) 289-0908

125TH STREET, 224 East 125th Street; (212) 534-5050

AGUILAR, 174 East 110th Street; (212) 534-2930

EPIPHANY, 228 East 23rd Street; (212) 679-2645

HAMILTON FISH PARK, 415 East Houston Street; (212) 673-2290

MACOMB'S BRIDGE, 2650 Adam Clayton Powell Jr. Boulevard; (212) 281-4900

OTTENDORFER, 135 Second Avenue; (212) 674-0947

ROOSEVELT ISLAND, 524 Main Street; (212) 308-6243

TERENCE CARDINAL COOKE-CATHEDRAL, 560 Lexington Avenue; (212) 752-3824

WEBSTER, 1465 York Avenue; (212) 288-5049

YORKVILLE, 222 East 79th Street; (212) 744-5824

WEST SIDE

115TH STREET, 203 West 115th Street; (212) 666-9393

ANDREW HEISKELL LIBRARY FOR THE BLIND AND PHYSICALLY HANDICAPPED, 40 West 20th Street; (212) 206-5400; voice mail (212) 206-5425; TDD (212) 206-5458

BLOOMINGDALE, 150 West 100th Street; (212) 222-8030

COLUMBUS, 742 Tenth Avenue; (212) 586-5098

COUNTEE CULLEN, 104 West 136th Street; (212) 491-2070

DONNELL LIBRARY CENTER, 20 West 53rd Street; (212) 621-0618

FORT WASHINGTON, 535 West 179th Street; (212) 927-3533

GEORGE BRUCE, 518 West 125th Street; (212) 662-9727

HAMILTON GRANGE, 503 West 145th Street; (212) 926-2147

HARLEM, 9 West 124th Street; (212) 348-5620

INWOOD, 4790 Broadway; (212) 942-2445

JEFFERSON MARKET, 425 Avenue of the Americas; (212) 243-4334

KIPS BAY, 446 Third Avenue; (212) 683-2520

MORNINGSIDE HEIGHTS, 2900 Broadway; (212) 864-2530

MUHLENBERG, 209 West 23rd Street;
(212) 924-1585

RIVERSIDE, 127 Amsterdam Avenue;
(212) 870-1810

ST. AGNES, 444 Amsterdam Avenue;
(212) 877-4380

SEWARD PARK, 192 East Broadway;
(212) 477-6770

WASHINGTON HEIGHTS, 1000 Street,
Nicholas Avenue; (212) 923-6054

DOWNTOWN

CHATHAM SQUARE, 33 East
Broadway; (212) 964-6598

**EARLY CHILDHOOD RESOURCE &
INFORMATION CENTER (ECRIC),**
66 Leroy Street; (212) 929-0815

HUDSON PARK, 66 Leroy Street;
(212) 243-6876

NEW AMSTERDAM, 9 Murray Street;
(212) 732-8186

TOMPKINS SQUARE, 331 East 10th
Street; (212) 228-4747

STATEN ISLAND

ST. GEORGE LIBRARY CENTER, 5
Central Avenue; (718) 442-8560

DONGAN HILLS, 1617 Richmond
Road; (718) 351-1444

GREAT KILLS, 56 Giffords Lane;
(718) 984-6670

HUGUENOT PARK, 830 Huguenot
Avenue; (718) 984-4636

NEW DORP, 309 New Dorp Lane;
(718) 351-2977

PORT RICHMOND, 75 Bennett Street;
(718) 442-0158

RICHMONDTOWN, 200 Clarke
Avenue; (718) 668-0413

SOUTH BEACH, 21-25 Robin Road;
(718) 816-5834

STAPLETON, 132 Canal Street;
(718) 727-0427

TODT HILL-WESTERLEIGH, 2550
Victory Boulevard; (718) 494-1642

TOTTENVILLE, 7430 Amboy Road;
(718) 984-0945

WEST NEW BRIGHTON, 976
Castleton Avenue; (718) 442-1416

THE BRONX

FORDHAM LIBRARY CENTER, 2556
Bainbridge Avenue (at Fordham
Road); (718) 579-4244; Bronx
Reference Center, (718) 579-4257

ALLERTON, 2740 Barnes Avenue;
(718) 881-4240

BAYCHESTER, 2049 Asch Loop North;
(718) 379-6700

**BELMONT LIBRARY-ENRICO FERMI
CULTURAL CENTER,** 610 East
186th Street; (718) 933-6410

CASTLE HILL, 947 Castle Hill Avenue;
(718) 824-3838

CITY ISLAND, 320 City Island Avenue;
(718) 885-1703

CLASON'S POINT, 1215 Morrison
Avenue; (718) 842-1235

EASTCHESTER, 1385 East Gun Hill
Road; (718) 653-3292

EDENWALD, 1255 East 233rd Street;
(718) 798-3355

FRANCIS MARTIN, 2150 University
Avenue; (718) 295-5287

GRAND CONCOURSE, 155 East
173rd Street; (718) 583-6611

HIGH BRIDGE, 78 West 168th Street;
(718) 293-7800

HUNT'S POINT, 877 Southern
Boulevard; (718) 617-0338

JEROME PARK, 118 Eames Place;
(718) 549-5200

KINGSBRIDGE, 280 West 231st
Street; (718) 548–5656

MELROSE, 910 Morris Avenue;
(718) 588–0110

MORRISANIA, 610 East 169th Street;
(718) 589–9268

MOSHOLU, 285 East 205th Street;
(718) 882–8239

MOTT HAVEN, 321 East 140th Street;
(718) 665–4878

PARKCHESTER, 1985 Westchester
Avenue; (718) 829–7830

PELHAM BAY, 3060 Middletown Road;
(718) 792–6744

RIVERDALE, 5540 Mosholu Avenue;
(718) 549–1212

SEDGWICK, 1701 Dr. Martin Luther
King Jr. Boulevard; (718) 731–2074

SOUNDVIEW, 660 Soundview Avenue;
(718) 589–0880

SPUYTEN DUYVIL, 650 West 235th
Street; (718) 796–1202

THROG'S NECK, 3025 Cross Bronx
Expressway Extension; (718) 792–2612

TREMONT, 1866 Washington Avenue;
(718) 299–5177

VAN CORTLANDT, 3874 Sedgwick
Avenue; (718) 543–5150

VAN NEST, 2147 Barnes Avenue;
(718) 829–5864

WAKEFIELD, 4100 Lowerre Place;
(718) 652–4663

WESTCHESTER SQUARE, 2521 Glebe
Avenue; (718) 863–0436

WEST FARMS, 2085 Honeywell
Avenue; (718) 367–5376

WOODLAWN HEIGHTS, 4355
Katonah Avenue; (718) 519–9627

WOODSTOCK, 761 East 160th Street;
(718) 665–6255

BROOKLYN

CENTRAL LIBRARY, Grand Army Plaza
(Flatbush Avenue and Eastern
Parkway); (718) 230–2100;
www.brooklynpubliclibrary.org;
Telephone Reference, (718)
230–2100, ext. 5

ARLINGTON, Arlington Avenue at
Warwick Street; (718) 277–6105

BAY RIDGE, Ridge Boulevard at 73rd
Street; (718) 748–5709

BEDFORD, Franklin Avenue at Hancock
Street; (718) 623–0012

BEDFORD LEARNING CENTER,
(718) 623–0028

BOROUGH PARK, 43rd Street near
Thirteenth Avenue; (718) 437–4085

BRIGHTON BEACH, Brighton First
Road (near Brighton Beach
Avenue); (718) 946–2917

BROOKLYN HEIGHTS, 280 Cadman
Plaza West (at Tillary Street);
(718) 623–7100

BROWER PARK, St. Marks Avenue
near Nostrand Avenue; (718)
773–7208

BROWNSVILLE, Glenmore Avenue at
Watkins Street; (718) 498–9721

BUSHWICK, Bushwick Avenue at
Seigel Street; (718) 602–1348

CANARSIE, Rockaway Parkway near
Avenue J; (718) 257–6547

CARROLL GARDENS, Clinton Street at
Union Street; (718) 596–6972

CLARENDON, Nostrand Avenue near
Farragut Road; (718) 421–1159

CLINTON HILL, Washington Avenue
near Lafayette Avenue; (718)
398–8713

CONEY ISLAND, Mermaid Avenue near West 19th Street; (718) 265-3220

CONEY ISLAND LEARNING CENTER; (718) 265-3880

CORTELYOU, Cortelyou Road at Argyle Road; (718) 693-7763

CROWN HEIGHTS, New York Avenue at Maple Street; (718) 773-1180

CYPRESS HILLS, Sutter Avenue at Crystal Street; (718) 277-6004

DEKALB, Bushwick Avenue at DeKalb Avenue; (718) 455-3898

DYKER, Thirteenth Avenue at 82nd Street; (718) 748-6261

EASTERN PARKWAY, Eastern Parkway at Schenectady Avenue; (718) 953-4225

EASTERN PARKWAY Adult Learning Center; (718) 778-9330

EAST FLATBUSH, 9612 Church Avenue near Rockaway Parkway; (718) 922-0927

FLATBUSH, Linden Boulevard near Flatbush Avenue; (718) 856-0813

FLATBUSH ADULT LEARNING CENTER, (718) 856-2631

FLATLANDS, Flatbush Avenue at Avenue P; (718) 253-4409

FORT HAMILTON, Fourth Avenue at 95th Street; (718) 748-6919

GERRITSEN BEACH, Gerritsen Avenue at Channel Avenue; (718) 368-1435

GRAVESEND, Avenue X near West 2nd Street; (718) 382-5792

GREENPOINT, Norman Avenue at Leonard Street; (718) 349-8504

HIGHLAWN, West 13th Street at Kings Highway; (718) 234-7208

HOMECREST, Coney Island Avenue near Avenue V; (718) 382-5924

JAMAICA BAY, Seaview Avenue at East 98th Street; (718) 241-3571

KENSINGTON, Ditmas Avenue near East 5th Street; (718) 435-9431

KINGS BAY, Nostrand Avenue near Avenue W; (718) 368-1709

KINGS HIGHWAY, Ocean Avenue near Kings Highway; (718) 375-3037

LEONARD, Devoe Street at Leonard Street; (718) 486-3365

MACON, Lewis Avenue at Macon Street; (718) 573-5606

MAPLETON, 60th Street at Seventeenth Avenue; (718) 256-2117

MARCY, DeKalb Avenue near Nostrand Avenue; (718) 935-0032

MCKINLEY PARK, Fort Hamilton Parkway at 68th Street; (718) 748-8001

MIDWOOD, East 16th Street near Avenue J; (718) 252-0967

MILL BASIN, Ralph Avenue near Avenue N; (718) 241-3973

NEW LOTS, New Lots Avenue at Barbey Street; (718) 649-0311

NEW UTRECHT, 1783 86th Street (at Bay 17th Street); (718) 236-4086

PACIFIC, Fourth Avenue at Pacific Street; (718) 638-1531

PAERDEGAT, East 59th Street near Flatlands Avenue; (718) 241-3994

PARK SLOPE, Sixth Avenue near 9th Street; (718) 832-1853

RED HOOK, Wolcott Street at Dwight Street; (718) 935-0203

RUGBY, Utica Avenue near Tilden Avenue; (718) 566-0054

RYDER, Twenty-third Avenue at 59th Street; (718) 331-2962

SARATOGA, Thomas S. Boyland Street at Macon Street; (718) 573-5224

SHEEPSHEAD BAY, East 14th Street near Avenue Z; (718) 368-1815

SPRING CREEK, Flatlands Avenue near New Jersey Avenue; (718) 257-6571

STONE AVENUE, 581 Mother Gaston Boulevard at Dumont Avenue; (718) 485-8347

SUNSET PARK, Fourth Avenue at 51st Street; (718) 567-2806

ULMER PARK, Bath Avenue at Twenty-sixth Avenue; (718) 265-3443

WALT WHITMAN, 93 St. Edwards Street (at Auburn Place); (718) 935-0244

WASHINGTON IRVING, Irving Avenue at Woodbine Street; (718) 628-8378

WILLIAMSBURG, 240 Division Avenue (at Marcy Avenue); (718) 302-3485

WILLIAMSBURG ADULT LEARNING CENTER, (718) 302-3489

WINDSOR TERRACE, East 5th Street at Fort Hamilton Parkway; (718) 686-9707

QUEENS

CENTRAL LIBRARY, 89-11 Merrick Boulevard (between Eighty-ninth and Ninetieth Avenues); (718) 990-0700; www.queenslibrary.org; Telephone Reference, (718) 990-0714 or (718) 990-0728

ARVERNE, Beach 54th Street; (718) 634-4784

ASTORIA, 14-01 Astoria Boulevard; (718) 278-2220

AUBURNDALE, 25-55 Francis Lewis Boulevard; (718) 352-2027

BAISLEY PARK, 117-11 Sutphin Boulevard; (718) 529-1590

BAYSIDE, 214-20 Northern Boulevard; (718) 229-1834

BAY TERRACE, 18-36 Bell Boulevard; (718) 423-7004

BELLEROSE, 250-06 Hillside Avenue; (718) 831-8644

BRIARWOOD, 85-12 Main Street; (718) 658-1680

BROAD CHANNEL, 16-26 Cross Bay Boulevard; (718) 318-4943

BROADWAY, 40-20 Broadway; (718) 721-2462

CAMBRIA HEIGHTS, 220-20 Linden Boulevard; (718) 528-3535

CORONA, 38-23 104th Street (between Thirty-eighth and Thirty-ninth Avenues); (718) 426-2844

COURT SQUARE, 25-01 Jackson Avenue; (718) 937-2790

DOUGLASTON/LITTLE NECK, 249-01 Northern Boulevard; (718) 225-8414

EAST ELMHURST, 95-06 Astoria Boulevard; (718) 424-2619

EAST FLUSHING, 196-36 Northern Boulevard; (718) 357-6643

ELMHURST, 86-01 Broadway; (718) 271-1020

FAR ROCKAWAY, 1637 Central Avenue; (718) 327-2549

FLUSHING, 41-17 Main Street; (718) 661-1200

FOREST HILLS, 108-19 Seventy-first Avenue; (718) 268-7934

FRESH MEADOWS, 193-20 Horace Harding Expressway; (718) 454-7272

GLENDALE, 78-60 73rd Place; (718) 821-4980

GLEN OAKS, 256-04 Union Turnpike; (718) 831-8636

HILLCREST, 187-05 Union Turnpike; (718) 454-2786

HOLLIS, 202-05 Hillside Avenue; (718) 465-7355

HOWARD BEACH, 92-06 156th Avenue; (718) 641-7086

JACKSON HEIGHTS, 35-51 81st Street; (718) 899-2500

KEW GARDENS HILLS, 72–33 Vleigh Place; (718) 261-6654

LANGSTON HUGHES, 100–01 Northern Boulevard; (718) 651-1100

LAURELTON, 134–26 225th Street; (718) 528-2822

LEFFERTS, 103–34 Lefferts Boulevard; (718) 843-5950

LEFRAK CITY, 98–25 Horace Harding Expressway; (718) 592-7677

MASPETH, 69–70 Grand Avenue; (718) 639-5228

MCGOLDRICK, 155–06 Roosevelt Avenue; (718) 461-1616

MIDDLE VILLAGE, 72–31 Metropolitan Avenue; (718) 326-1390

MITCHELL–LINDEN, 29–42 Union Street; (718) 539-2330

NORTH FOREST PARK, 98–27 Metropolitan Avenue; (718) 261-5512

NORTH HILLS, 57–04 Marathon Parkway; (718) 225-3550

OZONE PARK, 92–24 Rockaway Boulevard; (718) 845-3127

PENINSULA, 92–25 Rockaway Beach Boulevard; (718) 634-1110

POMONOK, 158–21 Jewel Avenue; (718) 591-4343

POPPENHUSEN, 121–23 Fourteenth Avenue; (718) 359-1102

QUEENSBORO HILL, 60–05 Main Street; (718) 359-8332

QUEENSBRIDGE, 10–43 Forty-first Avenue; (718) 937-6266

QUEENS VILLAGE, 94–11 217th Street; (718) 776-6800

RAVENSWOOD, 35–32 21st Street; (718) 784-2112

REGO PARK, 91–41 63rd Drive; (718) 459-5140

RICHMOND HILL, 118–14 Hillside Avenue; (718) 849-7150

RIDGEWOOD, 20–12 Madison Street; (718) 821-4770

ROCHDALE VILLAGE, 169–09 137th Avenue; (718) 723-4440

ROSEDALE, 144–20 243rd Street; (718) 528-8490

ST. ALBANS, 191–05 Linden Boulevard; (718) 528-8196

SEASIDE, 116–15 Rockaway Beach Boulevard; (718) 634-1876

SOUTH HOLLIS, 204–01 Hollis Avenue; (718) 465-6779

SOUTH JAMAICA, 108–41 Guy R. Brewer Boulevard; (718) 739-4088

SOUTH OZONE PARK, 128–16 Rockaway Boulevard; (718) 529-1660

STEINWAY, 21–45 31st Street; (718) 728-1965

SUNNYSIDE, 43–06 Greenpoint Avenue; (718) 784-3033

WHITESTONE, 151–10 14th Road; (718) 767-8010

WINDSOR PARK, 79–50 Bell Boulevard; (718) 468-8300

WOODHAVEN, 85–41 Forest Parkway; (718) 849-1010

WOODSIDE, 54–22 Skillman Avenue; (718) 429-4700

MANHATTAN

CHIEF OF RECREATION'S OFFICE: (212) 408-0243

ALFRED EAST SMITH (LOWER EAST SIDE)

80 Catherine Street (off Cherry Street, between Madison and South Streets); (212) 285-0300
Hours: Monday through Friday, 7:00 A.M.–10:00 P.M.; Saturday, 9:00 A.M.–5:00 P.M.; Sunday, 2:00–6:00 P.M. (fitness room closed).
Dance classes, open basketball, badminton, gardening club, basic computer courses, kickboxing and karate classes.

ASSER LEVY (MIDTOWN EAST SIDE)

East 23rd Street and Asser Levy Place (at FDR Drive); (212) 447–2020
Hours: Monday through Friday, 6:30 A.M.–9:30 P.M.; Saturday and Sunday, 8:00 A.M.–4:45 P.M.
Indoor and outdoor pool, group fitness classes, martial arts classes, swim classes, guitar lessons, yoga, seniors programs.

CHELSEA RECREATION CENTER

430 West 25th Street (between Ninth and Tenth Avenues); (212) 255-3705
Hours: Monday through Friday, 6:30 A.M.–9:30 P.M.; Saturday, 8:00 A.M.–4:00 P.M.
Brand-new center with indoor pool, cardio and fitness strength-training equipment, basketball, volleyball, game room, computer resource center, and a variety of fitness classes.

EAST 54 (UPPER EAST SIDE)

348 East 54th Street (between First and Second Avenues); (212) 754-5411
Hours: Monday through Friday, 7:00 A.M.–9:30 P.M.; Saturday, 9:00A.M.–4:00 p.m
Extensive schedule of fitness, yoga, and dance classes; indoor pool, track; after-school and senior programs.

HAMILTON FISH (LOWER EAST SIDE)

128 Pitt Street (at East Houston Street); (212) 387-7687
Hours: Monday through Friday, 8:00 A.M.–9:00 P.M.; Saturday, 10:30 A.M.–5:00 P.M.; Sunday, 10:00 A.M.–3:00 P.M.
Olympic-size outdoor pool, game room, fitness room, basketball courts, wrestling, computer classes, karate class.

HANSBOROUGH (CENTRAL HARLEM)

35 West 134th Street (between Lenox and Fifth Avenues); (212) 234–9603

Hours: Monday through Friday, 9:00 A.M.–9:30 P.M.; Saturday, 10:00 A.M.–5:30 P.M.

Outdoor rooftop sundeck, indoor pool, outdoor and indoor track, aerobic classes, fitness room, seniors programs.

HIGHBRIDGE (WASHINGTON HEIGHTS)

Amsterdam Avenue and West 173rd Street; (212) 927–2012

Hours: Monday through Friday, noon–9:30 P.M.; Saturday, noon–6:30 P.M.

Basketball courts, game room, computer center, dance and martial arts classes, after-school program.

JACKIE ROBINSON (WEST HARLEM)

85 Bradhurst Avenue (at 146th Street); (212) 324–9607

Hours: Monday through Friday, 9:00 A.M.–10:00 P.M.; Saturday until 5:00 P.M.

Olympic-size outdoor pool, fitness room, computer classes, volleyball, teen cooking classes, after-school program.

J. HOOD WRIGHT (WASHINGTON HEIGHTS)

351 Fort Washington Avenue (at 174th Street); (212) 927–1563

Hours: Monday through Thursday, 9:00 A.M.–10:00 P.M.; Friday and Saturday, 10:00 A.M.–4:00 P.M.

Fitness room, computer center, softball and basketball tournaments, game room, two athletic fields, tennis court, handball courts, teen and seniors programs.

MORNINGSIDE PARK (WEST HARLEM)

410 West 123rd Street (at Morningside Avenue); (212) 280–0209

Hours: Monday, 8:00 A.M.–4:00 P.M.; Tuesday through Friday, 10:00 A.M.–6:00 P.M.

Operates primarily as an after-school and seniors center.

NORTH MEADOW (UPPER EAST AND WEST SIDE)

Central Park (midpark at 97th Street); (212) 348–4867

Hours: Monday through Friday, 10:00 A.M.–6:00 P.M.; Saturday and Sunday until 4:30 P.M.

Tai chi and yoga classes, youth adventure programs, climbing wall (open-climbing hours are free for eight- to twelve-year-olds; adults $5.00), basketball clinics, and Field Day Kits. (Borrow a sack of equipment from them for a fun day in the park. The kit includes a basketball, ten cones, three bats, a horseshoe set, playground ball, Nerf ball, football, Frisbee, two handballs, a soccer ball, jump rope, two Wiffle balls, and hula hoops.)

PELHAM FRITZ (WEST HARLEM)

18 Mount Morris Park West (at 122nd Street); (212) 860–1380
Hours: Monday through Friday, 8:30 A.M.–9:30 P.M.; Saturday, 10:00 A.M.– 4:00 P.M.
Outdoor pool, computer room, aerobics classes, dance classes, drumming, extensive seniors programs, game room, basketball courts.

REC 59 (MIDTOWN WEST)

533 West 59th Street (between Tenth and Eleventh Avenues); (212) 397–3159
Hours: Monday through Friday, 11:00 A.M.–10:00 P.M.; Saturday, 10:00 A.M.– 6:00 P.M.
Indoor pool, small fitness room.

THOMAS JEFFERSON (EAST HARLEM)

2180 First Avenue (at East 112th Street); (212) 860–1383
Hours: Monday through Friday, 10:00 A.M.–9:30 P.M.; Saturday, 9:00 A.M.– 3:30 P.M.
Olympic-size outdoor pool, fitness room, basketball courts, athletic fields, martial arts classes, aerobic classes, boxing, handball courts, game room.

TONY DAPOLITO RECREATION CENTER (WEST VILLAGE/SOHO)

1 Clarkson Street (near Seventh Avenue South and Houston Street); (212) 242–5228
Hours: Monday through Friday, 7:00 A.M.–10:00 P.M.; Saturday and Sunday, 9:00 A.M.–5:30 P.M.
Very popular center. Indoor and outdoor pools, handball courts, two fitness rooms, indoor track, boccie court, fitness classes, basketball and flag football leagues.

BROOKLYN

CHIEF OF RECREATION'S OFFICE: (718) 965-8941

BROOKLYN SENIOR CENTER (FORT HAMILTON)

9941 Fort Hamilton Parkway (at 100th Street); (718) 439–4296
Hours: Monday through Saturday, 9:00 A.M.–5:00 P.M.
Line dancing, tap dancing, social dancing, arts and crafts, day trips, bingo, computer access.

BROWNSVILLE

1555 Linden Boulevard (between Mother Gaston and Christopher Streets); (718) 345–2706
Hours: Monday, Wednesday, and Friday, 9:00 A.M.–10:00 P.M.; Tuesday and Thursday until 11:00 P.M.; Saturday until 6:00 P.M.
Indoor pool, computer center, aerobics classes, martial arts classes, game room, basketball clinics, handball courts, track and field, music studio.

METROPOLITAN POOL AND FITNESS CENTER (WILLIAMSBURG)

261 Bedford Avenue (at Metropolitan Avenue); (718) 599-5707

Hours: Monday through Friday, 7:00 A.M.-10:00 P.M.; Saturday, 9:00 A.M.-5:30 P.M.

Indoor pool, fitness room, computer center, computer and digital video classes, play schoolroom, and "arguably the best indoor pool in New York City," says the Village Voice.

RED HOOK

155 Bay Street (between Henry and Clinton Streets); (718) 722-3211

Hours: Monday through Friday, 10:00 A.M.-9:00 P.M.

Outdoor pool, computer center and classes, aerobics, martial arts, yoga.

ST. JOHN'S RECREATION CENTER

1251 Prospect Place (at Schenectady Avenue); (718) 771-2787

Hours: Monday through Friday, 9:00 A.M.-10:00 P.M.; Saturday, 10:00 A.M.-6:00 P.M.

Indoor pool, computer center and classes, fitness room, aerobics, tai chi, SAT classes, quilting, seniors programs.

SUNSET PARK

Seventh Avenue and 43rd Street (at 42nd Street); (718) 965-6533

Hours: Monday through Friday, 2:00-10:00 P.M.; Saturday, 10:00 A.M.-6:00 P.M.

Outdoor pool, computer center, fitness room, boxing room, aerobics classes, tae bo classes, game room.

VON KING CULTURAL ARTS CENTER

670 Lafayette Avenue (between Marcy and Tompkins Avenues); (718) 622-2082

Hours: Monday through Friday, 9:00 A.M.-9:00 P.M.; Saturday, 10:00 A.M.-6:00 P.M.

Computer center, aerobics classes, game room, dance room, athletic fields, handball courts.

THE BRONX

CHIEF OF RECREATION'S OFFICE: (718) 430-1858

HAFFEN PARK

Hammersley Avenue at Ely, Gunther, and Burke Avenues; (718) 379-8347

Hours: Daily, 7:00 A.M.-3:30 P.M.

Outdoor pool, tennis courts, seniors center, handball courts.

HUNTS POINT

765 Manida Street (between Lafayette Street and Spofford Avenue); (718) 860-5544

Hours: Monday through Friday, 9:30 A.M.-9:30 P.M.; Saturday, 9:30 A.M.-5:00 P.M.

Fitness room; dance, aerobics, and karate classes; volleyball and basketball courts; movies on the last Friday of every month.

KINGSBRIDGE

3101 Kingsbridge Terrace (between Perot and Sedwick Streets); (718) 884–0700

Hours: Monday through Thursday, 8:00 A.M.–10:00 P.M.; Friday, 8:00 A.M.–9:00 P.M.; Sunday, 9:00 A.M.–2:00 P.M.

After-school teen and seniors programs, computer and back-to-work classes.

MULLALY

East 164th Street (at River Avenue); (718) 822–4191

Outdoor skate park.

OWEN DOLAN

1400 Westchester Square; (718) 822–4282

Hours: Monday through Thursday, 9:00 A.M.–8:00 P.M.; Friday, 9:00A.M.–5:00 P.M.; Saturday, 8:00 A.M.–5:00 P.M.

Small facility with some family-oriented classes.

ST. JAMES

2530 Jerome Avenue (at 192nd Street); (718) 822–4271

Hours: Monday through Friday, 9:00 A.M.–10:00 P.M.; Saturday until 5:00 P.M.

Computer center, tennis courts, basketball courts, handball courts, teen and seniors programs.

ST. MARY'S

450 St. Ann's Avenue (at 145th Street); (718) 402–5160

Hours: Monday through Friday, 9:00 A.M.–10:00 P.M.; Saturday until 5:00 P.M.

Indoor pool, computer center, fitness room, basketball courts, aerobics classes, boxing, cooking, karate, tae kwon do, teen programs, scuba classes, tennis courts, athletic field.

WEST BRONX

1527 Jessup Avenue (at 172nd Street); (718) 293–5934

Hours: Monday through Friday, 3:00–8:00 P.M.; Saturday, 2:00–6:00 P.M.

After-school programs, basketball courts, weight room, and tae kwon do classes.

WILLIAMSBRIDGE OVAL

3225 Reservoir Oval East (between 208th Street and Bainbridge Avenue); (718) 543–8672 or (718) 822–4508

Hours: Monday through Friday, 9:00 A.M.–8:00 P.M.; Saturday until 5:00 P.M.

Fitness room, tennis courts, basketball courts, handball courts, outdoor track, play schoolroom, karate classes, twenty-two-acre playground, seniors programs.

QUEENS

CHIEF OF RECREATION'S OFFICE: (718) 520–5936

DETECTIVE KEITH L. WILLIAMS (JAMAICA)
   173rd Place and Liberty Avenue (at 106th Street); (718) 523–6912
   Hours: Monday through Friday, 10:00 A.M.–6:00 P.M.
Outdoor pool, tennis courts, handball courts, cooking classes, garden, arts and crafts.

LOST BATTALION HALL (REGO PARK)
   93–29 Queens Boulevard (at Sixty-second Avenue); (718) 263–1163
   Hours: Monday through Friday, 9:00 A.M.–10:00 P.M.; Saturday, 10:00 A.M.–
   5:00 P.M.
Computer center, boxing room, fitness center, karate, kickboxing, rhythmic gymnastics, Gymboree, seniors program.

LOUIS ARMSTRONG (CORONA)
   108th Street and Northern Boulevard; (718) 446–8010
   Hours: Monday through Friday, 9:00 A.M.–5:00 P.M.
Fitness room, karate classes, dance classes, boxing, GED program, community groups, basketball, handball.

PASSERELLE
   Flushing Meadows Corona Park (between National Tennis Center and
   Shea Stadium); (718) 699–4236
   Hours: Open by appointment; call for details.
Fitness room, computer center, REACH program for people with disabilities. "We are more like a visitor center. We invite groups to come to us—school groups, organizations, seniors, et cetera."

ROY WILKINS FAMILY CENTER (ST. ALBANS)
   177th Street at Baisley Boulevard; (718) 276–8686
   Hours: Monday through Friday, 10:00 A.M.–10:00 P.M.; Saturday until 5:00 P.M.
Indoor pool, fitness room, outdoor track, extensive seniors program.

SORRENTINO (FAR ROCKAWAY)
   18–48 Cornaga Avenue (at Beach 19th Street); (718) 471–4818
   Hours: Monday through Friday, 9:00 A.M.–9:45 P.M.; Saturday until 4:45 P.M.
Fitness room, computer center, double Dutch program, computer classes, play school, seniors programs.

STATEN ISLAND

CHIEF OF RECREATION'S OFFICE: (718) 390–8020
CROMWELL CENTER
Murray Hulbert Avenue at Pier #6; (718) 816–6172
Hours: Monday through Friday, 7:30 A.M.–9:45 P.M.; Saturday and Sunday, 8:30 A.M.–4:00 P.M.
Fitness room, aerobics classes, computer classes, wood carving and ceramics classes, kid and teens programs.

INDEX

About the Author

Born and bred in New York City, **Rob Grader** is a writer, actor, and massage therapist and has lived in four out of the five boroughs (he'll make it to Staten Island one of these days). Rob's other writing credits include the soon-to-be-published book *The Cuddle Sutra* (Sourcebooks, 2007), scripts for the National Public Radio series Jazz From Lincoln Center, as well as articles for local newspapers and magazines. He has also created and produced the A&E reality show *House of Dreams*. As an actor, Rob has appeared at many regional theaters across the country; on the television shows *Law & Order, Law & Order: SVU, The Job, All My Children, Who's the Boss;* in the HBO film *American Splendor;* and in a number of national commercials. He's a graduate of the American Repertory Theater's Institute for Advanced Theater Training at Harvard University. As a massage therapist, he has rubbed many sore and aching backs around New York. Rob currently lives, works, and does his darndest not to spend any money in Manhattan.